STRATEGIC THINKING

Gordon J. Pearson

Prentice Hall
New York   London   Toronto   Sydney   Tokyo   Singapore

First published 1990 by
Prentice Hall International (UK) Ltd,
Campus 400, Maylands Avenue, Hemel Hempstead
Hertfordshire HP2 7EZ
A division of
Simon & Schuster International Group

Printed and bound in Great Britain by
BPC Wheatons Ltd, Exeter

Typeset in 10/12 pt Plantin by
Photoprint, Torquay

Library of Congress Cataloging-in-Publication Data

Pearson, Gordon J., 1939–
    Strategic thinking / Gordon J. Pearson.
        p.   cm.
    Includes bibliographical references.
    ISBN 0-13-852153-0 : £15.95 (Gt. Britain)
    1. Strategic planning.   2. Performance.   I. Title.
HD30.28.P347   1990   90–6956
658.4'012—dc20   CIP

British Library Cataloguing in Publication Data

Pearson, Gordon, *1939*–
    Strategic thinking.
    1. Management. Techniques
    I. Title
    658.4

    ISBN 0-13-852153-0

3 4 5 94

For My Father

Contents

Preface

Currently, the thrust of management development and education is very much on practical competence. The key question to be asked after any management training or teaching session is, 'what can participants *do* as a result of the training, that they could not do before?'. The former, rather more academic question, 'can they remember enough to pass an exam?' is increasingly recognized as irrelevant.

So far this emphasis on competences has tended to focus more on the skills required by junior and middle managers: communications skills; the ability to work effectively in, and lead, a team; the ability to delegate and motivate team members. There has been little emphasis on competency at strategic management level.

Yet there seems to be no intrinsic reason why training in strategic management should not also be competency-based. My experience on the academic side of management has only served to reinforce this view. Strategic thinking can be learned as a practical skill, just as can team-building or effective presentations. At any rate this is the point of view I have taken in writing this book.

I have not written primarily for those young men and women with a high quality first degree under their belts but no significant managerial experience, who pause to collect an MBA *en route* to a high flying job in finance or the City. It is written rather for those business managers on whom our industry depends for its future. They are likely to have several years' experience and wish to extend their theoretical and practical knowledge and expertise. Many of them achieve this through their own individual efforts, while others may take a formal qualification such as an MBA, a DMS or a professional diploma appropriate to their own functional responsibilities. Typically, they achieve this on a part-time basis while fulfilling their normal day-to-day managerial jobs.

When they have read this book they should be able to think about the strategy of their business from several different perspectives and understand which of these is likely to be more important to their business and its particular situation.

Thus, I hope it will be received by these practising managers as a contribution, however small, to competence in doing strategy.

Plan of the Book

The prologue to the book takes a broad view of the current business environment so that the various perspectives on strategic thinking discussed throughout the subsequent text can be considered against this backdrop.

Chapters 1 and 2 then introduce some of the basic concepts of strategy and seek to clarify some definitions and confusions currently apparent.

Chapters 3 to 9 suggest a number of different strategic thinking frameworks which have been widely used in practice. Each framework has its own strengths and weaknesses fitting it for particular circumstances. Moreover, each framework is both a way of looking at the

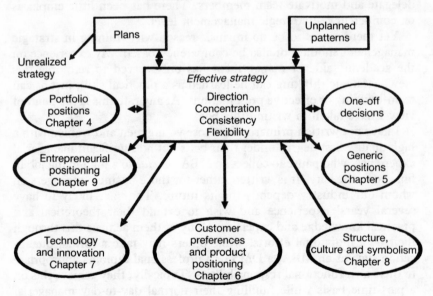

Inputs and outputs of effective strategy.

process of strategy and also represents both the inputs and outputs of strategy as indicated in the summary figure below. In many cases the inputs to strategy are likely to involve aspects of several frameworks, and the outputs from the strategy process are also likely to impact on the position of the business relative to several frameworks. However, for the sake of clarity, each framework is discussed separately, chapter by chapter.

Chapter 10 provides some pointers as to the relevance of the various strategic perspectives and provides a simple model of organizational characteristics which highlights many of the key issues discussed in previous chapters.

At the end of each chapter is a short discussion case where the reader is invited to consider a set of circumstances from a variety of viewpoints. These discussion cases are not orthodox case studies and do not include quantitative data – there are no balance sheets or profit and loss accounts, or even quantified sales forecasts. There is therefore no calculation or quantitative analysis of any kind. The aim is to focus the reader's thinking on some of the essential strategic issues, and in particular on how different people in different roles or circumstances may be pressured to take a particular decision. They have all been found useful in interactive management training sessions where the aim is to provide the opportunity for group discussions of these real life situations.

Acknowledgements

I am hugely indebted to three categories of people who have helped, directly and indirectly, with the production of this book.

Firstly, there are those management writers, researchers, consultants and practitioners whose work I have been influenced by and who, I hope, I have overtly acknowledged in the text. A book like this inevitably leans on, and is to some extent derived from, the work of some individuals more than others. Amongst the great and good in management literature I owe a particular debt to Drucker, Mintzberg and Porter. In addition I must also acknowledge the work of the Boston Consulting Group whose thinking influenced my practical work at an early stage of my management career. I am grateful to them for permission to reproduce Figures 4.2 to 4.7. Experience curves and business portfolios are now part of history and do not reflect the thrust of Boston's current approach to business strategy, but they have been extremely influential and encapsulate a number of important strategic concepts.

Secondly, there are those professional people with whom I have enjoyed personal contact over the years and particularly during the completion of my doctoral research at Manchester Business School. Notable among these are Jack Clyde, formerly of Urwick Orr and Mills & Allen, and my supervisors at Manchester, Alan Pearson and Derreck Ball, both of the R&D Research Unit at Manchester Business School.

Thirdly, and most importantly, a more personal debt of gratitude is owed to Eileen Pearson of Pearson Kirk Management Research and Training. Her expertise in management development and training has been a continuous spur to practicality in dealing with a topic which sometimes risks becoming too academic.

Finally, I must acknowledge Susie, William and Robert for their stoic good humour.

PROLOGUE

A view of the strategic context

We are cursed, as the Chinese would have it, by living in interesting times. There is a revolution in technology caused by the coincidence of an unprecedented number of fundamental inventions and discoveries which are reaching the stage of commercial exploitation more or less together. Businesses will either participate in this revolution or be swept aside by those that do. But investment in innovation – the decision to invest in something new in order to change the business and improve it – is, by definition, long term.

Simultaneously, and in no small part resulting from the technological revolution, there is also a revolution in financial practices and institutions. Markets which were set up to provide long term finance, have become so efficient that the long term can be measured in weeks or even days. Taking a long term view on a stock exchange, in the face of severe short term volatility, can be regarded as irrational, even irresponsible.

The requirement on businesses to maximize short term profits inevitably inhibits decisions to invest long term in innovation and leads to cut backs in the 'change functions' such as research and development (R&D). Consequently a technological gap opens up between those businesses which invest long term and those which are forced to the short term view. The outcomes of both sets of decisions are self-fulfilling and so the technological gap widens further.

The effects of the technological revolution are all-pervasive, affecting our quality of life, eliminating work, stimulating tremendous economic growth and providing business with exciting new competitive weapons. A new approach to strategic management is needed which will help firms grasp the opportunities, rather than slide down what Hayes and Garvin (1982) referred to as the 'disinvestment spiral'.

Innovation, the process of invention and its commercial exploitation,

1

is the strategic competitive tool of today and it is available to all businesses, no matter how small or how mature. For now, and perhaps the next ten or fifteen years, innovation will be *the* vital ingredient of business success.

However, much of manufacturing industry has been unwilling, or unable, to make long term commitments, afraid to be involved in risk if it can possibly be avoided. Management has adopted the philosophy of the accounting profession; conservatism, prudence and the avoidance of risk have become aims in their own right. The hard-nosed financial realist regards innovation with cynicism, and the cynicism is consequently fulfilled.

The validity and usefulness of any particular approach to strategic management depends very much on the situation in which it is to be used. Planning systems devised in the 1960s are not likely to be the most appropriate for managements in the 1990s simply because the world has changed. Mass production of standard product is now rarely an adequate response. Innovation is no longer concerned with putting stripes in toothpaste or bigger fins on automobiles. Growth is no longer guaranteed positive. Market dominance is no longer an end in itself and may even be a source of vulnerability, implying as it does a professional, financial and psychological commitment to today's technology, or yesterday's. The world is changing and management's approach to strategy needs to change with it.

The financial environment

Business is subject to almost irresistible short term financial pressure from the financial sector which originally existed to serve the purposes of industry. Now that sector has developed so extensively that the roles appear to have become reversed. Industry, and particularly manufacturing, is in danger of becoming almost an incidental pretext for the transactions of the financial sector.

The dominance of the financial world restricts the extent to which strategic management can exploit the opportunities now presented. Strategies are necessarily being shaped to provide quick returns. Shareholder wealth can more easily be increased, it seems, by opportunistic acquisitions than by persevering in the development of product manufacture. Thus, innovations are not available to a management who are instructed to milk their cash cow to the last. Organic growth is of little interest to many such firms, and the long term is discounted to insignificance.

The more efficiently financial markets work, the more it pays to take a short term view. This simple fact is the basic reason why the financial sector works against the long term interests of industry. As the City of London and Wall Street have become relatively more efficient, so they have become less able to support the manufacturer of products. Who wants to invest in developing the next generation of technology? How can the manufacturer persuade shareholders to remain patient for five or ten years while the development is completed and brought into profit, when their concerns are with weeks, days and sometimes even hours? What do neutral shareholders do if they can change £100 into £150 overnight?

This tension between industry and the financial world has long existed in New York and London, but has not existed to the same extent elsewhere in the world. Anglo–Saxon manufacturers have consequently learned to be increasingly sceptical of financiers. This is not because of the rogues who occasionally come to the surface, but because the interests of the manufacturing and financial sectors no longer coincide. Financial institutions may have come into existence to raise finance for long term and risky ventures such as merchanting expeditions across the high seas, or large scale investments like the railways, but this mutual interest no longer works. These institutions cannot now be relied on to provide the necessary stability in their financing. Their very efficiency has undermined their original purpose. Equity finance is no longer long term.

The New York and London markets are the most efficient and are also conducted in the international language. By comparison, the German market is unsophisticated and relatively inefficient. There are no quick Deutschmarks to be made, no well-oiled machine to induce the German investor to take the short term view. The same used to be true of Tokyo, where artificial restrictions have in the past been operative. As a consequence these countries have enjoyed more stable and fruitful capital investment records. However, because of its industrial success Japan's problem is less to do with taking a long term view in its financing decisions, than to do with trying to find a stable long term home for its surplus funds.

The efficiency of the financial markets is based on more information, available faster and cheaper. Dealing is easier, faster and cheaper. Big investors use short term performance measurement surveys to make fast returns and would be widely regarded as eccentric and irrational if they based their investment decisions on other than purely financial grounds. Inevitably they take the corporate raider's money as soon as anyone else's. The innovative business can expect scant support from the financial world if its requirements are for long term finance.

The financial culture is becoming increasingly dominant and is hostile to the long term investments required to participate in the progress of technology.

The technological environment

Looking at the past it is easy to see how dramatic technological progress has been and how, once started, it seems to go forward with an ever quickening momentum. We either participate in it, or we let it steamroller over us.

At the beginning of the nineteenth century no country in Europe had yet reattained the living standard of Imperial Rome. But over the past hundred years or so, real income per head rose by 700 per cent on average, labour productivity by 1,200 per cent and median exports by over 6,000 per cent (Madison, 1982). The real per capita income in the United States in 1870 was about the same as it is in the Philippines today, and slightly below that of Egypt. Growth rates in this period have exploded by comparison with anything ever achieved before. The explanation is simple, technological innovation. Otherwise, as Baumol put it, 'the economic history of the period, and its contrast with the world's economic performance in the previous, say, fifteen centuries, is difficult to account for' (Baumol, 1986).

Technological innovation, whether it is the product itself or the process of its production, is the engine which drives economic, social and organizational change. In the past, war has also been a stimulus and some such changes may also have resulted from the effects of plague. But today technological innovation is the key.

The connection between innovation and economic growth has been widely accepted since the original work of Kondratiev which was developed by Schumpeter in the 1930s (Schumpeter, 1939). Economists may disagree in detail, but most analysts associate the great expansions with periods when major innovations coincided (see Ray, 1980). Piatier (1984), for example, in his study for the European Commission identified three such 'revolutions' as illustrated in Figure 0.1.

The first, the eighteenth century industrial revolution, was based on innovations in coal energy, steel and the steam engine which gave rise to the mechanization of textiles and other manufacturing industries,

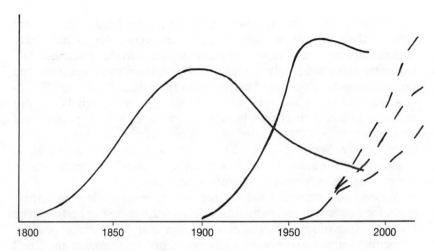

Figure 0.1 *The three industrial revolutions.*

plus the development of railway transport on a massive scale and the launching of inorganic chemistry. The ingredients of this revolution and its results in terms of economic growth are readily identifiable and dramatic.

> Coal, steel, railways, textiles and inorganic chemistry grew up and grew old together: the 1930s depression was neither a short term economic crisis, nor a crisis of capitalism, but signalled the end of a great wave of major innovations. (Piatier, 1984)

The second had its embryonic phase in the 1930s and was based on oil, motor vehicles, aircraft, sheet steel, organic chemistry and synthetic materials. The growth from this revolution was interrupted by the second world war, but was realized in the period of post-war reconstruction in the 1950s and 1960s, slowing down in the 1970s, perhaps being brought to an early maturity by the oil price crises of the mid-1970s, but definitely in decline by the 1980s.

The third revolution, still in its growth phase, is based primarily on electronics, information technology, new forms of energy and energy substitute, biotechnology, molecular engineering, genetic engineering, ocean development and possibly new forms of transport or transport substitute.

Differing forecasts have been made for this third revolution. It is uncertain when the period of rapid growth will peak, though the general consensus is that it will be before the turn of the century. As yet biotechnology and genetic engineering have hardly started but already their impact on agriculture is apparent. Researchers have successfully inserted a gene into plants which provides resistance to a commercial herbicide, glyphosate, and the probability is that protected crop seeds and herbicide will in due course be sold as a package. Breakthroughs are being achieved with the injection of foreign DNA into monocot plants such as cereals. Already massive grain surpluses, beef mountains, wine lakes, butter mountains and the like are commonplace in the West. If only 2 per cent p.a. productivity gain is maintained then around a third of today's farmland will be surplus to agricultural requirements in twenty years' time.

Molecular engineering will in due course make no less an impact with, for example, new synthetic materials surpassing the performance characteristics of steel at an inherently lower cost. The current practice of melting metal could eventually be consigned to museums and small craft units.

The electronics and information technology strands of the revolution have reached the stage of commercial exploitation, but even now this is still in an early phase. Commercial exploitation is rippling out from a core which is still bubbling with primary innovations, e.g. breakthroughs in high temperature superconductivity (i.e. conduction of electricity with zero power loss), a potentially more revolutionary and far-reaching innovation than the transistor itself.

The results of these innovations are that products and services are becoming cheaper, more reliable, more flexible, more sophisticated and intelligent. Flexibility and variety will be instantly available. Oneoffs will be as cheap as standard products. Labour costs will become largely irrelevant. The implications will be revolutionary for all firms, large or small and whether at the forefront of technology or languishing in the maturest of mature industries.

This third revolution is also changing the nature of work. The jobs that remain by the turn of the century are likely to be either ultra highskilled manufacturing jobs, high-skilled professional services associated with production, or in distribution and personal services. Inevitably shorter hours, shorter working lives and more part-time work are resulting. Some of these effects are already being experienced across manufacturing as a whole, not simply the new, high technology industries.

Thus changes in technology are causing other organizational and social changes, which will themselves feedback into industry generating needs for further new products and services. The revolution is all-pervasive.

Mature business is full of potential for innovation, just as are the new industries themselves. What are the chances of setting the stock-markets alight with a hamburger chain? Or a barber shop? Or a chain of dentistry offices? Or making and selling living room furniture, doughnuts, high quality chinaware, writing instruments, household paints or textile yarns? Yet, as Drucker pointed out (Drucker, 1985), all these mundane, and certainly mature, activities have yielded the sort of profits growth that the popular imagination has been led to associate only with the newer 'high tech', high growth industries.

Major changes in the structure of markets usually result from the efforts of one or more participants to improve their position by aggressive pricing strategies. Such improvements are generally only available at a very substantial cost so that only the biggest firms can afford to do this. Thus there is a natural tendency for the big to get bigger and the smaller firms to be driven into small niches of the market. The market structure is therefore set firm. However, during the course of a technological revolution, when all manner of new products and new processes are becoming available, competitive positions become less rigid, the market structure becomes fluid and individual firms can achieve major changes in their position at a relatively low cost.

The present technological revolution will, over the next decade or so, present just such a window of opportunity. But it will not continue indefinitely. As with the previous revolutions, the new technologies will grow up and mature together. By the turn of the century the competitive jelly will have set and major inroads to new markets will then again only be achieved at great cost. Right now the opportunities are there for the taking. As commercial applications of the current wave of new technologies become available, so opportunities will multiply. Each of the strands of new technology, electronics, information technology, biotechnology, genetic engineering, molecular engineering, ocean development, etc., will all offer opportunities for changing the competitive rules and structures. Some businesses will make huge strides while others will be blasted out of existence.

Globalization

A third contextual issue with which strategic management of the 1990s must contend is globalization. This is implicit in much of what has been said about the technological revolution. It is not a new phenomenon.

The impact of global competition has long been apparent in Britain. The story has often been recounted by the Engineering Council and others. Britain started the machine tool industry, but by the 1980s had less than 3 per cent of the world market. Similarly she once had 100 per cent of the textile machinery market, but now only 7 per cent. Thirty years ago Britain was number three in world steel production, but is now tenth in the world. Britain used to export motor cycles to a hundred foreign markets; now there is no British motor cycle industry left. The picture is the same in shipbuilding, cotton, automobiles and trucks, and many other markets.

While there has been a significant upturn in British manufacturing productivity over the past ten years there is little indication that the long term relative decline has been reversed. By comparison, America's decline, at the hands of global competition, is comparatively recent and possibly not chronic. But it is nevertheless apparent. For example, in 1979 American holdings abroad exceeded the value of foreign-owned assets in the United States by over $100 billion. By the end of 1986 the position had reversed and the trend was clear.

In 1970 the import share of the US automobile market was 7 per cent. By October 1985 this figure had hit 31 per cent and the main reason for this was identified as inferior relative quality, a problem no longer affecting Japanese products. Again, there is a depressingly long list of industries which used to be dominant, if not in world markets then at least on the domestic scene, but which now appear to be losing

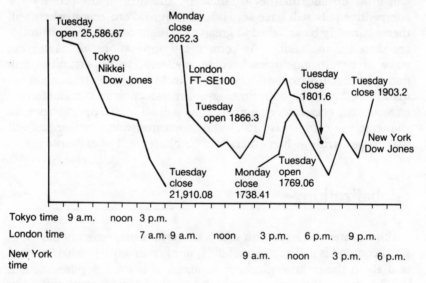

Figure 0.2   *The global stock exchange.*
Based on Chambliss and Peston, 1987.

the battle against competitors on the other side of the globe. In 1989 Japan finally overtook the United States as the wealthiest nation on earth in terms of asset ownership.

There is some political will behind the process of free trade and globalization, expressed through the General Agreement on Tariffs and Trade (GATT) agreements and through such organizations as the European Community (EC) which will have eliminated all statutory barriers on trade within the member countries by the end of 1992.

Nor is the process restricted to product markets. Stock-markets themselves are now truly global. Computerization of dealing has resulted in New York, London and Tokyo becoming so closely intertwined as to form, in effect, a single electronic global stock exchange. The trend to a global market has been progressive with many major stocks being quoted on two or more of the national exchanges. Computerization has completed the process. The global market operates not so much across national boundaries – these have become increasingly irrelevant – but across time zones. The perpetual, 24-hour-a-day market has almost been achieved as can be seen in Figure 0.2.

The 24-hour period shown in Figure 0.2 is Day 2 of the 1987 'October crisis'. Day 1 had seen 20–25 per cent written off share prices. Day 2 shows further falls at the start amounting to almost 15 per cent during Tokyo's market hours, a continued fall at the start of London's period followed by a rally which collapsed at the end of London's time but which recovered again during Wall Street's period. The period of overlap when both Wall Street and London were open shows how closely related the markets are. The size of the movements over the two-day period further highlights how short term the market's orientation had become.

Technology, product markets and finance are now all global. The world is, in effect, a smaller place. The technology is in place now for a customer in, say, Birmingham, Alabama to connect directly to a knitting machine in a Taiwan factory and instruct it in detail about the number, pattern and colour of garments to be produced. Long production runs, high value work in progress and finished goods stocks are things of the past – global just-in-time is now feasible.

Organizational responses

These environmental issues – technological pressures for essentially long term development despite financial pressures for a short term return, set against an increasingly global backdrop – are not new. Similar problems were confronting the businesses studied by Burns and Stalker (1961) as they tried to adapt old cultures to the imperatives of new technologies. They developed the much-quoted distinction between mechanistic and organic systems of management. 'Mechanistic' was the term Burns applied to the firms they studied which almost entirely failed to innovate. They were adapted to stable conditions. Their management tasks were broken down into precisely defined specialisms. They had a clear hierarchy of control, vertical communications, overall knowledge and coordination only at the top of the hierarchy and an insistence on loyalty and obedience. In short they were bureaucracies.

The organic organization was more difficult to define. It was the organization form which Burns found effective at innovating, used to dealing with unstable conditions, continually confronting new and unfamiliar problems, to which specialists contribute as and when needed. They enjoyed open communications, leadership by expertise and a much higher degree of commitment to organizational goals. Formal organization in the shape of charts, job descriptions and so on, just did not exist in the organic firms.

The two types of organization were distinguished also in terms of their age, the mechanistic form being mature while the organic forms were invariably young, rapidly developing organizations. It appeared therefore, that there might be a natural ageing process which inexorably led to older organizations becoming mechanistic or bureaucratic. Using this biological analogy such a process seems entirely plausible.

When a business is first formed its structure is simple. There are few coordination problems that are not handled by direct supervision. There is little opportunity, let alone need, for job specialization. There is initially no need for formalization of behaviour in operating instructions, job descriptions, company rules and so forth. The small entrepreneurial business has none of the big company problems of extended lines of communication and command. The dilemma of how far to decentralize control does not arise. In short, most of the structural problems which have puzzled practitioners over the years simply do not exist.

However, as the organization grows all these issues inevitably emerge. Early writers on organization, confronting a world that was changing only relatively slowly, developed certain basic principles of organization which applied in their times.

Fayol (1916) is generally credited with the first theoretical analysis of the job of management which he saw as being to forecast and plan, organize, command, coordinate and control. In order to achieve these roles he proposed a set of fourteen principles which largely prescribe the elements of organizational structure. These included such concepts as unity of command, unity of direction, centralization : decentralization, job specialization based on expertise, scalar chains or hierarchical organization and so forth.

Subsequent writers developed Fayol's principles further (e.g. Urwick, 1947 and Brech, 1957). Sometimes rather rigid and naive sounding rules were developed governing such matters as the maximum number of levels in a management hierarchy, the maximum span of control of an individual manager, the distinction between line and staff, and so forth. This 'classical' analysis seems often to revolve around questions which can be represented on a traditional organization chart.

Questions related to the overall shape of the chart – whether it is a tall, thin pyramid with many hierarchical levels, or low and wide with many people reporting to a single boss – may seem somewhat simplistic. However, these problems are real enough in practice. As a firm grows and employs more people it is forced to change its structure in order to remain manageable. The size of a firm necessitates the subdivision of responsibilities and the delegation of authority.

Many firms progress through various evolutionary phases as they grow. Typically, the first phase after the firm has outgrown the simple structure, is to adopt a functional organization, based on the primary tasks such as production, marketing, finance, etc. This enables the firm to accommodate functional professional specialists at senior levels of management and it also enables relatively short lines of communication to operate.

However, functional structures are not best suited to managing diversified activities. Typically, as firms grow they tend to diversify into new product market areas. Diversification brings with it an explosion of complexity which is generally contained by setting up an organization of more or less separate businesses, either as divisions or as separate subsidiaries under a holding company organization.

Thus structure appears to depend directly on the firm's phase of development and, in particular, its size. However, there are various other factors which exert influence. Researchers have found that production technology was a key determinant of structure (Woodward, 1958), that the most appropriate structure depends on the firm's environment (Lawrence and Lorsch, 1967), or that structure results more from changing pressures in the market place (Chandler, 1962).

From all this one might conclude that the firm's organization structure is an almost involuntary reaction to its various circumstances, rather than the result of overt top management decision. But structure is not a natural phenomenon; it results from specific management decisions. In many cases these decisions are simply reactive, changes in the formal organization merely reflecting changes that have already occurred in the real organization.

Mintzberg (1983) traced this development of organization from the simple structure to various forms of bureaucracy and in particular defined three bureaucratic forms.

Firstly, machine bureaucracy is typical of the older industries with large scale production providing large numbers of highly specialized, low skill jobs, many staff analysts to maintain the systems of standardization, rigid departmentalization and a large scale middle management hierarchy. It requires a stable environment to function which leads it firstly to seek out stable environments and secondly to impose stability, for example, by vertical expansion into activities that more entrepreneurial organizations would simply buy in. Machine bureaucracies provide dull repetitive work, alienated employees, an obsession with control and an inability to adapt.

Secondly, the professional bureaucracy, which is a rapidly growing organizational form as the technological revolution spreads, relies on standardization of skills rather than organizational processes or products. It relies on trained professionals and has to cede to them, and their external professional affiliations, much of its power. Thus the structure is highly decentralized with a high degree of participation and autonomy for the professionals themselves, but with an autocratic, non-participative structure for the substantial support staff which carries out the functions the professionals have shed.

Thirdly, the divisionalized form, the result of diversification, is a composite structure containing within it different structures, e.g. machine bureaucracy, at 'divisional' level. Divisionalized form is a means of setting up market-, or product-based subunits with a considerable degree of autonomy, but nevertheless subject to central control exercised through certain performance control systems and additionally through certain centralized functions. It is this central control which in effect imposes a structure of machine bureaucracy within the divisions because neither simple structure nor adhocracy (discussed on p. 159) would respond to central control.

A type of divisionalized structure, sometimes referred to as the 'M form', has predominated over the past twenty years. This structure has a relatively small corporate headquarters responsible for the formalization of strategy and for allocating resources to operating divisions whose performance is monitored through regular financial returns.

Not only does this impose machine bureaucracy on the divisions, but by formally denying them discretion over strategy, it more or less ensures that they will adopt simple risk avoidance behaviour, inevitably retreat from seriously contested markets and concentrate all on satisfying the short term financial targets demanded of them.

Machine bureaucracy, fundamentally unsuited to innovation, is being seen increasingly as inappropriate to contemporary needs for flexibility and speed of response. Its dominance of large scale business is nevertheless more or less complete, not only within the older industries, but also in the new industries which large scale business has bought into. There is a natural tendency to seek out stability and set up an organizational form that would prosper in such conditions. Bureaucratization is therefore, for all its faults, an almost inevitable process, which will only be avoided or reversed as a result of great and deliberate effort.

The tendency to bureaucratize is not necessarily because it is thought to be an inherently more efficient structure, but because it apparently makes management's role easier by allowing large parts of the organization to be put on to 'autopilot'. If the autopilot system worked well enough to cope with the volatility and uncertainty of the real world this would be an admirable solution. But this is clearly not the case. Nevertheless, the autopilot system, bureaucracy, is easier for managers to handle if they ignore its shortcomings.

Moreover, the pressures on divisional managers to conform to bureaucratic norms are immense. The rules, the customs and practice, and culture of the firm all lead to the conclusion that conformity is the most rational form of behaviour. Non-conformity is essentially high risk behaviour which places salary, career and pension very much on the line. Despite the many stories of the exceptions (e.g. Pinchot, 1985), most managers do in fact conform, thus further reinforcing the predominance of the bureaucratic form.

The predominance of bureaucracy at divisional level creates severe problems for the effective divisional manager at the business face. Innovation is needed to achieve the strategic objective, but the bureaucratic organization inhibits this. There are three options: the manager can become a bureaucrat; an attempt can be made to change the organization as a whole; or a small suborganization may be set up within the main business where different rules apply and where individuals can be given the freedom to innovate.

Adding further weight to this trend within manufacturing industry, has been the increasing domination of management by the accounting profession. Increasingly business is being managed according to the rules and norms of professional accountancy. Conservatism, risk avoidance, strict budgetary control and the principle that time is money are the dominant rules of most businesses.

Dominance of strategic management by the accounting philosophy has resulted in a rejection of creativity and innovation, and a belief that success comes simply from 'hard work and achieving budget' (Norburn and Schurz, 1984). This leads to a repressive, cost-oriented style of management and a professional ignorance about technology and markets. A board of directors dominated by this mode of thinking, as so many are, would be peculiarly unsuited to making decisions about strategy, though that is their task.

Accounting-dominated leadership has coincided with a dramatic industrial decline in Britain and the same picture has recently been emerging in America. The inevitable result is a buy and sell philosophy of business. Rather than solving business problems, such managements dispose of problem businesses. Rather than investing in innovations and physical assets to exploit business opportunities, such managements focus on investing in quickly realizable stocks and shares. Rather than make any long term commitments which involve risk, such managements prefer to borrow long and lend short. Such a philosophy is well suited for managing a unit trust, but not a business.

The tendency to bureaucratize and the increasing dominance of the accounting philosophy are complementary and together lead managements almost inevitably to adopt a planning-oriented approach to strategy. Planning is itself an essentially bureaucratic activity. Financial planning satisfies the requirements of both bureaucracy and accounting. Long range financial planning therefore emerges as the natural format for the expression of business strategy in most large scale businesses and, through the requirements of the banking system, in small businesses also.

Getting round bureaucracy

The technological revolution and its requirements for flexibility and speed of response have encouraged many attempts to circumvent the bureaucracy and tight accounting control of existing businesses. In recent years there has been a great deal of interest in setting up an organization within the organization, specifically charged with the task of 'entrepreneuring'. The main organization continues to be managed on a more or less bureaucratic basis because this is still believed to be the most efficient mode for stable conditions, the implicit assumption being made that conditions continue to be stable.

Under these dubious assumptions, product innovation is regarded as disruptive of the ongoing activities of the firm. Production systems may have to be altered to accommodate new products; selling skills may have to be augmented to promote new products. Sometimes a firm may be so locked into manufacturing and marketing its existing products that there is little or no expertise for product innovation. The case for separate organizations for innovation rests on three main assumptions:

1. It is essential to separate the function from the ongoing business to ensure it gets sufficient attention.
2. It is necessary to provide the appropriate climate and structure which is radically different from the climate and structure of ongoing business.
3. It is necessary to insulate the new business from the dominant values and norms of the existing business.

As Drucker puts it:

For the existing business to be capable of innovation it has to create a structure that allows people to be entrepreneurial . . . the new has to be organized separately from the old and existing. Whenever we have tried to make an existing unit the carrier of an entrepreneurial project we have failed. (Drucker, 1985, p. 148)

The ways of achieving this separation are various. Some firms set up separate subsidiary companies for the sole purpose of innovation. Others may hive off innovation to a separate division. Others may formally make use of matrix management structures. Less adventurous, but widely practised options that have been identified (Johne, 1985) are summarized below:

Permanent arrangements
- New venture group or department
- Standing new product committee
- New product department
- Marketing department
- Technical department

Temporary arrangements
- New venture team
- Temporary new product committee

- Marketing department led project team
- Technical department led project team
- Inter-departmental project team

Thus firms have sought to achieve freedom from bureaucratic norms in prescribed ways and to precisely limited extents through these various temporary and permanent devices. Kanter's investigation of more than a hundred American firms (Kanter, 1983) showed that such parallel organizations can operate successfully. However, this is far from automatic. The case of matrix organization – where individuals fulfil two roles: a 'normal' line function reporting to the line boss, and a project or team function reporting to the team leader – was considered by Peters and Waterman (1982). Their unequivocal verdict was that matrix organization is confusing.

> The organization gets paralyzed because the structure not only does not make priorities clear, *it automatically dilutes priorities*. In effect, it says to people down the line: 'everything is important; pay equal attention to everything'. The message is paralyzing. (Peters and Waterman, 1982, p. 307)

In essence these are all attempts to get round the existing organization. Some such efforts are even made underground by small independent groups working to circumvent, or even sabotage the formal systems. These underground 'skunkwork' teams routinely bootleg company resources or steal company time to make things happen. By contrast, 'The functional monolith is almost by definition, bureaucratic, not commitment/small team/skunkwork/action oriented.' (Peters and Austin, 1985, pp. 145–6)

Exciting, even noble, though these 'skunkworks' may be, it is surely regrettable when an organization has become so inept that such undercover 'intrapreneuring' has become a corporate necessity.

The strategic agenda

This brief examination of the strategic context of business suggests a number of specific strategic management concerns which are the main subject matter of this book.

Management's main strategic initiatives must be aimed at breaking out of the short termist vicious cycle and participate in the opportunities being presented by the technological revolution. Only proactive, offensive strategic management will make businesses fast and effective innovators.

Getting round bureaucracy is an inadequate response to the problem it poses. Burns and Stalker (1961) had accepted the widely held view, first expressed by Max Weber (1947), that bureaucracy is the most efficient way of operating in stable conditions. Weber defined such conditions as being where all tasks are unambiguous, routine and repetitive, and where all decisions can be made by reference to a rule book. But that world has now largely gone, and where the last vestiges remain, the work involved can be performed by microprocessors, computers, robots and so forth.

The current instability of more or less all technological and product market environments appears to make an organic form of organization universally more desirable, and the particular requirements for innovation underwrite this desirability. In this era of change, there is no longer a valid role for bureaucratic forms of organization, if indeed there ever was. Getting round them is therefore an insufficient answer; they must be made more organic.

Burns and Stalker's bleak and unacceptable conclusion was that mechanistic, bureaucratic organizations are unable to change into organic, innovative ones. Many attempts to make this fundamental change have undoubtedly failed. Nevertheless, in this era of innovation, many firms which have till now enjoyed relatively stable environments for generations are suddenly *having* to change. Such firms have enjoyed all the conditions that are both necessary and sufficient for the evolution of mechanistic structure. Yet they are now innovating in order to survive.

Changing an organization from mechanistic to organic may not be easy, but it is possible. However, few managers apparently desire to change the structure of the *whole* organization, or if they do, few are in a position to do very much about it. Moreover those that do in the main change their organizations by imposing structure and control, for example, Alfred Sloan at General Motors, they are thus acting as agents of the process to bureaucracy.

Deliberate change of the whole organization in the opposite, liberating, direction is much less common and perhaps more difficult, but certainly not impossible. Strategic management must achieve this change if they are to exploit the technological opportunities being presented.

Positive strategic management remains the key to long term business success even though planning appears to have little measurable effect. The need to know what the business is about, what it is trying to achieve and which way it is headed, is a very basic requirement determining the effectiveness of every member's contribution. Every successful entrepreneur has this business self-awareness and every successful business seems to have this clarity of vision, even though it does not arise from a formal planning process.

The aim of this book is to identify different ways of approaching strategy, so that managers can reap all the benefits of a strategic frame of reference without getting bogged down in some antistrategic, bureaucratic planning process. In this way it is intended that managers may adopt ways of strategic thinking which are appropriate to their situation and on which to base decisive strategic action.

CHAPTER ONE
Introduction to strategy

1.1 Introduction

A few years' management experience may well engender a view of strategy, if such a thing exists, that is confused and incomplete. Its theory seems muddled and its practice often a mess. For a lot of people strategy is simply whatever is written down on a fat document entitled 'Corporate Plan' or something similar. For others it may be a plant replacement programme, a long term market projection, or even a five-year cash forecast. Most conceptions of strategy would subsume a long time scale, a broad significance or a recognizable structural change of some kind. More or less all conceptions would include the idea that strategy is, in some way or another, important – if it's unimportant it's not strategic.

However, at the battle of Flodden Field it turned out that a horseshoe nail had strategic significance. For the Titanic the position of icebergs proved to be a trifle strategic. In certain circumstances and at certain times almost anything can be strategic. Moreover, one person's strategy is another person's tactics; what seems tactical today may be strategic tomorrow. Strategy can be about anything: products, processes, customers, citizens, etc., etc.

Moreover, the terminology used in strategy is imprecise and confusing. Strategy clearly means different things to different people in different situations. There appear to be few universal truths about strategy, but the notion remains that it is about the most important of management responsibilities, capable of the most profound impacts on corporate development and success.

The strategy business is further confused by the fact that it has always been prone to fads and fashions. Techniques of strategy formulation and control have their day, are often oversold both by theoreticians and practitioners, and are then discredited. Sometimes, it seems, planning techniques are used symbolically as a way of packaging a decision so that it is depersonalized and the decision-maker avoids the risky business of nailing their colours to the mast and saying 'it was my decision'.

However, techniques are not as clinical as they may appear. Even numbers may be psychologically loaded! Most important accounting calculations, for example, are based on substantial value judgements. Profit itself can be largely a matter of opinion.

Techniques and quantifications can contribute to strategic decision-making, but they are not the foundations of sound strategy. Giving a scalpel to a greengrocer wouldn't make him an effective brain surgeon. It is vital to understand the business (or the brain) and what it does and how it works, before the tools and techniques can be used effectively on its improvement.

In the strategy business, techniques have tended to focus on the process of planning. Planning seems logical and the likelihood of it being effective seems entirely plausible, but conclusive empirical evidence is distinctly absent, despite researchers repeatedly trying to identify evidence of business success arising from strategic planning.

Perhaps strategic planning is a contradiction in terms. Planning is an essentially bureaucratic process – to do it well requires the organization to excel in the administrative virtues. Strategy, on the other hand, is essentially entrepreneurial, even opportunistic – an entrepreneurial business would be unlikely to devote much effort to planning.

In summary, there is confusion over the terminology of strategy; the subject is prone to fads and fashions; it seems to be driven by the techniques of planning; and strategic planning itself appears not to work. Is it possible to develop an effective strategy without the stultifying process inherent in most approaches to strategic planning? To achieve that, at least, is the main thrust of this book. Strategy is not about planning, but about thinking and doing. It is not a technique, but a way of managing the business according to a strategic understanding and perspective.

There is no single best strategic perspective – strategic thinking can be structured in various ways. None provides the answers to every situation, but in most approaches there is something of value. They have relevance in particular circumstances or to do a particular job. If they are understood and the circumstances are recognized, it may be possible to formulate a strategy which is effective and incisive.

These opening two chapters seek to clarify the basic concepts of strategic thinking while subsequent chapters review the various different perspectives that have been most widely adopted in practice.

1.2 The purpose of strategy

Intuitively it might appear obvious that strategy is only worth while inasmuch as it contributes to the profitability of a business. At the same time it is equally obvious that strategy is to do with the longer term and is unlikely to contribute much to the current year's profit and loss. Herein lies a problem. Orthodox financial measures, with an impeccable logic, accord the greatest value to the quickest gain. A pound now is worth more than a pound in a year's time. Yet strategy is very often concerned with a five- or ten-year horizon or even longer.

Strategic considerations frequently result in very different evaluations from those produced using orthodox accounting criteria. For example, when Blue Circle Industries put its sand and gravel business up for sale in 1982, the business had a balance sheet total net asset value of around £9 million. A professional revaluation of the land and minerals in the business produced a surplus over book value of almost £10 million, implying an asset value of £19 million. An alternative valuation was made by estimating the maintainable level of earnings multiplied by the then current sector price : earnings (P : E) ratio plus a 50 per cent premium to reflect the bid situation. This produced a valuation of almost £20 million. A third valuation was based on an estimate of future cash flows from the business discounted at 15 per cent to a present value of £16.8 million. These three different methods of valuing the business showed an average valuation of £18.6 million. The business was actually sold for around £30 million.

The justification for the premium was strategic. The Blue Circle Aggregates business included large deposits of minerals in the West Midlands region. Many of these were not currently being exploited – some appeared unlikely to be used for as long as forty years. The value now of £1 in forty years' time, discounted at 15 per cent, is a mere 0.373 pence. The strategic value of having a secure business for the next twenty years is immense. Strategic value, whether it is invested in minerals under the ground, long term research and development, or a structural or positioning change in the business, is not strictly measurable in orthodox financial language.

Strategy is to do with long term prosperity. It is to ensure that the business is still around in ten or twenty years' time. It is concerned with long term asset growth, not short term profit.

Focusing on short term profitability, to the exclusion of any strategic considerations, leads organizations to make short term opportunistic decisions which whilst financially rational in themselves, may lack any coherence or consistency and thus lead to the business becoming widely diversified and highly complex, and in the end unmanageable.

Thus businesses need strategy in order to ensure that resources are allocated in the most effective way. This is particularly important when it comes to major resource allocation decisions such as large capital expenditures, disposals or divestments and all forms of diversification, including acquisitions.

When such decisions arise, consideration of the strategic issues involved is more or less unavoidable. Such decisions themselves serve to clarify strategic thinking and overtly planned strategy usually focuses on these major resource allocations. However, resources are also allocated by a thousand and one minuscule decisions, mainly taken by default, every day by every organization member. Cumulatively these decisions may be far more important than the occasional one-off large scale investment. The important question is whether all these thousands of mini 'strategic' decisions get taken in a way which reinforces the organization's strategy, or whether they are taken more or less randomly with regard to strategy.

The purpose of strategy is therefore not best conceived in terms of its impact on 'the bottom line'. Instead it can be identified in more operational terms as setting the direction of a business and achieving a concentration and consistency of effort. In this way inconsistent flitting from short term opportunity to short term opportunity is avoided and business expertise and leadership can be built up. Finally, the purpose of strategy must also be to ensure an awareness of when change is necessary and thus the ability to be flexible.

1.2.1 Setting direction

The strategist's role can be seen in terms of the corporate navigator and the strategic plan as the charts by which direction is set and progress measured. This is perhaps the most commonly used analogy. We wouldn't leave London along the Edgware Road in a random attempt to get to Canterbury.

Thus, the familiar idea underlying strategy:

In order to get there we need to know
 where we are now,
 where we want to get to, and,
 how we can get there.
We then need to start moving and, finally,
 we need to monitor progress and, replan as necessary.

The directional idea is far from being the whole story, but it is nevertheless surely crucial. Once the direction is set, it becomes possible to take decisions in a consistent manner with regard to strategy. Only when direction is set is it possible for all members of the business to know which way they are headed, and only then can they shape their own efforts accordingly. With no direction, members may well allocate their efforts and enthusiasm in random and conflicting directions and investments be made similarly.

1.2.2   Concentrating effort

The second main purpose of strategy is to achieve concentration of effort. Drucker and others have continuously highlighted the power of concentration. 'Concentration is the key to real economic results' (Drucker, 1964).

'Managers must concentrate their efforts on the smallest number of products, product lines, services, customers, markets, etc.' (Drucker, 1964, p. 10)

Such statements have continuously highlighted the power of concentration and the need for strategic focus.

Concentration does not just apply to the small number of large scale capital investments, it applies equally to the million and one mini decisions about apparently unimportant jobs and work priorities, that are taken every day by people at every level in an organization. Cumulatively these mini decisions may far outweigh the few big capital items, but in most firms they are taken pragmatically with little regard to strategy and receive little attention unless catastrophe threatens.

Concentration seems to be one of those concepts about which there is a high degree of consensus, but with only few exceptions, businesses continually fail to put it into practice. The 80 : 20 rule and the name of Pareto are monuments to the failure to concentrate. Resources tend to get misallocated and spread thinly across all activities, products, customers, etc. No other principle of effectiveness is violated as constantly as the basic principle of concentration.

The reasons for lack of concentration are various, but one of the most important is the fact that where there is no direction there can be no agreement as to what to concentrate on. Most organizations do not have simply stated, unifying strategic objectives such as 'our business is service'. Few businesses really understand what their particular specialism is. Most formally stated strategies are not simple, but reflect the complex world in which the business operates. As a consequence strategy statements often appear to convey conflicting messages and strategic managements seem reluctant to acknowledge the simplicity of effective strategic concepts.

Peters and Waterman found concentration was a prime requirement of 'excellent' business performance (Peters and Waterman, 1982); operating with a simple structure and a lean staff so that efforts can be concentrated on 'the knitting', i.e. the core business. Concentration remains one of the key determinants of business success, but with no direction there can be no concentration.

1.2.3 Providing consistency

The third main purpose of strategy is to provide consistency. All that has been said of concentration applies to consistency. Consistency is simply concentration over time. Like concentration it applies to the big one-off investment decisions and it applies to the myriad of mini strategic decisions which determine how an individual's time, effort and enthusiasm will be allocated.

Without consistency the organization will continually change direction, flitting like a butterfly from one project to another, developing no critical mass of expertise or even proficiency let alone any form of leadership position.

Direction, concentration and consistency, extremely simple ideas in themselves, are the essence of strategy. However, they are not necessarily simple to implement. They require determination and commitment on the part of management, to overcome the natural 'Pareto'-type processes which result in a thin spread of resources across a wide front. They require that management reject an apparently natural attitude to risk, the risk of putting all your eggs in one basket. They require courage to overrule the almost inevitable resource allocations suggested by the orthodox accounting and administrative processes which otherwise control the business.

1.2.4   Ensuring flexibility

An appropriate direction on which resources are consistently concentrated is the key to long term prosperity. It can lead to the establishment of a leadership position, based on a continually developing body of knowledge, skill and expertise which generates economic results.

The successful behaviour patterns which are regularly reinforced, the successfully established position and effective culture of the organization gradually become more deeply imprinted on organization members and more rigid and automatic. Individual members become expert and make heavy personal and psychological investments in their expertise and the organization as a whole accumulates substantial investment in, and commitment to, the existing and successful technology, customers, competitive positions and ways of doing things. The successful strategy has a built-in obsolescence and will tend gradually to blinker the organization and render it less capable of noticing, let alone creating, change.

As Drucker pointed out, 'any leadership position is transitory and likely to be short-lived [and] what exists is getting old' (Drucker, 1964). If it was true in 1964 it is far more true in the 1990s, and the need to be flexible and responsive to these changes is more vital than ever before.

Strategy needs to set direction, concentrate effort and provide consistency, but at the same time, it needs also to ensure organizational flexibility.

The concepts of direction, concentration and consistency are simple, perhaps too simple, but flexibility is rather more complex. A flexible strategy may be almost a contradiction in terms, yet this is the other main purpose of strategy.

Direction, concentration and consistency do not arise from any natural process but require determined management action for their achievement. And when achieved, they militate against flexibility. Thus the purpose of strategy is rather subtle: a balance between commitment to a successful direction and the ability to change direction when required.

1.3   The inputs to strategy

Strategy is most often thought of as being deliberately *planned*, usually written down with the intention of being implemented. However, as Mintzberg (1987) suggested and as is common experience, strategy can also emerge progressively over time and become a well recognized, though *unplanned*, pattern or recipe, an ultimately agreed way of doing things, that may or may not be written down. It may be a pattern peculiar to a particular organization or it may be a recipe that is widely used throughout an industry.

1.3.1 Planned strategy

The rationale for planning strategy is compelling. Planning seems to provide management with a means of understanding their business. Firms have to adapt continually to their rapidly changing environments. Many firms adapt continually and progressively to change, but many others take the apparently easier route of diversification, in search of greener grass. Diversification has become so frequent for some firms that they completely lose sight of their original aims so that there is no longer any single unifying purpose relevant to the different parts of the business. In this situation, managers feel the need for *the* definitive planning system to reduce the complexity of the business and bring back the feeling of coherence that it now lacks and the sense of direction and focus it so badly needs.

Moreover, in a world that is subject to increasingly rapid change, exploding with new technology and financed by a sort of international game of roulette, it seems vital to have a clear idea about where you are now, where you want to get to and what there is likely to be along the way. And, every so often, it is surely important to know how far you have got and how much further there is to go. Sales, marketing, market share, manufacturing, technology, profit, cash, earnings per share and a score of other factors need to be planned in such an unstable and basically hostile environment.

If there is likely to be a weak point in your company's cash flow profile sometime over the next five years, the sooner you know about it – how deep the shortfall is and how long it will last – the sooner you can draw up plans to cover the situation in some way.

If your company's production technology is likely to become obsolete sometime in the relatively near future, you must know about it and overtly plan whether to raise the finance to replace the plant, to withdraw from the market, to buy into some entirely new business, etc. Drifting planless into such situations is clearly a prescription for disaster.

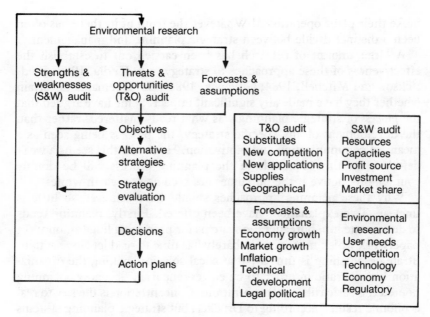

Figure 1.1   *Typical SWOT-based planning system.*

The search for a satisfactory strategic planning system has progressed through several phases. Early approaches tended to be simply extensions of one year financial budgets. Mostly they projected forward five, or in some cases, even ten years.

In the early 1960s strategic planning became fashionable. Planning departments, employing specialist planners who often reported direct to the chief executive, developed sophisticated systems based on exhaustive analyses of the strengths and weaknesses of the firm and the threats and opportunities in its environments (known as the SWOT analysis), and the development of formal plans for every function, timescale and purpose. Figure 1.1 shows a typical flow chart of such a system. All the possible actions that could be taken were identified and, typically, top management were presented with explicit alternatives to choose from.

Over the past ten years or so, the term 'strategic management' has become more widely used. Previously, strategy and management appear to have been theoretically divided. Either, management used the skills and techniques of the planners in order to identify strategy. Or, as frequently appeared to happen, planners used management to make their plans operational! Whatever the truth of it, there has often been a distinct divide between strategic planning and management.

A large amount of research has been carried out to establish the effectiveness of these approaches to strategy (e.g. Kudla, 1980; Fredrickson and Mitchell, 1984; Greenley, 1986), but it remains uncertain whether they have made any significant impact. Some have argued that the *process* of strategic planning was what really mattered, rather than the development of any specific strategy, the process being seen as a means of communication and motivation. However, this seems a weak defence: the time demands of the planning process will be doubly counter-productive if the outcomes are seen as not worth while.

Why these planning approaches should have achieved so little is unclear. Two explanations have been offered. Firstly, planning tends to degenerate into bureaucratic systems for producing huge amounts of paperwork which management barely has time to read let alone action. Strategic planning is thus a paradoxical solution making the organization bureaucratic in order to be entrepreneurial. Secondly, planning flouted the basic rule of concentration. 'Concentration is the key to real economic results' according to Drucker, but strategic planning systems often generated exhaustive lists of actions to exploit strengths, rectify weaknesses, grasp opportunities and avoid threats. The almost inevitable result of such systems was a thin spread of resources across a very wide front, with consequently very little being achieved.

Moreover, the idea of forecasting the future and meeting budget on which many strategic plans were based (Norburn and Schurz, 1984), is clearly no longer an adequate response. If a business is to grasp the opportunities of new technology, rather than being defeated by others who do, its management must not only think strategically, but must also create the future.

1.3.2 Unplanned strategy

Plans represent an overt and deliberate attempt by management to impose a certain strategy. However, as indicated in Figure 1.2, they do not necessarily succeed, i.e. the intended strategy may not, for a variety of reasons, be realized. At the same time, many firms which appear to have very clear strategies, apparent and understood by company members and the outside world alike, may have never made any attempt to develop a formal strategic plan of any kind. In such firms the realized strategy has emerged, rather than being planned.

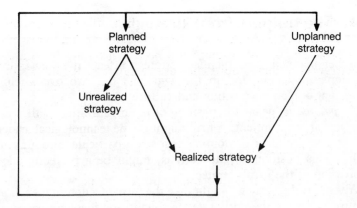

Figure 1.2 *Planned and unplanned strategy.*
Based on Mintzberg, 1987.

Unplanned strategy may take place in any number of ways, often in response to customer needs. This can happen either overtly when, for example, a customer specifically demands some new product attribute which may become the cornerstone of future business, or more typically through a process of prolonged trial and error during which the firm progressively identifies what is most profitable, or what it is best at producing or selling. Such strategy emerges slowly as the successful approaches gradually merge into a pattern of action that becomes the strategy. For example, Henry Ford's 'any colour so long as it's black' became that company's strategy, symbolizing an attitude to standardization and an attitude to the customer, even to the man on the shop floor, which was for a long time the source of Ford's great strength.

Unplanned strategy that is realized in this way is likely, by its very nature, to be robust; those that are not robust are unlikely to be realized. A firm with such a realized strategy will have established a pattern of behaviour, or recipe, which ensures both concentration and consistency, even though it is not formally planned.

Such unplanned strategies are often inferred by outsiders, notably journalists, who seek to identify a pattern in corporate behaviour. Identification of the pattern offers a means of making sense of corporate behaviour and thus predicting future behaviour. The pattern may be real or it may be a rationalized myth, willed into existence by the need to explain 'strategy'. Managers may infer strategies about a competitor. They may go further and impute intentionality where none exists, or is only rationalized subsequently.

1.4   The outputs from strategy

Whether planned or unplanned, strategy affects the way individual decisions are taken, and in the aggregate has two overwhelmingly important outcomes: position and culture.

By *position* is meant the position of the organization with regard to its external environment. A firm might be the technological leader, the lowest cost producer or dominant in some particular product market niche. This position, whatever it is, might be a perfectly adequate expression of the firm's strategy.

Alternatively, strategy might take the form of a dominant *culture*. By culture is meant the corporate personality or ideology as perceived collectively by organization members.

1.4.1   Individual decisions

Individual strategic decisions are usually thought of as the big one-off investments, diversifications, divestments or acquisitions. These are the decisions which, because of their scale or structural impact, are clearly of strategic significance and warrant the most careful scrutiny as such. In most businesses they would be treated as strategic whether or not any system of strategic planning was actually in place. With an effective system that has identified the strategic direction of the business such decisions can be taken in a concentrated and consistent way so that the strategy is progressed.

In addition there are other less obvious decisions that can be guided by a clear strategic direction. For example, when a new product is introduced, special arrangements may be made for the sales force to give it special attention. In some cases additional sales personnel may be recruited dedicated to the new line. During the introductory phase this may be appropriate, but it may not remain so. Unless overt decisions are taken to reallocate the time of the sales force to the whole product range, it is probable that the new product will continue to consume a disproportionate amount of resource, not just in selling, but in marketing, production and even administration. Thus resources will tend to become misallocated unless explicit management decisions are taken to avoid this happening. With a clear direction such decisions can readily be taken, without it they are improbable. The end result of such processes would be for resources of all kinds not to be concentrated on the few products, customers, technologies, etc., which will earn the greatest return.

Whilst influencing individual decisions is not the key end result of effective strategy, its importance should not be overlooked.

1.4.2 Strategy as position

Position refers to how an organization is located in its various environments. The most obvious example is the market niche the organization occupies. A niche is a place that is occupied in order to shelter from and avoid competition. Product market niches may be defined in terms of the existing and potential customers, geographically determined, or fixed by the age, sex and income, or by their life style, etc. Alternatively, product market niches might be defined in terms of product attributes such as price, quality, design, etc.

For some organizations, technology niches, or even financial market niches, may be equally as important as product market niches. For one firm the ability to develop new products quickly may be the vital ingredient that sets it apart from potential competitors; for another, technical sophistication in the product itself may be the unique selling point.

Being the lowest cost producer is also a position strategy, though the niche in this case may be defined as industry-wide. The strategy of Bic, for example, whether planned or unplanned, is clearly imprinted on the public imagination as a producer of high-utility, low-cost disposable plastic products, whether it be ball-point pens, razors or cigarette lighters. Their strategy, in terms of position is perfectly clear. Bic's position would not be properly exploited by competing with names like Cross or Mont Blanc. Bic is a cost leader.

Even though all but one of an industry's intended cost leaders are bound to fail, this strategy still attracts many firms. Cost leadership implies direct confrontation with competitors in the most direct way, and there is mounting evidence that such strategies are frequently counter-productive leading to disinvestment and rising unit costs. By contrast differentiation, or nichemanship, is competition avoidance and appears to offer good prospects of economic performance.

Competition avoidance is the most potent aim of strategy as position. The organization is located in its environment so as to minimize competition. The organization's boundaries with its various environments are so managed as to avoid competition. Thus strategy becomes the match between the organization and its environment.

Positional strategies have long been acknowledged as a prime concern of top management. Throughout the last 100 years, one of the most important strategic functions of large company top management was the setting up of global competition avoidance arrangements, through the auspices of trade associations, international technology exchange organizations, joint ventures, interlocking directorships, long-standing customs and practices as to who competed in which markets, and, where all else failed, by the formation of covert constraints on competition. The globalization of markets over the past twenty years probably results more from the collapse of these international cartels than from the market and technological pressures more widely acknowledged.

Currently the limits on international competition are again being painstakingly rebuilt through international strategic alliances, based on overt agreements covering the exchange of technology and often involving an exchange of shares. Global competition avoidance is again assuming great strategic importance.

1.4.3 Strategy as culture

The other outcome of strategy is culture. Whereas position defines the organization externally, culture defines what the organization is internally. Culture explains how people in the organization perceive the organization, and consequently determines how they behave.

Culture has been defined variously as:

The behaviour patterns and standards which bind a social group together and which are built up over many years and is a unifying philosophy, ethic and spirit. (White, 1984, p. 14)

Behaviour, beliefs, values and learned recipes. (Schein, 1984)

A family of concepts like symbol, language, social drama and ritual. (Pettigrew, 1979)

The way we do things around here. (Bower, 1966)

Potentially culture offers a way of combining concentration and consistency with the flexibility essential to effective strategy. At the same time, it can contribute to the sense of direction and climate of success, far beyond what could be achieved through more orthodox management approaches. The meaning that these phrases convey is essentially subjective. To one manager they may seem to get to the core of what a business is all about. To another, they may seem to be meaningless. The concept of culture seems still to be riddled with such ambiguities.

Organizational culture is not simply homogeneous, but the sum of many subcultures, each of which contributes its own nuances of meaning and its own rituals and images. Those working on the shop floor clearly belong to a different subculture from the company's directors; the accountants belong to a different subculture from the marketers; managers in the United Kingdom belong to a different subculture from their counterparts in overseas subsidiaries. Thus although organizational culture is often held to be a powerful cohesive force giving members a feeling of belonging and coherence, this is not necessarily the case. With no managerial control, different subcultures are likely to conflict and compete and the inevitable result will be a loss of organizational cohesion. Management has to ensure that the desired cultural norms predominant over all others.

Peters and Waterman recounted how

> stories, myths and legends appear to be very important, because they convey the organization's shared values, or culture. Without exception, the *dominance* and *coherence* of culture proved to be an essential quality of the excellent companies. (Peters and Waterman, 1982, p. 75)

The implication is that culture can in some way be controlled to make management's desired culture both coherent in itself and dominant over other subcultures.

In management literature there are many stories, even legends or myths about the great and good, or not so good, originators of such organizations as IBM, Hewlett Packard, NCR, ITT, McDonald's etc. These businesses all share 'strong', deliberately established and maintained, coherent, dominant 'cultures'. They have gained the active participation of all their members, the consistent concentration of effort on exploiting their organization's distinctive position.

The distinctive feature of strategy as culture is that it is shared by organization members. The shared assumptions about the organization and the way to behave in the organization represent a powerful means of getting strategy implemented via the 'hearts and minds' of all organization members.

1.5 Interrelating the inputs and outputs of strategy

The inputs and outputs of strategy are indicated in Figure 1.3.

As already noted the inputs, i.e. planned and unplanned strategy, are independent of each other. Plans may go unrealized, patterns not

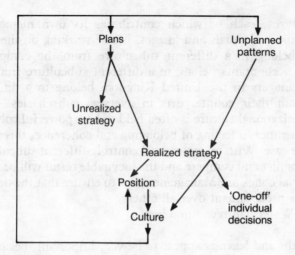

Figure 1.3 *The inputs and outputs of strategy.*
Based on Mintzberg, 1987.

be preconceived. But for a strategy to be successfully realized, planned and unplanned strategies need to be compatible with each other, if not directly complementary. Similarly, the outputs of realized strategy may comprise simply a few operational commitments or individual decisions, but may more importantly also include the definition of various positions and cultures as suggested in the preface figure and outlined in later chapters. But, for the most potent strategy, the outputs must all be consistent.

Plans and patterns can be altered but positions and cultures are much less easy to change. Plans and patterns must therefore be made compatible with position and culture. Mintzberg (1987) examples the McDonald's EggMcMuffin as a strategically consistent new product introduction, and contrasts this nicely with a delightful inconsistency: the McDuckling à l'Orange by candlelight!

Strategic planning will not work if it is inconsistent with the unplanned patterns and recipes which emerge over time. Nor will it work if the plans are inconsistent with the position and culture of the organization. All four aspects of strategy are needed and they need to be made compatible with each other.

1.6 The strategic context

The theory of management has come a long way since the days of

F. W. Taylor and the certainties of scientific management. Nothing is certain any more. There is no one best way of doing anything.

Yet strategy, more than most areas of management, has its panaceas, tools and techniques, patent medicines of more or less dubious origin. Moreover, none appears to have any strong connection with corporate success (e.g. Prescott *et al.* 1986 and Miller, 1988). As Miller put it, 'strategies must be matched with complementary environments and structures to promote success' (Miller, 1988, p. 280).

To do this requires the ability to think strategically, not simply to apply the currently fashionable tool or technique of strategic planning. Thinking strategically requires an awareness of alternative strategy frameworks, alternative strategic purposes and the ability to recognize critically different environments. In addition it requires the ability to diagnose an organization in terms of various critical characteristics and to be able to shape those characteristics so that the organization is best fitted to its environment in order to achieve its strategic purpose.

In the prologue to this text three particular features of the current environment were highlighted:

1. We are at the exciting stage of the technological revolution which is changing *every* industry and *every* business and making long term investment in new technology imperative.
2. The world of finance is becoming ever more efficient and consequently demanding ever shorter term returns and so orthodox financial arrangements are becoming progressively more hostile to investing long term.
3. We are in an increasingly more competitive world, firstly because competition comes from all over the globe and, secondly, new technology permits large scale production to be sufficiently flexible to attack relatively small sheltered markets.

There may be other environmental characteristics which will gain similar importance. For example, some might argue that green issues are already paramount both in terms of the threats to existing technologies and business activities and, more importantly, in terms of the opportunities they present for the generation of new business.

Clearly, these various factors impact differently on different businesses, so there is no one best way of approaching strategy. Management must diagnose its own situation and circumstances and work out its own prescription.

These may seem merely to be business truisms, but nevertheless they are different from the fundamentals of twenty years ago. Then the main concerns were with standardization not change, and market share not competition. Twenty years from now the dominant issues will no doubt be different again.

1.7 Summary

This chapter has briefly reviewed some ideas about strategy which are beginning to gain consensus among practitioners and theoreticians.
Businesses need strategy in order to:

(a) set direction;
(b) concentrate effort;
(c) achieve consistency; and
(d) ensure flexibility.

Strategy may be planned or unplanned.
Some strategies emerge progressively as patterns of behaviour, or recipes, which appear to produce satisfactory results.
Moreover not all planned strategies are realized in practice.
Whether planned or unplanned, strategy that is realized may take the form of:

(a) specific decisions,
(b) a business position, or
(c) an organizational culture.

Strategies must be matched to their complementary environments if they are to be successful.
The current business environment is characterized by the following three features:

(a) rapidly changing technology which is changing *every* industry and *every* business;
(b) rapidly increasing competition which will eventually envelop *every* market niche, no matter how sheltered;
(c) increasingly efficient financial markets requiring ever shorter term returns.

DISCUSSION CASE: VALDERVERNIK FABRICS LTD

Valdervernik Fabrics was a medium-sized warp knitting company producing fabrics from man-made yarn for household and apparel markets. They grew large during the 1960s producing knitted nylon fabric for men's shirts and bed-linen. These products had provided a very large volume of business. At the peak more than 60 per cent of men's shirts were made of knitted nylon fabric. However, both products had quite suddenly lost consumer acceptance and in a matter of a few months were eliminated from the market. The impact on Valdervernik had been profound. They had survived only by closing two of their five factories and making 60 per cent of their employees redundant. They then sought another mass market application of knitted fabric, but none emerged.

Valdervernik's main products were now lining materials for clothing and curtains. These were high volume, low cost fabrics made on fast, simple machines which ran more or less continuously producing the same standard product. Whilst the quality standard of fabric was important the main selling point was price.

At the other end of the market, warp knitters were beginning to produce high quality lace which, for all but the most elaborate designs, was indistinguishable, to all but the most knowledgeable eye, from traditional twist lace, and at a fraction of the cost. Having failed to discover a new mass market to replace sheeting and shirting, Valdervernik considered whether to diversify into this high price, high quality, high margin knitted lace market.

Discussion points
- What would be Valdervernik's main strategic problem with this diversification?
- From the information provided what appears to be Valdervernik's competitive specialism?
- How relevant is that to the proposed new product?

At first Valdervernik sought to achieve the diversification through the acquisition of an existing lace warp knitter.

Discussion points
- Would Valdervernik do better to run the lace business separately or as an integral part with their existing business?
- What would be the main problems of integrating the two businesses?

In the event they were unable to identify an acquisition candidate that was both available and had the desired high quality reputation, so they decided to set up the new business from scratch. They considered two options: operating out of one of their existing factories, or starting from a green field site.

Discussion point
- What are the main pros and cons of these two options?

They decided to operate from an existing plant, but as far as possible to separate the two businesses. The lace knitting business was pre-dominantly made up of relatively short runs, the product was high priced and high quality and the patterns were extremely intricate, some dating back to the mid-Victorian era, others being created specially for an individual customer.

On traditional equipment, patterns were developed using manually produced artwork and systems for converting artwork to machine patterning instructions. These were then converted into patterning chains which controlled the way the fabric was knitted. For the more elaborate patterns these chains could weigh several tons and take up to three weeks to build, during which time the machine would be unable to produce. This amount of down-time was one of the main elements of cost and meant that the producer had to run the machine on any pattern for a lengthy run, whereas the customer probably only wanted a small amount of this very expensive lace. Consequently the producer also became a substantial stockist of finished product.

Using new technology it was possible to develop patterns at a computer terminal. Old patterns could very often be produced automatically by 'scanning' items of old lace. The patterning instructions could then be transferred to the machine by a computer tape rather than a pattern chain in a matter of seconds rather than weeks. The new machines cost around £250,000, around ten times the cost of Valdernervik's existing knitting machines.

Valdernervik invested in four of the new electronically controlled machines. This immediately made them among the three best-equipped lace manufacturers in an industry which totalled around forty.

Discussion points
- What was Valdervernik's competitive specialism in lace manufacture?
- Would this accord with the strategic position of their traditional business?

Valdervernik found that the new lace knitting machines provided some interesting possibilities. They were able to develop patterns on computers and dump the patterning instructions direct to the machine in a matter of seconds. Additionally they also had a system of production control which monitored each electronically controlled machine on a continuous basis and provided continuous status reports. This system also allowed making instructions to be passed to the machine from the production control office. In addition, to Valdervernik's surprise, they found that any customer with an IBM compatible PC and a modem could ring up a machine direct and give it making instructions including full patterning details. This appeared to be the ideal from the point of view of flexibility and responsiveness to customer requirements. In addition it seemed to offer the potential of running the new machines on three-shift continental working with only a very small skeleton staff to oversee night operations.

Discussion points

- You are Valdervernik's Production Director. Why do you feel so strongly against offering customers the extra facility of being able to ring up the machine and instruct it what to make?
- Can you see any possible application of this idea to the traditional Valdervernik business?
- From the point of view of the customer is there any advantage to the possible new arrangements?
- Are there any other advantages that might flow from such arrangements in the longer term?
- What are the disadvantages of such an arrangement?
- Are there any implications in such systems for the globalization of markets?

Although Valdervernik did not make this facility available to customers, they did provide a computerized access to the production control system so that order information could be logged and progress checked continuously. The new business was very successful and in due course became the main profit earner.

Discussion points

- Would the new lace business be likely to have had any impact on the traditional Valdervernik business in terms of marketing? Production? People?
- If so, what?

CHAPTER TWO
Strategies and objectives

2.1 Introduction

The terminology of strategy causes great confusion. 'Corporate', 'long range' and 'business' are all terms which are applied to strategy or strategic planning, sometimes distinctively and sometimes interchangeably. In addition some terms have different meanings for different functional specialists. For example, what some marketeers regard as marketing strategy is regarded by others as business strategy. What is strategy to one person is merely tactics to another. The nuances of different meanings are often ignored or left unclear. This is so not simply in every day discussion, but also in the strategy literature.

However, some consensus is starting to emerge and be placed on record by some of the leading proponents (e.g. Mintzberg, 1987; Porter, 1987) and the distinctive meanings of the various terms identified below are intended to reflect this.

2.2 Corporate strategy

Corporate strategy refers to the strategy of the company as a whole, whether it is a multibusiness, multinational conglomerate, or a single site, single product business. It is concerned with the development of the company as a whole in terms such as total profits, asset growth, price : earnings performance, earnings per share growth, return on equity and so forth.

Corporate strategy is not simply the summation of the strategies of the different businesses in the company – it is different in kind from business strategy. Nor is corporate strategy concerned directly with the details of any particular business strategy. However, it is concerned with maintaining a balanced portfolio of businesses, balanced in terms of such concepts as growth, cash flow and profit.

The decisions of corporate strategy are therefore mainly concerned with:

(a) the acquisition of individual businesses;
(b) levels of new investment in those businesses and the returns obtained,
(c) the liquidation and/or disposal of individual businesses, and
(d) the maintenance of a balanced portfolio of businesses.

The corporate strategist adopts the perspective of the shareholder, or potential shareholder. Responsibilities for corporate strategy are more like those of unit trust management than they are those of business management.

If a subsidiary business does not perform, the corporate strategist has a relatively limited array of options which should be considered:

● The top management of the business can be changed.
● New investment can be increased or curtailed.
● The business can be sold or closed down.
● The results of the business can be monitored more closely.

However, corporate management should not normally be concerned to become involved in, or take over, the management of the subsidiary business. The way the subsidiary business operates or serves its customers is the specific responsibility of the subsidiary business management.

In practice, however, it often happens as a result of simple hierarchical pecking orders, that the corporate strategist has the power to interfere in the day-to-day running of subsidiary businesses and the temptation for such interference is often not resisted. It is often done by simply directing how the subsidiary business should be run, or by dictating the direction of future capital investments. Very often it is achieved through the simple means of requiring over-demanding cash and profit targets to be met by the subsidiary business. This necessarily prevents the subsidiary business management taking a truly strategic view of their business, having instead to concentrate on short term targets. Whether overt and deliberate or implicit and unintended the result of corporate management dictating subsidiary business strategy is to undercut and constrain the effectiveness of subsidiary business management.

2.3 Business strategy

Business strategy is concerned with how to make an individual business survive and grow and be profitable in the long term.

The main considerations are as follows:

(a) the creation of customers;
(b) the identification of appropriate market niches where no competition exists;
(c) the identification of customer needs and how best they can be satisfied;
(d) the application of technology and its future development or substitution;
(e) the understanding of competitors and how direct competition may be avoided;
(f) the motivation of people to put their efforts and enthusiasm behind the strategic aims of the business.

These are matters of considerable complexity and detail. If they were to be fully managed by the corporate centre of a company of any significant size, they would require a huge and costly headquarters staff which in the end would be self-defeating. On the other hand such things are meat and drink to the subsidiary business management, in constant contact with their customers, expert in their technology and intimately knowledgeable about their competitors.

This separation of corporate and business strategies is relatively simple as stated above, but the dichotomy raises a fundamental question. Which is the more important in running a company: corporate strategy, or the multiple business strategies of its component parts?

This question gets to the core of an individual's business philosophy. For people such as Sir James Goldsmith, Jim Slater and to a rather lesser extent, Lord Hanson, for example, corporate strategy is all important. Their companies are, or were, deliberately and overtly in the business of buying and selling assets, being primarily concerned with matters of wealth ownership. The individual businesses matter only as contributors to the corporate balance sheet. Each plays a transient role in the ever changing portfolio of businesses making up the corporate whole, but their individual business strategies are largely irrelevant. The existence of such financially-oriented companies arises mainly because of the increasing failure of financial markets to provide secure long term finance for industry. Proactive corporate strategy of this kind is, however, not the present concern. This book is concerned with wealth creation rather than ownership.

For wealth-creating companies, the individual businesses matter much more and such companies make up the vast majority in the United Kingdom. For them corporate prosperity is the summation of the prosperity of the individual businesses and it is individual businesses that matter most. Such corporate managements mostly try to give subsidiary businesses maximum autonomy, support and long term commitment in order to assist the wealth creation process.

2.4 Marketing strategy

A basic tenet of marketing theory is that marketing management is concerned with the controllable variables of product, price, promotion and distribution, i.e. the marketing mix. Consequently, marketing strategy should logically be concerned with the long term development of these four very important issues. If this is so, then marketing strategy appears to be much the same as business strategy outlined above.

However, in practice, most businesses operate along rather different lines. It is almost universally the general manager of a business who has the final responsibility for profit, and one of the key determinants of profit is product price. Thus, although marketing management may recommend price levels and changes, it is usually general management that holds price responsibility and takes the final decision. Moreover, there are usually considerable constraints over marketing management's discretion with regard to product decisions. They may recommend product changes or product developments, but again it is most often general management who has the ultimate decision responsibility.

Thus there seems to be a substantial divide between the theory and practice of marketing. Theoretical literature seems to suggest that marketing management has more or less total responsibility at the business level. In practice marketing strategy is very much concerned with promotion and distribution strategies and with the initiation and introduction of new products. Thus defined, marketing strategy is a subset of business strategy, though the most important subset.

The problem arises because marketing can be a set of techniques, a function or department or a philosophy, and it is often not clear which definition is being used. The marketing strategy which is the direct responsibility of the marketing function is much more limited than the strategy arising from the marketing philosophy. In a marketing-oriented business this latter will be essentially the same as the business strategy already outlined.

2.5 Operations strategy

Operations strategy might at first seem to be almost a contradiction in terms – an issue can be operational or strategic. However, direction, concentration and consistency are likely to be achieved through the implementation of operations, be they the production of a product or delivery of a service. Moreover, during this period of rapidly developing technology, operations and the maintenance of their competitive edge, may be the most costly and organizationally traumatic of all aspects of strategy.

Technological developments have over the past ten years been so fundamental that they have allowed competitive structures which have been set rigid for decades suddenly to be dissolved. They have eliminated huge tranches of unskilled labour and their associated costs, and they have permitted the economic production of entirely new products and services specifically designed to satisfy specialized customer needs.

While these possibilities are available, operations strategy is a vital source of competitive strength. A survey of manufacturing strategy in Europe, America and the Far East suggests further, that the next global competitive battle is likely to be over the issue of manufacturing strategy (Meyer *et al.*, 1989). Too many European and American businesses still appear to be focusing their operations efforts on cost reduction programmes and the improvement of quality, but the Japanese are already concentrating on achieving cost efficiency based on flexible manufacturing as opposed to cost efficiency based on standardization and long production runs. In this way it appears the Japanese are likely to be better equipped to handle the ever shorter product life cycles and more volatile product demand that seem inevitable.

Operations strategy is concerned with service decisions just as much as production and the investment in new technology; systems and structures to improve the level of efficiency of customer service will become relatively more important in the next decade.

Thus operations strategy, like a tightly defined marketing strategy, is a subset of business strategy identifying a set of management actions required to achieve the overall business strategy.

2.6 The integration of strategy

All these different aspects of strategy are separate. Corporate strategy relates to the company's interface with the providers of its capital, while business strategy and its two main substrategies in marketing and operations are concerned with what makes the business prosper in relation to its customers, competitors and technologies.

Though separate, if strategy as a whole is to be effective, the separate elements must be consistent with each other and reinforce each other, rather than incompatible or even competitive. If corporate strategy and business strategy conflict, as they not infrequently do, it often tends to be the business which is prevented from achieving its potential as a result of corporate constraints. This problem is almost inevitable in a large multibusiness company. One way of achieving a more satisfactory balance is through an explicit system of objectives.

2.7 Business objectives

The debate about objectives has continued right through the history of management literature, and before that the literature of classical economics. If the objectives of a business are known, the balance between corporate and business criteria may be established. Objectives play a key role in the strategic management of any business. However, no really coherent theory of objectives has ever achieved any consensus.

Classical economics was based on the mathematically convenient concept of profit maximization. The entrepreneur was held to equate marginal revenue with marginal cost, at which point the level of profit would be maximized. The beauty of this was its mathematical simplicity – for economists, basic calculus solves the problem of management. However, the theory only works if it is accepted that the only factors of importance are the price of the product and the volume produced and sold; that the entrepreneur's costs are identical to everyone else's; that the product is also identical; and that everyone else's volume, price and cost are known, and all the other underpinnings of perfect competition. The purpose of this completely unreal theory remains obscure to both the management theorist and practitioner.

Slightly more realistic ideas were developed, such as sales revenue maximization (Baumol, 1959), management utility maximization (Williamson, 1973) and so on. At each stage *en route* to reality the economists lost something in mathematical tractability, until they ended up with the behavioural model of Cyert and March (1963) which indicated that major decisions tended to be made by compromise between coalitions of managers aiming to satisfy at least the minimum requirements of all interested parties. Whilst seeking to be realistic this behavioural model defied any attempt to make it mathematically, or practically usable.

Accountancy has had a major impact on both the theory and practice relating to business objectives. Accounting considerations lead to multiple financial objectives which may have an internal focus such as return on assets, asset turnover, margins on sales, etc., or an external focus such as share performance targets (price : earnings ratios, dividend yields, etc.). Increasingly these objectives are being adopted by economists and financial models of the firm are becoming part of economic orthodoxy.

In practice, objectives have remained more diffuse. Since the days of Henri Fayol, whose main working experience was in the last century, multiple objectives have been the common ground. More than thirty years ago Drucker (1955) cited the necessity for objectives in the following eight areas:

- Market standing
- Innovation
- Productivity
- Physical and financial resources
- Profitability
- Manager performance and development
- Worker performance and attitude
- Public responsibility

This practical approach to multiple objectives presents a complex picture where often objectives will be in opposition to each other. Maximizing one would inevitably mean failure with another. A balance has to be achieved, but there is no indication as to how this should best be done. Drucker's concept was an unstructured checklist. Management's job was to achieve the balance between conflicting objectives, but they were given no guidance as to how this should be done.

The systems approach (Emery and Trist, 1965) presented the firm as a complicated open system having a constantly changing relationship with its various environments. These are the firm's product markets, its suppliers, technological, financial and labour environments, government and society. Management's job was to control the boundary conditions of the firm, i.e. its relationship with these various environments.

The idea of boundary management and of constantly changing relationships cast some new light on the subject. The idea of managing the firm's relationship with, for example, its financial environment, implies managing the firm's share price. This would not simply be a matter of maximizing the shareholders' wealth, but managing the share so that its performance was sufficient to permit adequate performance in other boundary areas. Increasing the shareholders' wealth by more than is necessary, would be just as wasteful as over-designing a product (i.e. giving customers something they neither want nor are prepared to pay for). The idea of balancing the firm's performance in its various, and often competing environments, still implies management's role is basically a balancing act.

Unstructured multiple objectives, which require trading off against each other, only serve to confuse and paralyse. What is required is a system of objectives which can be used to focus effort and guide the firm towards a unified strategic approach.

2.8   The hierarchy of objectives

Translating boundary ideas into a set of objectives might produce targets in each of Drucker's eight objective areas. The systems approach implies that the firm ought to set financial objectives, for instance, which would ensure the share price performed well enough to safeguard the firm's continued independence, together with its ability to raise such finance as would be required to perform on other objectives, such as market standing and innovation. Thus the corporate objectives need to be achieved in order that other objectives could be aimed for.

This seems to imply a hierarchical ordering of objectives, analogous to Maslow's now hackneyed work on intrinsic human needs (1943).

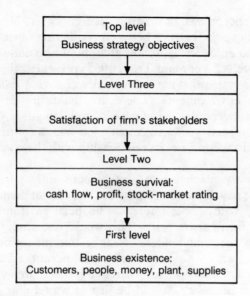

Figure 2.1 *The hierarchy of business objectives.*

Maslow suggested a hierarchy of needs going from the lowest level of physiological needs (food, sex, sleep, etc.) through safety needs, love needs, eteem needs, up to the highest level, what he called the need for self-actualization. As each need level in the hierarchy was satisfied so the next level up become potent. Thus if physiological needs were satisfied, the need for safety became dominant, and if at any time a lower level need ceased to be satisfied then that lower level need would again become prepotent.

Business objectives seem to follow a similar pattern as shown in Figure 2.1

At the lowest level the business needs basic resources of customers, people, money, machines and raw materials. Without these it could not exist. Above these, analogous to Maslow's safety needs, are the needs for solvency and to avoid being taken over. Above these are the needs to satisfy the stakeholders in the firm, including its customers, employees, suppliers and including a responsibility to satisfy the *minimum* requirements of society at large. The top level need, analogous to self-actualization, has been labelled simply 'business strategy objectives'. These are to do with the firm doing what it is uniquely good at, exploiting its distinctive competence. An operational definition of the business strategy objectives will be developed later.

As with Maslow's system, when a low level need has been satisfied the business moves up to the next level. When liquidity and profitability are sufficient to provide safety, and when this reality is being reflected in the price level of the company's shares, then the business is able to turn its attention to satisfying its own members, for example, through opportunities for self-development through both training and promotion, satisfactory working conditions, equitable payment and so on. Of course this by no means exhausts the ways in which a firm can satisfy the needs and aspirations of its employees. As is indicated later, many of the possibilities related to this overall objective, cost nothing and do not necessarily mean trading off other objectives. However, where management is involved in making trade-off decisions, the priority accorded to the satisfaction of its internal stakeholders is at Level Three. That is, it is not in itself the object of the business, but it represents a higher level of aspiration than mere survival.

The idea of social responsibility has received considerable attention in recent years. Being at an intermediate level in the hierarchy it is clearly not the main purpose of the business to maximize the amount of social good it does. Nevertheless, a complete disregard for social responsibility is not a valid strategy. At Level Three the business should aim to satisfy the minimum needs of society, wherever there is a direct contact, and having done sufficient to satisfy those needs, it should then address itself to the higher level objective.

If at any time the business is threatened by shortage of cash, or any basic resource, this immediately becomes prepotent and dominates the whole business activity. When the threat has been overcome and survival is no longer a problem, then the business can resume aiming to satisfy the higher level need.

Thus, all objectives have their place in the hierarchy, and the way they are defined will depend on what they are. Financial objectives will be expressed quantitatively and they will be set at a level where their satisfaction ensures the independent survival of the business. The whole hierarchy is ever present, though the levels which are operational at any one time will change.

None of the objectives that have been discussed are maximization objectives. They only require some minimum level of achievement in order that the business may then seek to satisfy the next higher level in the hierarchy. Thus the business is focused on achieving its top level, business strategy objectives, which are the only maximization objectives. Anything more than satisfaction of needs at lower levels merely serves to inhibit the firm in its attempts to satisfy the business strategy objectives. From time to time the lower level needs become prepotent and then the firm has to shift its attention, for example, away from the long term strategy on to short term survival. This is a common enough experience when managements may find it prudent to ration capital, postpone long term developments, slash R&D expenditure and so on. In an accounting culture, such actions can take on an almost heroic aspect, almost as though the aim of the business is to cut costs and operate efficiently. In reality these are the means to the end. Sometimes they become dominant, but they should be recognized as an interruption in the pursuit of the strategic goal.

The hierarchical view of objectives provides a systematic way in which a firm may balance the conflicting priorities of various opposing interests. In particular, it helps management to balance the long term interests of the business itself against the short term interests of the firm's financial environment.

2.9   The business unit

The hierarchical system of objectives has direct implications for the way in which a firm should be structured.

The distinction has already been made between the 'business' and the 'firm' or 'company' without any precise definitions having been made. The term 'business' refers to the individual unit which produces and/or sells a product or service to known customers. It is often referred to as the 'strategic business unit', though a perhaps more appropriate term might be 'entrepreneurial unit'. The company is the legal entity which may comprise one or more businesses.

Where the business units are independent companies, the system of objectives can clearly be applied directly. Top management have control of all business decisions and define their objectives autonomously. However, most such units are not actually independent companies, but wholly-owned parts of larger legal/financial entities. For these businesses there are additional difficulties. Who defines the objectives, the business unit or the parent company? Over what decisions does the business unit management have control and what is the role of the corporate headquarters?

It is now widely seen as desirable to take decisions as near to the front-line as possible. Local management are inevitably more in touch with the pertinent realities, so better decisions get taken locally. Decisions can also get taken faster the closer they are to the action.

Moreover the devolution of responsibility and authority has a powerful motivational effect.

However, the 'simple form and lean staff' which are the aims of most large companies today, has mainly served to preserve the bureaucratic form. Typically the lean staff at headquarters impose control on subsidiary, or divisional businesses, firstly by retaining responsibility for strategy and, secondly, through a small number of financial performance measures, usually set at levels which include some 'stretch'. The practical result of this is that the divisional level business operates as the most rigid form of machine bureaucracy (Mintzberg, 1981). There are immense pressures on divisional managers to conform to the performance rules, customs and practice and culture of the parent organization. Their salaries, careers and pensions depend on conformity. The attempt to give divisions the benefits of autonomy together with the muscle of financial security has in the main failed, because the autonomy is not compatible with control and control is extremely difficult to devolve.

The hierarchical system of objectives suggests a rather different approach to organization. It implies that the parent company might specify what *minimum* levels of performance it requires the entrepreneurial unit to achieve on all but the business strategy objectives. The financial requirements should be set at the minimum level required to ensure survival. If they are set higher than this minimum they will inhibit the business unit concentrating on its business strategy, i.e. they will force the business management to take short term decisions – a common enough complaint throughout industry.

Moreover, the hierarchy also confirms what has already been suggested, that the parent should take no part in identifying the business unit's strategy. This is a knowledge-intensive activity and the parent, with its multiplicity of subsidiary businesses, would not be, or should not be, sufficiently knowledgeable in this area. The only way it could achieve this degree of detailed understanding is by setting up large scale staff functions at head office, thereby becoming a top heavy bureaucracy.

The hierarchy of objectives implies the parent company would provide central finance and treasury services, acting rather like a preferred banker. In addition, corporate headquarters might also require entrepreneurial units to satisfy *minimum* requirements of internal and external stakeholders, in accordance with a corporate policy. Otherwise the business unit would be given maximum autonomy, and in particular total strategic autonomy.

This concept of the relationship between the unit and its parent is not widely practised. In most multibusiness companies the executive at corporate headquarters controls strategy while the business unit managers, being expert in their field, control the short and medium term business operations.

Few parent companies appear to be prepared to delegate authority for strategy to the subsidiary business. Few parents set the business unit financial objectives which are substantially below the level it can clearly achieve. Very few parent companies delegate responsibility for surplus cash to subsidiary business units. These are real problems. A high degree of suspicion still surrounds the simple idea of devolution. The parent company that would do these various things is the company that has retained a business unit management it respects and trusts.

The business unit is the wealth producer on which the rest of the company depends. The problems of balancing a portfolio of business units are of secondary importance compared to the prime business function of wealth creation. Thus though business unit management may report to corporate management and though business strategy is essentially a subset of corporate strategy, it is important to recognize that it is the business unit that matters. Getting business strategy right is the key to long term financial results.

2.10 Summary

This chapter has sought to clarify some distinctions between various levels of strategy and objectives.

Corporate strategy is essentially concerned with the relationship between the company, which is the legal/financial entity usually comprising a multibusiness organization and its shareholders. It is concerned with such measures as earnings per share, dividend yields, etc.

Business strategy is essentially concerned with the relationships between the particular business unit and its customers, its technology suppliers and its competitors.

Marketing strategy is essentially concerned with the long term control of the marketing mix, i.e. product, price, promotion and distribution.

Operations strategy is essentially concerned with the application of technology to the business.

To be effective each level of strategy must be compatible with all others and ideally the nature of that compatibility should be specified. This balance can be achieved by adopting a hierarchy approach to business objectives.

The lowest level objective is to achieve the basic requirements for the business to exist – customers, suppliers, people, plant, etc.

The second level is for the business to survive – liquidity, stockmarket performance, etc.

The third level is for the business to satisfy other stakeholders – employees, society.

The fourth level is concerned with the business strategy objective and is about exploiting the firm's distinctive competence whatever it happens to be.

The business is driven by its business strategy, but has first of all to satisfy the lower level objectives, which are all set at *minimum* levels. Should any lower level objective cease to be satisfied at any time, it immediately becomes dominant.

Adoption of the hierarchy of objectives implies certain organizational requirements for the multibusiness firm if the parent company wishes to avoid its subsidiary companies adopting the worst aspects of bureaucracy. Firstly, the parent company must only impose *minimum* financial targets on subsidiary businesses. Secondly, the parent company must allow the subsidiary business to define and follow its own business strategy.

The hierarchical system of objectives has direct implications for organizational structure. It suggests that a multibusiness unit would be managed most effectively by delegating all authority and responsibility to business unit management and retaining only treasury and ultimate hire and fire decisions at corporate headquarters.

DISCUSSION CASE: COOPER SOFT DRINKS LTD

Cooper, a Midlands-based soft drinks business, was until recently under family ownership, but is now a separate division of a large financially-oriented conglomerate. Cooper has a strong market position in the Midlands region, being much the largest independent with sales through general retail outlets and supermarkets, public houses and off-licences. They sell under the Cooper brand and under various own labels, but they do not have any arrangements with major national or international brands such as Pepsi-Cola. They have over the past few years expanded by achieving national distribution through several supermarket chains.

Each April Cooper are required to submit a 'Five-Year Business Plan'. This document extends to around 120 pages and includes numerous five-year financial projections. These are intended to indicate the extent to which Cooper contributes to the parent company's stated objectives of:

- 15 per cent return on capital employed, and,
- 10 per cent growth per annum in earnings per share.

In addition Cooper has exacting annual cash generation targets imposed by the parent company.

Cooper express their own business objectives in what is described as a 'mission statement'. These include the following:

1. Being the lowest cost producer in the region.
2. Achieving national coverage through all main outlets.
3. Providing 'excellent' customer service in terms of:
   (a) delivery
   (b) quality
   (c) manufacturing flexibility.

In the past year Cooper opened the world's most advanced automated soft drink bottling plant which permits it to respond flexibly to changes in demand. In the press release announcing the opening of this new facility the Chairman said,

> In this industry, flexibility means tripling production because of a heat wave. It means a special promotion for a single retail store wanting, say, pink bottles with a special label. It means producing ten lines of 1,000 bottles as cheaply and quickly as one line of 10,000 bottles. It means delivering the same high Cooper quality to the customer no matter what the product.

Discussion points

You are a senior executive at Cooper Soft Drinks Ltd and are currently involved in preparing the next 'business plan'. As part of this process you have to consider the following questions:

- What business are we in? Soft drinks? Bottling? Distribution? Transport?
- What information, if any, would be required to answer this question?
- On the information provided, how would you answer the question?

- Does it matter what business Cooper is in?
- What would be the implications of your answer for Cooper's business strategy?
- Given that the UK soft drinks market is only low growth, how can Cooper achieve continuous growth after obtaining national coverage with the existing product range through the existing types of outlet?

Over the years Cooper have tried many times to introduce distinctive new products in an attempt to replicate the Coca Cola story. In this quest they have recently unearthed the recipe for a soft drink which had been highly successful in the Midlands region between the wars but had been discontinued when its producer was taken over and closed down in 1953. This product was previously called Spa Tona Iron Brew. It contained a reduced amount of sugar, was rich in iron and had a distinctive 'dry' flavour. It had been popular both as a normal soft drink and as a component of beer shandy. Cooper had seen old advertisements for the product emphasizing its health-giving properties. A test market had been encouraging in terms of consumer acceptance of the product, particularly amongst adults.

Cooper propose to produce Spa Tona and promote it as a health product, distributed nationally through chemists and health food specialists, and priced with a substantial premium. Once established in this market niche, Cooper envisaged exploiting its premium image by wider promotion through all the main existing outlets.

Discussion points
You are a director of Cooper's parent company and have been shown a dossier on the proposed new product 'Spa Tona'. The proposal includes an interesting but costly promotion campaign including a level of advertising many times higher than any previous product.

- What are your immediate views for the prospects of success for the new product?
- What information would you require Cooper to provide before you could reach any decision about the validity of the proposal?
- How do you feel the proposal lines up with Cooper's stated strategy?
- Is the proposal likely to fit in with the parent company's requirements?

CHAPTER THREE
Long range budgeting

3.1 Introduction

This chapter describes the first tentative approaches to the development of formal strategic planning. It is not, therefore, directly concerned with strategic thinking as such, but rather with the beginnings of explicit management concern for the problem of strategy.

Entrepreneurs and managers have been implicitly concerned with strategic issues since ever large scale business started. The actions, writings and sayings of the great entrepreneurs such as Ford, Sloan, Watson and many others, show how sensitive they were to strategic issues. Even before them, their counterparts in other large scale organizations, such as the state, the church and the military, had also been similarly concerned.

Organizations which remain successful over the long term have continually had to adapt to the ever-changing world. This has always been the case. Based on his experience of the nineteenth century French mining industry, Fayol identified forecasting and planning (*prévoyance*) as one of the key managerial functions (Fayol, 1916).

In many firms *prévoyance* led inexorably to diversification in search of greener grass through entry into different and often unrelated businesses. A firm that diversifies away from its original business, risks losing sight of its real strategic objectives. It has no single unifying purpose relevant to the different parts of the business. In this situation, managers may feel the need for a suitable planning system which will help to reduce the apparent complexity of the business and bring back the feeling of coherence that it may lack and the sense of direction and focus it needs. So deliberate, formal concern with business strategy as a systematic management discipline coincided with the emergence of conglomerate multibusiness companies not much more than thirty years ago. The strategic planning of business first came on the scene in the mid-1950s, along with the early commercial computers and Drucker's *The Practice of Management* (1955). It was a time when the new analytical methods promised definitive answers to all business problems, strategic or otherwise.

Some of the main strands in the developing methodologies of business strategy are described below. The strategic impact of most of them fell far short of expectations. However, a lot was learned and today's strategists have the benefit of that learning: the early approaches to strategy and the reasons why they largely failed to deliver. It is a significant thread in the contemporary fabric of strategic thinking.

3.2   Accounts-based budgeting

Thirty years ago most company accounts were prepared without the help of electronic computers. Most companies of any size made use of a variety of accounting machines for the processing of purchase and sales transactions and for running payroll systems. These machines, however, were totally dedicated to carrying out one specific function and had no flexibility and no development potential. They eliminated considerable clerical work, but could not produce a set of accounts. This was a labour intensive task of considerable proportions, exceeded only by the production of management accounts. Accounts departments were commonly split into two main sections: financial accounts and management accounts and, in terms of numbers employed, the management accounts section was usually much the most significant.

At that time most accounts departments were concerned only with the current year's operations. Nevertheless consolidation of subsidiary company accounts into the corporate whole gave the accounting function the only formal 'handle' on the whole organization. So it was perhaps natural that the first forays into formal strategic planning should have been accounting-based.

One approach that was widely practised was to make projections of the consolidated accounts along lines that would have been satisfactory from the shareholder's viewpoint and then to deconsolidate the projections back to separate subsidiary companies which were then given the resultant figures as targets.

Even for quite small businesses this approach generated huge amounts of paper, mainly detailed accounting schedules, usually based on a single long range sales forecast. For even a small single business company, the annual budget might well extend to twenty or so full page schedules. A five-year budget on a similar basis would comprise five times that amount of data and a company comprising ten businesses would therefore comprise fifty times the data of a single business annual budget, without considering the additional data generated through consolidation for the company as a whole. Such systems, far from simplifying matters, only served to confirm the already apparent truth that a multibusiness company is highly complex.

Inadequate as this system was, it represented a step forward for many businesses. The real strategic content was extremely small, though the process of long range sales forecasting might have highlighted particular problems or opportunities which might otherwise have been missed. The strategic value of most of the detailed accounting schedules was probably minimal.

The availability of computerized accounting systems reduced the manpower required to produce such budget-based 'plans' and increased their flexibility by making sensitivity and 'what if?' analysis quick and cheap. Many high quality proprietary computerized planning systems became available and they became progressively more sophisticated. But the strategic value of such systems was probably not very great. In terms of direction, concentration and consistency, a budget-based plan remained more or less silent. Such models were not, in any significant sense, strategic.

One part of the financial budget, however, was potentially of greater strategic value and that was related to the allocation of capital expenditure. A capital budget typically comprises a number of specific and relatively large items of expenditure. Though the financial justification for committing funds may be made on an individual basis, as and when the project has been appraised in detail, the broad strategic decision as to whether the item is appropriate in principal may be taken at the time the capital plan is put together. Thus capital budgeting, or planning, was the key strategic item in the long range budgeting approach to strategy.

The process of capital planning forced senior management to consider strategic issues and the way capital decisions were taken clearly had a strategic impact in terms of direction, concentration and consistency. However, the process offered no guidance to management as to which direction would be appropriate.

Few companies nowadays produce full accounting budgets projected five or ten years ahead, presumably because the value of such a process was found to be limited. However, detailed long range capital plans with summary accounting projections, produced on a rolling annual basis, is still a widely used approach to strategic planning.

3.3   Forecast-based budgeting

The accounting approach to strategic planning, with all its short-comings, served to highlight the need for a practical, strategically relevant planning system. The old dictum of 'garbage in – garbage out' encouraged a focus onto the quality of information being input to the strategic planning process and the emphasis therefore moved naturally away from the production of accounting schedules onto the processes of analysis and forecasting, i.e. the generation of data inputs.

Table 3.1   *Typical strengths and weaknesses checklist.*

1. *Market structure*
   Products and product characteristics
   Product missions
   Customers

2. *Growth and profitability*
   History
   Margins and liquidity
   Forecasts
   Phase of life cycle

3. *Technology*
   Basic technologies
   Technical innovation history
   Rate of development
   Importance of technology

4. *Investment*
   Cost of entry to industry
   Cost of exiting from industry
   Rate of obsolescence of plant
   Importance of capital investment

5. *Marketing*
   Methods of selling and distribution
   Importance of service and field support
   Importance and method of promotion
   Basic determinants of demand

6. *Competition*
   Market shares
   Degree of concentration in industry
   Strength of leading competitor

7. *Trends*
   Demand
   Market structure
   Technology

Source: Ansoff, 1965.

The intention is to be objective and clinical and to formulate strategy on a wholly rational analysis of the business and its markets. This involves a detailed, exhaustive assessment of the strengths and weaknesses of the business and the opportunities and threats presented by its markets and other environments such as the financial community, technology suppliers, etc.

An audit of the company's strengths and weaknesses might include the items indicated in Table 3.1.

The company audit involves a review, product by product, function by function, department by department of the strengths and weaknesses of each area both in absolute terms and also in terms relative to competitors.

Similarly, the environmental analysis, identifying threats and opportunities facing the business, looks at each environment with which the business interacts, e.g. the financial environment (i.e. the stockmarket and banking community, the political environment, tech-

Table 3.2   *Typical environmental audit checklist.*

1. *Product market*
   Size, shares, segments, trends
   Distribution channel structures
   Changes in usage and expectations
   Price/cost/volume relationships
   Competitive positions
   Potential substitute products

2. *Technology*
   Developments and applications
   Obsolescence
   Research and discoveries
   Potential substitute technologies

3. *Financial*
   Sector price : earnings ratios and trends
   Earnings/share and trends
   Takeover threats and opportunities

4. *Social, economic and political*
   Trade cycles, inflation, interest rates
   Balance of payments and exchange rates
   Employment levels, trade union activity
   Government policy, political stability
   Demographic changes
   Wealth and income distribution
   Education, atitudes and life styles
   Environmental regulation and trends

nology, etc., etc.), as indicated in Table 3.2. Again the intention is to be exhaustive, to identify every threat and every opportunity in each environment.

Strengths and weaknesses, opportunities and threats, familiarly known as SWOT analysis, forms the basis of the analytical planning systems as outlined in Figure 1.1. The simple prescriptions derived from this analysis are summarized in Figure 3.1. Where a company strength coincides with a market opportunity there is the potential for successful exploitation. Where a weakness coincides with a threat there is potential for disaster. In the two intermediate positions it is suggested the problem is given careful consideration, there being no inbuilt solution.

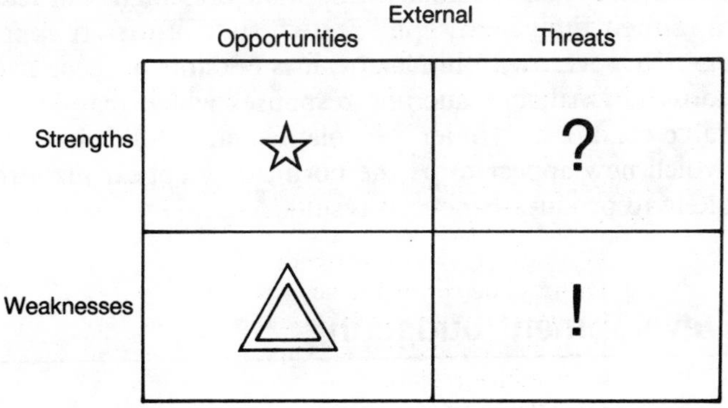

Figure 3.1 *SWOT Analysis.*

Superficially appealing, this model is oversimplified and in practice has only limited use. SWOT analysis sometimes draws management's attention to important strategic issues but, as with accounting-based systems, it generally fails to help management to any discriminating view of the business. Nor does it provide any coherence or focus, or any contribution to the decision on strategic direction. Without this there are no criteria for recognizing which SWOTs were important and which trivial. Thus the essential element of selectivity is not available. The critical management skill is to decide which SWOTs to attend to and which to ignore – if you're trying to get to Canterbury you can ignore the SWOTs that would lead you down the Edgware Road.

The problem is made worse because any thorough-going SWOT analysis will reveal innumerable strengths and weaknesses and threats and opportunities. If the attempt is made to address them all, as is often the case in practice, the inevitable result will be that resources are spread extremely thinly across a very broad front and, as a consequence, very little of substance will be achieved.

One way round this problem is for the staff planner to present management with a number of alternative scenarios to choose from. Alternative possible environmental futures are considered and the planner selects a small number of different resource allocations for each and presents the simulated results of these to management who simply select the preferred outcome. This may make management's role easier, but the danger is that it is the planner, rather than management, who are making the important strategic decisions.

SWOT-based systems, with or without the presentation of scenarios, appeared in their time to be sophisticated, state-of-the-art approaches to strategy. However, with hindsight, it is possible to recognize them as orthodox, rational, bureaucratic responses which may be relevant under stable conditions. Under the volatile and rapidly changing conditions which now appear to be the norm, they appear inappropriate and unlikely to produce beneficial results.

3.4   Development budgeting

The necessity to be selective in the allocation of resources is addressed in development budgeting, sometimes referred to as programme budget planning.

The aim of this approach is to identify the resources available for business development, i.e. not required for maintaining the existing business, and then to allocate these resources, mainly manpower and capital, to various programmes within the development plan. Each programme is aimed at achieving certain broad thrusts, e.g. market penetration, production cost reduction, substitute raw material development, etc.

There are a number of variations on development budgeting, but typically the process is administered by a professional planner. The essence of the system is to involve all management in the process of developing the business. Each senior manager is invited to propose development projects for inclusion in the development plan. To do this they specify each proposed project in both qualitative and quantitative terms as well as estimating the amount of development resource the project would require. In the main the development resource of greatest concern is time: man weeks of research, development engineering, production engineering, marketing research, management accounting, etc. The managers of each of these resources would specify the total amount of time that could be made available for development projects, as opposed to the day-to-day business. Additionally, during the course of preparing the plan, each resource manager would prepare their estimates of the amount of time each proposed project would take of their department.

The planner's role in the above process is typically administrative. The planner ensures that proposals of projects and bids for resources are submitted and coordinated at the appropriate time and in the prescribed formats. When this is completed, the planner takes a more proactive role in the process. The ultimate strategic management decision is to choose the preferred allocation of resources to development projects. The planner facilitates this decision by offering a number of alternative allocations for consideration. Typically each alternative allocation is described by the planner in qualitative and quantitative terms in order to make the implications, risks and possibilities of each allocation quite clear.

This approach to planning combines a number of virtues. Firstly it involves the whole of the management team, both in terms of being able to propose development projects and in working on them. Secondly, it provides top management with explicit alternatives from which to choose. Thirdly, it is so organized as to eliminate much of the clerical effort from line management and give it to the staff specialist planner.

However, there is a danger that in this proactive role, the planner is in fact playing the most influential role in deciding the resource allocation; more influential, for example, than the top management of the business who would normally be regarded as responsible for strategy.

Moreover, the system does not contain within itself any guidance as to direction and thus, despite the benefits of the process, provides only a limited contribution to concentration and consistency. Indeed there are certain aspects of development planning which make the achievement of concentration from this process exceedingly unlikely.

Formal decision-making of this sort, can tend to be prone to what Cyert and March (1963) referred to as satisficing. When decisions are taken by groups, they tend to be taken by compromise, i.e. in such a way as to satisfy the minimum requirements of every member of the group, rather than in a way which might be in the group's overall best interests but possibly be detrimental to the interests of one or more members. In this way, no member will achieve their target, but all will have grounds for some minimum level of satisfaction.

Development planning makes this process highly formal. Each senior manager proposes a number of projects and each manager's lowest level of development involvement might be discussed quite openly. An acceptable allocation may be one which includes at least all the projects which meet this lowest level of involvement for each department. Additionally there will be other projects for which there was a clear corporate, or business, need. Thus the inevitable result of the process is a large number of development projects in the plan. This means in most circumstances that there will be a relatively small amount of resource devoted to each project and consequently only limited development progress achieved in any time period. In other words, without direction there can be no concentration and consistency and the result will be that resources are allocated across a wide front and thus little is achieved.

3.5   The bureaucratic tendency

All the systems referred to in this chapter share a generic organizational failing, the tendency to become 'routine-ized', bound by rules and regulation, by the completion of pro-formae, in short to become bureaucratic.

Such systems are still widely used, despite their effectiveness being questionable. Various writers have advocated such systems. For example, Jones (1974) advocates a system based on the completion of twenty-three detailed pro formas per business. These provide predominantly quantitative information. However, strategy is a qualitative concept; it may find quantitative expression in some ways, but its essence – the direction, position or culture – can only be expressed in words. Thus to adopt Jones' approach with a strategic commentary produces a document which for the simple one business company would be extremely long. The length of such a company plan involving six or seven businesses would become a severe problem to managers expected to read it, understand it and take decisions based on it. The significance of a strategic plan extending to four or five hundred pages is likely to be much less than the significance of a plan that is expressed on a single side of paper.

Nevertheless the bureaucratic tendency persists. Shaw (1981) suggests thirty-eight schedules per planning unit. The assertion is made that standard planning forms are used in order that all planning units can submit plans in the same format so that it can be accumulated on a hierarchical basis, line by line, 'to give the total for the next higher level and, ultimately, for the company as a whole' (Jones, 1974, p. 165).

The idea that plans can simply be added together is an acceptable idea when related to simple accounting pro formas, but makes nonsense of business strategy. Two business strategies can no more be added together than can apples and pears. The action that results from the summation of business strategies is not made clear, nor could it ever be so with any coherence.

By and large the systems described in this chapter fail to make any fundamental strategic impact except in the case of the large one-off capital investment decisions. Capital budgeting systems can serve to focus management's attention on the issues concerned and give cause for consideration of the strategic impact of the relevant decisions. However, there is no guidance as to direction, and consequently no significant impact in terms of concentration or consistency, in any of the systems discussed. Moreover, they are all absolutely silent in regard to flexibility which was not an issue in the days when these approaches to strategic planning were first devised.

In the current highly competitive and technologically volatile environment, these issues are crucial. Hence the concern for a valid way of strategic *thinking*, rather than the production of sound, exhaustive paper plans.

3.6 Summary

Whilst the leaders of large scale organizations have probably always demonstrated a concern for key strategic issues, it is only over the last thirty or so years that business managements have made these concerns explicit in the form of long range plans.

The first approaches to formal long range planning were generally accounting-based and amounted to the projection of annual budgets over five- or even ten- or twenty-year periods.

These systems sometimes highlighted particular issues, but generally fail to achieve any proactive strategic effect. Moreover, they also failed to provide any significant understanding of the business through valid simplification.

One of the problems with accounting-based long range plans was that insufficient emphasis was placed on the analysis and interpretation of company and environmental data and consequently the forecasts on which long range projections were made were often of low quality.

Forecast-based planning, where effort was concentrated on corporate and environmental analysis, aimed to identify all the threats and opportunities presented by the environment and all the strengths and weaknesses relevant to the business.

Such systems did not in themselves contribute any sense of direction and as a consequence very often led to a broad and thin spread of resources in order to address all SWOTs. Thus they actively discouraged concentration of effort.

Development budgeting sought to focus attention on decisions and resources specifically aimed at developing the business, as opposed to its day-to-day running. Again, the systems most widely used did not contribute to the identification of strategic direction and also tended naturally to result in widespread and thin allocation of resources.

The risk in all these systems was that they might become processes in their own right and a recognized part of the corporate bureaucracy, having an apparent but unjustified importance. They could not be justified by their contribution to direction, concentration, consistency and flexibility.

Nevertheless, they represented a stage in the learning process along the way to strategic thinking.

DISCUSSION CASE: INCA CONSTRUCTION MATERIALS LTD

Inca Construction Materials was established at the start of this century as a manufacturer of mineral fibre-reinforced corrugated building board, for which it held various patents and enjoyed a virtual monopoly until the early 1930s. Even after the patent protection had lapsed, the high costs of setting up production limited entry to the industry, and up to 1950 there were still only two producers in the United Kingdom, Inca having over 80 per cent of the market which was almost entirely concerned with the external cladding of industrial and agricultural buildings. Inclad, Inca's proprietary name, was generic for what had become more or less a commodity, lacking any significant differentiation from one manufacturer to another.

During the 1950s and 1960s excess demand encouraged two overseas producers to establish plants in the United Kingdom. However, despite the loss of market share, Inca continued to work at full capacity and enjoyed high profitability.

Exceptional cash generation during this period encouraged Inca to broaden its product range. The first substantial new product was a highly successful range of thermal insulation boards, called Insheet, which became the market leader in internal cladding of industrial buildings. The technology used in producing Insheet was quite different from that of Inclad, being more like paper manufacture. This led to further diversification into electrical insulation papers and subsequently into phenolic and polyester resin-impregnated papers for a wide variety of technical applications. These developments were expensive, but during Inca's years of plenty, such investments presented no problem.

By the late 1960s the company was employing around 6,000 people in seven factories, four of which were predominantly engaged in producing building board, two being devoted exclusively to the newer technical product ranges and the seventh factory, the biggest, handling the entire product range.

Inclad's loss of market share was at first regarded almost with relief by the top management – being too dominant was regarded as unsustainable and the company's reliance on a single product line for profit and cash was regarded as having a 'high risk'.

New competitors therefore came into the market without any active discouragement from Inca. Transporting Inclad long distances was regarded as uneconomic, so new competitors were allowed to pick off geographically specialized areas. The first of these was in Scotland where Inca did not have a manufacturing plant. As a result of this one change Inca lost 10 per cent of its sales volume.

By 1970 the excess demand for cladding materials had ceased and Inca recognized that future growth for the main products would be slight. This realization put more emphasis on the various diversifications that had been made and were being considered. Inca were already peripherally involved in plastics through impregnated papers and further commitment to plastics appeared tempting.

Thus while still very liquid, Inca set up a well-funded development programme, the aims of which were to reduce the company's reliance on fibre and buy its way into new growth markets.

A corporate planning department was set up comprising eleven high calibre, graduate professional specialists. A thorough SWOT appraisal was carried out and presented to the Inca board of directors with an exhausive study of the company's strategic options, including no less than twelve different ten-year scenarios.

The result of this work was the institution of a development plan which included an extensive programme of new product development and diversification. The plan was seen as a race against time as the existing markets waned and then collapsed in the oil price crisis of 1973. By 1976 Inca had completed two green field developments to manufacture lightweight aggregate blocks, had acquired three high quality facing brick manufacturers and taken its first tentative steps into thermoplastic resins. Meanwhile, its main product, Inclad, had lost further market share to around 40 per cent and the company as a whole was starting to record losses.

Discussion points
- Consider what action Inca could take to improve its financial performance.
- What more information would you require in order to develop a specific programme of action?
- Consider the problem from the point of view of:
  the Marketing Manager responsible for Inclad;
  the R&D Manager responsible for the resin-impregnated papers and other new technical products;
  the Chairman of Inca; and
- Inca's new Corporate Planning Manager.

Profit analysis showed the Inclad and Insheet ranges generated 90 per cent of Inca's profit and 150 per cent of cash. The development plan comprised the following four programmes:

- Profit improvement
- New product development
- Diversification
- Acquisitions

In total there were over 250 individual projects in the plan and apparently being worked on. However, only 20 projects were 'completed' in a year, 'completion' including projects taken out of the development plan because of failure of some sort – either technical or economic. Failure was itself a controversial issue and the elimination of a project that had not reached successful completion was never agreed unanimously. Always there would be one manager who felt that, in view of the efforts made and costs already sunk in the project, success would be relatively quick and cheap to achieve.

Discussion points
- What can Inca do to improve the results from the development plan?
- Consider how the development plan has contributed to Inca's strategic direction, the achievement of concentration of effort and consistency.

Inca top management decided to close down all the development plan programmes apart from 'profit improvement' and 'new product development' and to reduce the total number of projects supported in the development plan to a maximum of twelve.

Discussion points
- In the light of the limited amount of information provided above, does this seem an appropriate action for Inca management to take?
- What do you envisage would be the impact of this decision on personnel morale?
- How would this be manifested and by which categories of personnel?
- What further action might Inca management consider taking?

CHAPTER FOUR
Strategic thinking frameworks: life cycles and portfolios

4.1 Introduction

The approaches to planning described in the last chapter provided little guidance on fulfilling the key purposes of strategy: direction, concentration, consistency and flexibility. They tend not to be truly strategic. Moreover, they tended to become excessively bureaucratic, creating additional work rather than providing a focus for the work already done. There was thus a widely felt need for a more informed and efficient approach to strategic planning.

The search for such a planning system has progressed through several phases, but *the* definitive system has not yet emerged. Nor is it ever likely to. No system will serve adequately for the formulation of strategy in all circumstances. What was appropriate at times of high growth is less relevant when the aim of strategy is to win a game of competitive relationships.

In this and the next few chapters a variety of different models are discussed. Some may be regarded as business concepts or theories, others as planning techniques. What they all have in common is that they each provide some additional insight and contribute to the development of strategy and the achievement of its purposes. They provide frameworks for strategic thinking. They represent different ways of viewing a business and shaping its future. Some were developed many years ago and may now be falling out of use as the world changes and imposes new imperatives. Others may be more appropriate to a business environment which is only now starting to emerge. They all have relevance and application to some businesses in some situations. Profitability from standard products and long production runs has been replaced by profitability from manufacturing flexibility and responsiveness to customer needs. Yet the McDonalds hamburger is undoubtedly a long production run and its success is surely based on the very strictest standardization, not only of the product, but also of plant layout, service, quality and every other conceivable factor. Yesterday's model of manufacturing may well be of value in understanding tomorrow's problems of customer service.

All the different strategic thinking frameworks have their applications. The popularity of any particular approach may wax and wane but its validity for particular circumstances may nevertheless be retained. Informed strategic thinking is likely to be far more powerful than any individual planning approach or technique.

4.2 Product life cycles

Life cycle curves have often been used in the search for a simplifying model of a business and its long term position. Life cycles have much common sense appeal, look plausible and have attracted considerable interest, so that now there is a standard explanation of the growth, maturity and decline phases of a product, business or industry as idealized in Figure 4.1.

In the early stages of the development of an industry, so orthodox wisdom has it, growth is slow. Basic feasibilities and economic viability are being investigated and demonstrated, the development resources are being built up and commitments to longer term support being

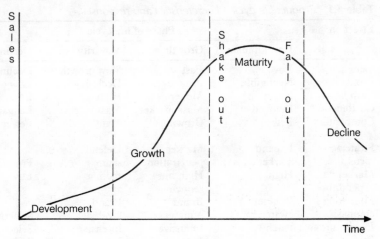

Figure 4.1 *The industry life cycle curve.*

made. The development of semiconductors and integrated circuits are examples from the recent past, while molecular engineering and biotechnology are examples where a body of knowledge and expertise is currently being built up.

Once commitment has reached a certain critical mass then growth takes off. During this phase innovation efforts tend to centre around the product. New technology is applied to produce genuinely new products and radically improved products with more features and better performance. Participants in the industry focus all their development efforts on producing the latest technology product. The past ten years has seen this phase in the development, for example, of the personal computer (PC) market. Growth took off with the 8-bit machines such as the Apple II, Tandy TRS80 and Commodore Pet, followed by hundreds, possibly even thousands of others, all different and more or less all incompatible. New products were introduced almost daily. Innovation was clearly focused on the product.

In due course, generally accepted standards of performance for the product emerge as the industry moves into the slower growth mature phase. During this transition there will be a radical reassessment of growth projections and several participants will realize that the volumes required in order to be profitable, will not be available. Consequently there may be a period of fierce competition, during which a number of the weaker participants will decide, or be forced to withdraw. The emergence of the CP/M operating system followed by 16-bit technology and the introduction of IBM's PC operating system was such a phase in

Table 4.1 *Product life cycle characteristics and responses.*

Effect on:	Phase of life cycle			
	Development	Growth	Maturity	Decline
Sales	Low	Fast	Slow growth	Decline
Profits	Negligible	Peak levels	Declining	Low or zero
Cash flows	Negative	Moderate	High	Low
Customers	Innovative	Mass market	Mass market	Laggards
Competitors	Few	Growing	Many rivals	Fewer
Strategic focus	Expand market	Market penetration	Defend share	Productivity
Marketing expenditure	High	High but reducing	Falling	Low
Marketing emphasis	Product awareness	Brand preference	Brand loyalty	Selective
Distribution	Patchy	Intensive	Intensive	Selective
Price	High	Lower	Lowest	Rising
Product	Basic	Improved	Differentiated	Rationalized

Table 4.2   *Strategies and life cycle phases.*

Competitive position	Phase of life cycle		
	Growth	Maturity	Decline
Leader (high market share)	Build share by price cuts to discourage new competing capacity. Add capacity to anticipate future requirements.	Hold share by improving quality and increased sales effort and advertising.	Harvest: maximize cash flow by cutting investment in advertising and R&D.
Follower (low market share)	Invest to increase share. Concentrate on segment.	Withdraw or hold share by lower prices and costs than leaders.	Withdraw.

the PC market. Most names associated with 8-bit technology are now distant memories, relatively few having survived the shake-out period.

During the ensuing, relatively stable mature phase, the emphasis of innovation tends to move from product to production process, where innovations are largely aimed at reducing costs and improving efficiency. For some industries the mature phase may last a long time: several decades, or even centuries.

The mature phase comes to an end when either a new technology takes over or eliminates the existing business. Again the reduction in expectations of future business will be accompanied by increased price competition which forces the marginal businesses to be quickly eliminated through either closure or amalgamation.

The implications of the product life cycle are summarized in Table 4.1.

From this analysis it is possible to prescribe certain strategies as being appropriate for different participants at different phases as shown in Table 4.2.

Life cycle curves are the product of general systems theory and are analogous to the life cycle of a biological cell which exhibits the four phases with the change from one phase to another generally accompanied by periods of volatility. Systems theory also indicates that the mature phase steady-state is the period of maximum efficiency or, in biological cases, maximum energy conversion. Koehler illustrated system life cycles with the graphic example of a candle being lighted, its flame flickering into life and quickly growing to its maximum size where it burns steadily for a prolonged period until it starts to putter before declining and eventually going out (Koehler, 1938).

Perhaps an even better analogy can be made with the theory of chaos. The changes from one more or less steady state to the next being signalled by intervening periods of chaos which have unpredictable outcomes which may be exciting or terrifying. Shake-out will see the demise of many, but the dawn of a new period of prosperity for the few who survive. The British iron foundry industry appeared to go through a phase of terminal chaos in the early 1980s. For around three years foundries were closing at the rate of almost one a week. For the few businesses which survived, however, the late 1980s have been extremely prosperous. Clearly there is considerable value in survival to fight another day. Yet some strategic models explicitly deny this, notably the Boston portfolio, discussed later.

In the case of business life cycles the phases of volatility are clearly discernible. Also the period of steady-state maturity and maximum energy conversion is recognizable as the period when industries generate the maximum surplus cash flow.

Life cycles appear to have a wide validity and they seem at an intuitive level to offer satisfactory explanations of system behaviour. The same ideas can be applied to businesses and to products, just as readily as to industries. However, the problem with life cycles, as with general systems theory itself, is their very generality which makes it difficult to know how valid they are as explanations of particular situations. For example, in any particular industry at any particular time, is it possible to deduce, using a life cycle curve, which phase has been reached?

There is no definitive solution. Building bricks made of clay have been around now for upwards of three thousand years and might therefore be thought of as mature. The IBM PC, on the other hand, is a relatively new product, only now in its third edition, and using relatively (compared to the clay brick) new technology. But which of the two is furthest along its life cycle? Which is the more mature product? Which will last longer? Which will generate more wealth from this point on? Which represents the greatest opportunity for innovative development? The answers are not certain.

The important thing about mature business is not its maturity but its potential. Individual firms, whole industries and even entire economies depend, and will continue to depend, on products which have been around a very long time. They will change in detail, be developed and enhanced to achieve higher quality, improved performance, lower costs and greater acceptability, but they will remain, as they have for long ages past, fundamentally the same products satisfying fundamentally the same customer needs. In so doing such products may appear to refute entirely the life cycle curves of systems theory.

There is one further problem with life cycle curves which should be noted: they can become self-fulfilling prophesies. This is not peculiar to life cycles, but is a particular problem if the diagnosis of position is inaccurate. For example, if a business is diagnosed as being in the decline phase, it may well be starved of new investment and consequently decline. An alternative diagnosis, suggesting a continuity of the mature, maximum energy conversion (cash generation) phase, might suggest the level of investment needed to maintain the business.

Life cycles, though intuitively valid, may be fraught with difficulty in particular circumstances. Even after a clearly defined cycle has reached well into what appears to be the decline phase, there may still be potential for major new business. There is no reason why a curve should follow the smooth idealized shape of Figure 4.1. Nevertheless, in some situations life cycle concepts may apply and be identifiable, and they may be a useful aid to strategic thinking in many situations.

4.3 Experience and costs

Life cycle curves suggest that maximum efficiency is only reached during the phase of maturity. This is partly because it is not until maturity that attention is focused on efficiency, but also because of the effects of the familiar learning curve. Efficiency is likely to go on increasing as more of a product is produced.

The Boston Consulting Group investigated these processes and

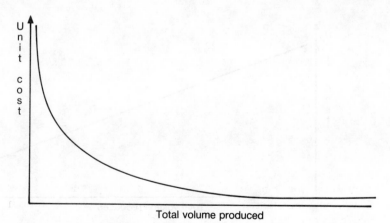

Figure 4.2   *The experience curve.*
Source: Boston Consulting Group, 1968.

found that there appeared to be a surprisingly consistent relationship between improved efficiency and production experience across a wide range of products and industries (Boston Consulting Group, 1968). They investigated twenty-four products and derived the total costs involved in their production. These were plotted against total volumes produced, as shown in Figure 4.2.

The smoothness of this cost–volume curve suggests an apparently stable relationship between the two. Based on Boston's twenty-four product analyses it appeared to be that unit costs tended to fall by between 20 per cent and 30 per cent every time total production doubled.

For simplicity the relationship is usually presented with both axes having logarithmic scales so that the smooth curve becomes a straight line as in Figure 4.3.

A reduction in costs of 20–30 per cent is potentially a very significant factor. If it occurred all at once it would be crucial. If it was spread over say ten years, i.e. on average some 2–2.5 per cent cost reduction per year its impact would be much less decisive. Assuming the Boston Group is correct in its estimate of 20–30 per cent reduction, then it is a simple matter of mathematics to calculate the cost reductions arising from experience in different industry situations. The two critical characteristics are firstly the cumulative production experience and secondly the growth rate. For a long established industry, such as clay bricks for example, it will clearly take a great many years before total production experience is doubled. For a younger industry, such as those originally studied by Boston, the

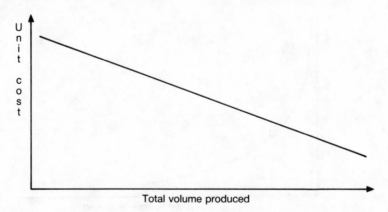

Figure 4.3 *The experience relationship (log : log scales).*
Source: Boston Consulting Group, 1968.

speed with which production experience will be doubled will be much quicker and depend critically on the growth rate of that industry.

The Boston Consulting Group suggested that these cost effects apply equally to industries as a whole as well as for individual producers. Thus an individual producer can achieve reduced costs by increasing cumulative experience more rapidly than the competitors, and this can be done by increasing market share. The bigger the increase in market share the more quickly a firm would increase its experience and thus enjoy the reduction in costs.

4.4 Costs and prices

The Boston Consulting Group suggested that prices follow the same pattern as costs so long as the competitive scene remains stable. Typically, new products would be introduced at prices fixed below costs in order to create a market as shown in Figure 4.4a. Once established, unit costs start to fall and in due course drop to a level which provides producers with an adequate margin. Subsequently costs and prices fall more or less together. Producers may attempt to hold prices up and so earn higher margins as shown in Figure 4.4b, but this is unlikely to be long lasting. If super margins are made then new competitors will be encouraged to enter the market. Consequently existing producers will be encouraged to reduce prices to levels which will discourage new competition to enter. Thus in either case a stable relationship between cost and price will ultimately prevail.

If cost is a function of accumulated experience then it follows that the competitor with the most accumulated experience, i.e. the biggest

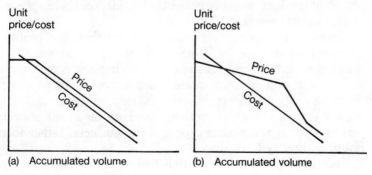

Figure 4.4 *(a) Stable relationship.   (b) Unstable relationship.*
Source: Boston Consulting Group, 1968.

cumulative market share, will have the lowest costs. The scale of this cost advantage will depend on how far the leading competitor's cumulative experience exceeds that of the nearest competitor. A good approximation to this would be to measure market share in relative terms, i.e. market share relative to the share of the leading competitor. This is the theoretical basis for the assertion that high relative market share would produce high profitability.

4.5 Market share and profit

The connection between profitability and market share is not at first surprising. The idea of economies of scale implies nothing else. Furthermore it was supported by empirical evidence from the influential and longstanding PIMS (Profit Impact of Market Strategy) databank of the Strategic Planning Institute. This suggests that 'a business's share of its served market (both absolute and relative to its three largest competitors) has a positive impact on its profit and net cash flow' (Schoeffler, 1977, p. 10).

If the market is growing rapidly experience is doubled in a relatively short period of time and consequently costs would fall quickly. Under these circumstances the value of increased market share would be considerable because it would result in increasing cost advantage over competitors. On the other hand, if the market was not growing, increases in market share would not be worth a great deal, and would ironically only be available at great cost. Thus Bostonian analysis suggests that during the growth phase of a product or an industry, the returns from increasing market share are very high. But for all other phases of product or industry life cycles, market share appears not to be particularly relevant.

However, the connection between market share and profitability is controversial, despite the PIMS evidence. The existence of a reliable correlation between market share and profitability is widely disputed. Even if it is accepted that there is a positive connection, the causal direction remains uncertain. It is at least as likely that dominant market share and high profitability are both the result of exceptional performance in some other aspect of the business, rather than profit resulting directly from share.

Even before the Boston analysis had emerged, Drucker wrote,

in many industries the largest company is by no means the most profitable one . . . the second spot, or even the third spot is often preferable, for it may make possible that concentration on one segment of the market, on one class of customer, on one application of the technology, in which genuine leadership often lies. (Drucker, 1964, p. 6)

More recently a survey into the connection between market share and profitability found that it very much depended on the particular situation. Eight environmental contexts were investigated and in five of these there was no positive relationship between market share and profitability (Prescott *et al.*, 1986).

Most analyses of the connection, and including the PIMS data, are essentially statistical and can only be very tentative when it comes to interpreting causes. Nevertheless, the idea that profitability stems from market share, for the plausible reasons explained, remains one of the foundations of the Boston analysis.

4.6 Business portfolios

There have been a number of variations on the portfolio approach, but they all rely on the work of the Boston Consulting Group, outlined

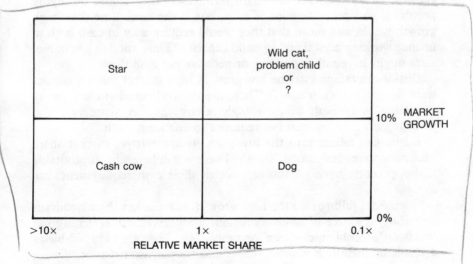

Figure 4.5 *The Boston matrix.*
Based on Boston Consulting Group, 1968.

above, for their theoretical and empirical underpinning. Boston's model is discussed in some depth while other variations are only briefly summarized.

4.6.1 The Boston matrix

According to Boston, the two most important factors which determine the long term profitability of a business are the rate of growth of its market and the share of the market that the business has relative to its largest competitor. Boston presented the model in the form of a simple two dimensional matrix as in Figure 4.5.

Relative market share of the business in question is assessed in terms of the market share of its largest competitor. This market share is expressed as a number of times that of the competitor. The break between the high and low market shares of the matrix was originally set at equality with the leading competitor, and the break between the high and low market growth rates was originally set at 10 per cent p.a. Both these dividing points were later relaxed and the matrix defined less mechanistically as being divided into high and low relative market shares and high and low rates of market growth.

Businesses falling into the high growth, high market share quadrant were designated 'stars'. They are tomorrow's breadwinners or cash earners. Being high market share businesses, they would be highly profitable and generate a lot of cash, but at the same time their high growth would also mean that they would require a lot of cash both to finance working capital and to build capacity. Thus, though profitable, stars might have either positive or negative net cash flow.

Businesses falling into the low growth, high market share quadrant were designated 'cash cows'. These are the real breadwinners, being profitable as a result of their high relative market share and also throwing off surplus cash not required to finance growth.

Businesses falling into the low growth, low relative market share quadrant were designated 'dogs'. These are inherently unprofitable and apparently have no future, though their cash requirements are low.

Businesses falling into the high growth, low market share quadrant are clearly a source of some confusion. They have been referred to as 'wild cats', 'problem children' or simply '?'s. They are unprofitable as a result of their low market share, and they consume a lot of cash merely to maintain their market position because of the high growth rate. However, when markets are growing fast, the Boston analysis

Figure 4.6 *The Boston matrix prescriptions.*
Based on Boston Consulting Group, 1968.

suggests that the value of increased market share is extremely high. Therefore, it may be worth a very large investment in order to convert these businesses into stars.

From this simple analysis, Boston developed equally straightforward strategic prescriptions as follows:

Stars Invest to maintain market share. Keep prices up only reducing them in order to maintain market share.

Cash cows Strictly ration new investments. Keep prices up but ensure no new entrants enter the market.

Wild cats Invest to convert into stars, or withdraw on the most advantageous terms by progressively pricing out of the market.

Dogs Manage tightly for cash and withdraw.

The overall model is summarized in Figure 4.6.

The strategic value of a business is thus defined simply by having regard to two factors: market growth and relative market share. The simple idea depicted on Figure 4.5, with its familiar menagerie, implies the anticipated direction of cash flows and the summary strategic prescriptions. Strategy is defined simply with regard to the management of cash flows in order to achieve a balanced portfolio over time. Cash is invested in stars to convert them into tomorrow's cash cows. It is extracted from cash cows to fund stars. Dogs are divested and wild cats, or problem children, either converted into stars or liquidated. In this way it is intended that a balanced portfolio of

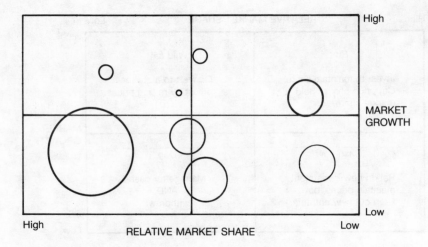

Figure 4.7 *A portfolio of businesses.*
Based on Boston Consulting Group, 1968.

businesses be achieved with an adequate succession of stars ready to take over from today's breadwinners, the cash cows. A typical portfolio is shown in Figure 4.7 where each circle represents a business, the size of the circle being proportional to annual sales revenue.

The strategic prescriptions derived from this analysis are extremely important. No decision to close or milk a business is taken lightly. Yet the factual basis for the prescriptions is restricted to knowledge about the market growth rate and relative market share. On the face of it this may seem to be an extremely superficial analysis for such important decisions. Clearly this view has been widely felt and a number of variations on the Boston theme have been devised in response; two of these are summarized below.

4.6.2   The directional policy matrix

A variation on Boston was published by the Royal Dutch Shell Group. Instead of having regard to only two factors the directional policy matrix (DPM) broke each down into groups of rather more detailed factors.

In the DPM market growth was replaced by 'business sector prospects', which comprised:

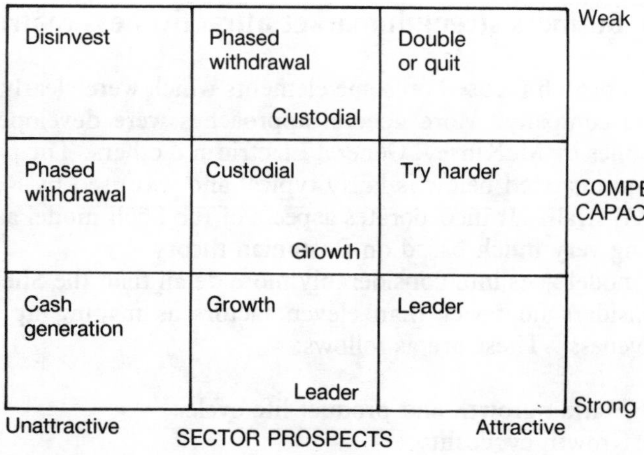

			Weak
Disinvest	Phased withdrawal	Double or quit	
	Custodial		
Phased withdrawal	Custodial	Try harder	COMPETITIVE CAPACITY
	Growth		
Cash generation	Growth	Leader	
	Leader		Strong
Unattractive	SECTOR PROSPECTS	Attractive	

Figure 4.8 *The directional policy matrix.*

- Market growth rates
- Market quality (i.e. stability and consistency)
- Industry feedstock situation (i.e. reliability of raw material supplies)
- Environmental aspects (extent of restrictions, etc.).

Also, relative market share was replaced by 'company's competitive capabilities', which comprised:

- Market position
- Production capability
- Product research and development.

The considerable debt to Boston is apparent in these categories, as well as in the resultant matrix shown in Figure 4.8.

To some extent the Shell matrix was a response to the over-simplification which was both Boston's main strength and, in the end, its greatest weakness. The analysis of sector prospects and competitive capabilities was a step forward in terms of a real assessment of what appeared likely to be important, but was considerably more complex than the Boston approach and represented also a step in the direction of a bureaucratic paper-chase. The outputs from this system offered slightly more variety than that offered from the Boston analysis, but it seems probable that full benefit is not obtained from the additional analysis involved.

4.6.3   Business strength/market attractiveness matrix

Shell's approach focused on some elements which were clearly specific to an oil company. More general approaches were developed along similar lines by McKinsey, General Electric and others. The particular model summarized below is fairly typical and was used by Readymix Ltd of Australia. It incorporates aspects of the Shell model as well as still being very much based on Bostonian theory.

The model goes into considerably more detail than the Shell model and considers no fewer than eleven factors as making up 'market attractiveness'. These are as follows:

1. Market growth and product life cycle.
2. Growth cyclicality.
3. Market size.
4. Industry profitability.
5. Ease of entry.
6. Business environment.
7. Feedstock availability.
8. Competitor concentration.
9. Marketing intensity.
10. Margin elasticity relative to quality.
11. Customer concentration.

The model considers the following thirteen factors as being important aspects of business strength:

1. Relative market share.
2. Change in relative market share.
3. Profitability.
4. Distribution.
5. Product differentiation.
6. Vertical integration.
7. Management calibre and depth.
8. Company reputation and image.
9. Process economics, plant age, obsolescence, etc.
10. Plant capacity.
11. Feedstock availability and price.
12. Investment intensity.
13. Product R&D and technical competence.

This approach gains considerably in realism by going into far greater detail in the business assessment than the original Boston

			100%
Invest to maintain dominance	Invest and grow	Dominate or divest	
Invest and grow	Invest and grow	Improve performance or withdraw	
Earn and protect	Earn and protect	Phased withdrawal	MARKET ATTRACTIVENESS
Earn and protect	Phased withdrawal	Divest	

100%   BUSINESS STRENGTH   0%   0%

Figure 4.9   *Business strengths/market attractiveness matrix.*

analysis. Much of the analysis proposed in these two lists is much the same as the analysis proposed by Porter in his competitive strategy model discussed in the next chapter. However, the penalty in terms of complexity, cost and paperwork, is substantial. And the difference in outputs between the various portfolio approaches is really only slight. Whilst the number of prescriptions implied by the matrix of Figure 4.9 is greater, the general tenor of the results is not much different from Boston or Shell. In all cases, a low share of a low growth market should be divested, a high share of a low growth market should be milked and a high share of a high growth market should be invested in.

If the purpose of the portfolio approach is to fix a position on the matrix and then read off the appropriate prescription, the Boston method is the most efficient. The more detailed analysis required in the other formats, relevant though it is to the formation of a business strategy, is not properly exploited within a portfolio system where strategy is more or less restricted to buy, sell or hold.

4.7 Limitations of portfolios

There are a number of problems with the portfolio approach which have tended to limit their usefulness in practice.

As Boston themselves pointed out, the basic rules of experience curves do not apply to mature or low growth business. If low growth is defined as 'below 10 per cent p.a.' (as it was originally), then there is no rational basis for applying portfolio concepts to more than 80 per cent of industry. This has, however, not stopped them being so applied in practice.

The outcomes from portfolios in terms of strategy development are extremely limited if the businesses concerned are mature or only growing slowly. 'Manage for cash and withdraw' may be provocative but is an inadequate and unduly pessimistic prescription to apply simply because the low growth business is not the market leader.

Clearly the prescriptions arising from portfolio positions are little help in themselves to the business management process. They are of no assistance in choosing between two or more potential investments *within the individual business*. They provide no feel for the appropriateness of a particular competitive strategy. From the business as opposed to corporate viewpoint, they provide little of strategic relevance. They offer no directional guidance and are of no assistance in the achievement of concentration and consistency. The categorization by corporate headquarters of any subsidiary business as a 'dog', with the concomitant strategic prescription, is likely to be counter-productive to the achievement of concentration and consistency. Since the majority of British businesses would be categorized as 'dogs' under this scheme, this is an extremely serious point.

There are also considerable practical problems of how to define the 'served market'. Should every individual product and every individual market it is sold into be regarded as a separate business unit and be given a separate matrix position? If so, it is difficult to see how the strategic prescriptions could be applied sensibly – it would be impossible, for instance, to divest one such business and expand another if they represented the same physical assets such as plant and buildings, etc. A way round this problem would be to aggregate products and markets in order to make the prescriptions feasible. This is how most firms operate the system, using the strategic business unit concept.

However, if this is done the whole system appears to become incoherent. What is meant by a low growth, low market share aggregated product? Such a 'dog' might in fact comprise a dozen or more separate products with very different share and growth characteristics. If so it is unclear what the strategic prescriptions should be. And if there are no strategic prescriptions there appears to be no point in the whole exercise.

Strategic business units (SBUs) can be defined according to the following (Roberts, 1986):

- product groups
- end-user groups
- distribution channels
- geography
- technology
- original equipment/replacement parts
- custom/standard parts
- manufacturing/marketing dominant
- established business/development business.

There is an almost infinite number of ways of defining units, and no clear guideline as to which is best. In many situations the use of portfolios is completely invalidated because there is no coherent way of defining any meaningfully, aggregate SBUs.

Finally, it should also be noted that portfolios fail to take account of the capacity of management to manage. Identifying market share and market growth as the sole determinants of corporate success, denies the possibility of managers affecting the position in any other way, e.g. through motivating people, effective marketing, efficient production and, most of all, through innovation. Yet many mature low growth businesses are highly profitable thanks solely to the efforts of effective and dedicated managers.

4.8 The uses of portfolios

Despite these limitations, which are fairly well understood, the portfolio approach is still widely used (Hamermesh, 1986). This is not done blindly in ignorance of the limitations, but cautiously in the full knowledge that the prescriptions may be wrong and need to be considered carefully before implementation.

The portfolio approach appears to have three main applications.

Firstly, it provides apparently objective strategic criteria for making, or influencing, business investment/divestment decisions. This is certainly one of the main benefits claimed by those who use the approach. However, caution is suggested since, if the approach is flawed, there is a danger that it will lead to the taking of bad decisions. Moreover, portfolios tend to encourage the adoption of diversification and acquisition strategies, there being no explicit, or implicit, commitment to any business: all are open to buy, hold or sell decisions. Flexibility and short term returns largely determine the choice of business strategy.

Secondly, many corporate managers have indicated that they obtain considerable benefit from portfolios through their simplifying of highly complex corporate situations. They help corporate headquarters 'get a handle' on many subsidiary businesses in a way that other approaches would not permit. Using portfolios corporate managers feel they know what makes the subsidiary businesses tick. However, caution is counselled since if portfolios themselves are problematic then the 'handle' may be illusory and the understanding entirely mistaken and superficial.

Finally, managers have indicated that portfolios are effective as an aid to strategic thinking (Hamermesh, 1986). This is why they have been dealt with at some length in this text. They represent a way of looking at business, which despite its flaws, has probably had more impact than any other strategic model and is still widely used even today. Being aware of the portfolio prescription for a particular business, whether or not it is accepted, serves to promote thinking along strategic lines. Running a business categorized as a dog will challenge most competent managers to develop an alternative strategic framework.

4.9 Summary

There is no universally applicable strategic management system. Each framework has particular relevance for particular circumstances.

The first approaches to strategic planning tended to be merely an extension of the annual budget and had little strategic relevance. As businesses grew and diversified, and became more complex, they used professional specialist planners to analyse the strengths and weaknesses of the business and the threats and opportunities posed by its environments and thus project alternative scenarios as the result of different resource allocations.

Products and businesses were also analysed in terms of their life cycle. Most products and businesses appear likely to progress through a four-stage cycle: development, growth, maturity and decline. For each phase of the cycle there appeared to be a rational set of strategic management decisions which would optimize the economic results from the business. Attractive and full of insights though this analysis is, it is often extremely difficult to locate a product or a business accurately in terms of its cycle phase. Consequently it is often unclear what the optimal decisions should be and there is a strong probability that such decisions become self-fulfilling.

Experience curves suggest a model where the likely long term profitability and cash flow performance of a business are largely determined by just two characteristics: the rate of market growth and the market share relative to the largest competitor. These ideas gave rise to the business matrix on which a portfolio of businesses could be positioned and the appropriate balance achieved.

The validity of experience curves is based on empirical studies of high growth products and appears only to have relevance to businesses which are growing at compound rates in excess of 10 per cent p.a. Moreover, though portfolio analysis appears to provide a feel for otherwise complex business organizations, this 'feel' may be illusory being based on an analysis of just two variables.

Various more sophisticated versions of the matrix have been developed and suggest using market attractiveness instead of simply market growth rates, and business strength instead of simply relative market share. Though these approaches may require a more in-depth analysis of the business, they are still based fundamentally on the original Boston analysis and are open to the same objections.

None of the models reviewed has been entirely satisfactory. None of them have looked clearly at strategy and none of them appear in any way concerned with people and the way their enthusiasm may contribute to organizational development.

DISCUSSION CASE: SIMMONDS INDUSTRIES PLC

Simmonds Industries is a medium-sized, diversified group of companies involved in four main business areas:

Simmonds Materials – building board and products
Simmonds Brick – clay building bricks

Simmonds Electrical – electrical insulation materials, and
Simmonds Electronics – specialized electronic components.

Materials and Brick are in mature low growth markets and are
profitable and generate good positive cash flow. Electrical markets were
growing at around double the rate of the economy as a whole and
Electronics at over four times.

Materials and Brick account for around 75 per cent of total sales
revenue and all the profit. Electrical make small profits which were
cancelled out by losses from Electronics.

Materials had proposed a substantial capital investment project aimed
at increasing its share of the European market by taking business mainly
in France and Belgium, currently being satisfied by German competitors.
The new plant would enjoy substantially lower costs than any existing
plant, so long as its utilization was above 60 per cent. The proposal was
supported by a financial assessment showing that at 60 per cent utilization, the rate of return would narrowly exceed the estimated cost of
capital. The sales would be gained as 50 per cent in France, 25 per cent
in Belgium and 25 per cent in the United Kingdom.

Discussion points
You are the Chief Marketing Executive of Simmonds Materials and have
been asked to attend a parent company board meeting to argue the case
for the proposed plant.

- What are the main items of additional information you would want
  to provide?
- What would your main supporting arguments be?
- What are likely to be the main weaknesses in your case?

At the same time, Simmonds Electronics has also requested a similar
large scale investment in a complete new factory intended to satisfy
the UK market growth requirements for the following five years. The
economies to be achieved with the new plant would enable the business
to be turned into profit. The alternative appears to be that the business
would eventually have to be sold or closed down, and Simmonds would
therefore lose the opportunity of being a leading competitor in a fast
growing high tech market. The comparison of these two alternatives is
reflected in the discounted cash flow assessment supporting the proposal
and it consequently shows a very high return on the investment.

Discussion points
You are the Chief Accountant of Simmonds Electronics and are asked to

attend the parent company's board meeting to support your case for the investment. You have already learned about the Materials proposal and regard the two as being likely to compete for scarce funds.

- What would be your main arguments to persuade the Simmonds Industrial PLC board members to decide in favour of the Electronics proposal?
- What additional information would you require?
- Would you require information on the Materials proposal and if so, what information?

Unknown to either subsidiary business, the head office strategic planning department have formally proposed that the leading competitor of Simmonds Electronics be acquired and the two businesses merged under the acquired company's management. This would result in Simmonds being much more advantageously placed in an increasingly international, high growth market. At the anticipated purchase price (based on an assumed 50 per cent premium over the current market valuation), this would have the effect of producing a short term dip in earnings per share, but it is argued this would be outweighed by the longer term benefits.

Discussion points
You are the head office Corporate Planning Manager and will also attend the same board meeting.

- What is your view of the relative merits of the three proposals?
- How will you make sure your proposal is accepted in favour of the other two?
- What is your view of the riskiness of all three proposals?
- What would you propose to do about the riskiness of your acquisition proposal?

Now put yourself in the position of a non-executive director of the parent company:

- What information do you require before you vote on these various proposals?
- From this non-executive viewpoint what are the main pros and cons of each?

CHAPTER FIVE

Strategic thinking frameworks: competitive strategies

5.1 Introduction

Economic growth, which had been continuous since the Second World War, came to a sudden halt with the oil price crisis of 1973. Through the 1970s and early 1980s many businesses had to adapt their strategies to cope with zero or negative growth. A planning framework based on growth rates of 10 per cent per annum or more became irrelevant to most business situations. The new focus of attention was on how the cake was divided rather than trying to increase its size. Thus attention was concentrated on competitive strategy.

Many of the ideas that Porter (1980) established in the competitive strategy model were evolutionary developments of Boston's basic portfolio model. The approach focuses on the following two key issues:

(a) the factors which determine the long term profitability of an industry, and
(b) the factors that determine a firm's competitive position in the industry.

Superficially, these are not dissimilar to the two dimensions of a portfolio matrix. The factors which determine the long term profitability of an industry are those which, in portfolio terminology, comprise 'market attractiveness'. Similarly, the factors which determine a firm's competitive position in an industry are those which comprise 'business strength'. However, the treatment of these two issues is very different.

Moreover, Porter adds a number of ideas which come directly from classical economics, and dispenses with the portfolio idea itself.

One of the most important differences is a change in orientation from one of corporate strategy, concerned with investment in the portfolio of businesses which would best strengthen the balance sheet, to a concern with how the individual business unit should be managed in order to ensure its long term prosperity.

5.2   Industry analysis

The approach is heavily dependent on the collection and analysis of detailed information about the firm's industry, its competitors, customers and suppliers. By comparison with portfolios, competitive strategy is neither superficial in its analysis nor simplistic in its prescriptions.

The analysis of industries is detailed and follows the SWOT approach in seeking to identify *all* the existing and potential threats and opportunities posed within an industry. Competition is seen as the crux of the firm's success or failure. The aim of business strategy is to establish a profitable and sustainable position in the face of the forces which determine profitability. This basically means understanding the

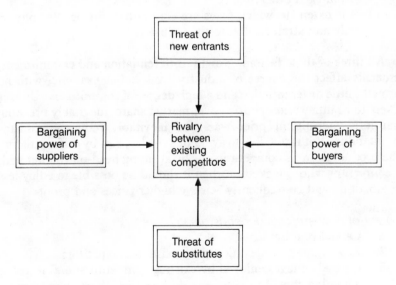

Figure 5.1   *Competitive forces shaping industry profitability.* based on Porter (1980).

industry and its various participants, existing and potential, so that competition can be managed in such a way that its profit potential can be maximized.

Industry profitability is determined by the competitive forces identified in Figure 5.1.

Each of the competitive forces is investigated in depth and the various competitive determinants of industry profitability are identified as below.

Competitive rivalry depends on:
1. Market growth rate.
2. Level of fixed costs.
3. Frequency of over-capacity.
4. Extent of product differences.
5. Strength of brand identities.
6. Cost of moving out of the industry.
7. Comparability of competitive rivals.

Broadly, these determining factors resolve into three main groups:

(a) the rate and shape of market growth;
(b) the degree to which products and firms are differentiated from each other;
(c) the extent to which firms are committed, financially, physically and strategically, to the industry.

All three of these factors, growth, differentiation and commitment, crucially affect the degree of industry rivalry. For example, with no growth, little differentiation and a high degree of commitment, there is likely to be intense competition over market share, inevitably breaking out into intermittent price wars and inevitably reducing industry profitability. If it is possible to avoid this rivalry, e.g. by differentiating the product from its competitors, or by avoiding head-on conflict with a competitor who is locked in, then it should be possible to enjoy less competition and consequently achieve higher prices and profit.

Threat of new entrants depends on:
1. Capital requirements.
2. Economies of scale enjoyed by existing competitors.
3. Cost advantages enjoyed by existing competitors: e.g. learning curve benefits.
4. Existing product differences.

5. Strength of existing product brand loyalty.
6. Access to distribution channels.
7. Access to appropriate technology.
8. Access to long term supplies of raw materials.

Prices and profitability can be extremely vulnerable to competition from new entrants. Consequently, the likelihood of increased competition from this source is similarly analysed. This depends on the cost of entering the industry, the degree to which a new entrant would suffer running cost disadvantages, and the degree to which existing products are differentiated and consequently enjoy a high degree of brand loyalty from their customers.

Entry costs include the scale of investment required for specialized plant, or for advertising or R&D to achieve competitive economies of scale, or to counter the high switching costs of existing customers.

Running cost disadvantages include the degree to which existing firms have tied up economic raw material supplies, or might have achieved cost reductions through 'Bostonian' experience.

Similar appraisals are made of the bargaining power of suppliers and buyers, and of the threat of substitute products, having regard to the relative importance of the business relationship to each participant, the existence of substitute products, the degree to which alternative products are differentiated, etc. The main factors are summarized below:

Bargaining power of suppliers depends on:
1. Monopoly power in supplier industry.
2. Degree of differentiation of suppliers' product.
3. Costs of switching from one supplier to another:
   (a) for the supplier,
   (b) for the firm in question.
4. Importance of volume to the supplier.
5. Importance of the supplier's product to the industry.

Bargaining power of buyers depends on:
1. Buyer volume.
2. Availability of substitute products.
3. Costs of switching.
4. Concentration of buyer's industry.
5. Price sensitivity.
6. Product differences.
7. Buyer information.

Threat of substitutes depends on
1. Relative price of substitutes.
2. Technical comparability of substitutes.
3. Costs of switching.
4. Speed of technological development in 'substitute' industries.

This multidimensional analysis is intended to indicate the likely long run profitability of the industry. It is the approach's unique contribution to thinking about strategy and contrasts vividly with the proposition that market growth is the sole factor of any significance in determining industry attractiveness.

5.3 Competitor analysis

A firm's relative position within the industry, and consequently its long run profitability, is determined by the degree to which it is able to establish a sustainable advantage over its competitors.

Analysis of competitiors is comprehensive and seeks to answer such questions as:

Who should we pick a fight with in the industry, and with what sequence of moves?

What is the meaning of that competitor's strategic move and how seriously should we take it?

What areas should we avoid because the competitor's response will be emotional or desperate? (Porter, 1980, p. 47).

The recommended analysis of competitors may be too detailed to be realistic for many businesses. It includes analysis of the competitor's future goals and assumptions, and current strategies and capabilities. Just looking at competitor capabilities, the analysis involves detailed appraisals of the following:

● competitor's products
● dealer/distribution
● marketing and selling
● operations
● research and engineering

- overall costs
- financial strength
- organization
- general manager ability
- corporate portfolio
- personnel turnover
- relationships with government bodies, etc.

The analysis in each of these areas is quite detailed. For example, just looking at operations, it is suggested that information is required on the following items:

- manufacturing cost position – economies of scale, learning curve, newness of equipment, etc.
- technological sophistication of facilities and equipment
- flexibility of facilities and equipment
- proprietary know-how and unique patent or cost advantages
- skills in capacity addition, quality control, tooling, etc.
- location, including labour and transportation cost
- labour force climate, unionization situation
- access to and cost of raw materials
- the degree of vertical integration.

Additionally, a detailed assessment is needed of the competitor's abilities to grow, to respond quickly and to adapt to change, as well as its staying power as indicated by such things as cash reserves, unanimity among management, long time horizon in its financial goals and lack of stock-market pressure.

The above relates only to the analysis of the *capabilities* of a competitor. In addition, it is suggested that with an adequate analysis of a competitor's future goals, assumptions, current strategies and capabilities, 'we can begin to ask the critical questions that will lead to a profile of how a competitor is likely to respond' (Porter, 1980).

The analysis is therefore exhaustive, not to say exhausting. Its pedigree in industrial economics, as opposed to practical management is apparent. The aim seems to be to obtain what economists refer to as perfect information, or as near to it as is feasible. The firm may have several substantial competitors that it needs to consider. Additionally, the business also needs to analyse its customers, its technology suppliers, and its suppliers of raw materials, etc., in similar fashion. It needs to carry out the analyses individually and it needs to consider the strategic groups which may lead to quite different responses.

Moreover, in this rapidly changing world, there is a need continuously to update substantial elements of the information base.

The information requirements defined by Porter (1980) are extremely pertinent to strategy, but they pose a severe problem in terms of the time and cost involved in obtaining, processing and continually updating such colossal amounts of data.

Moreover, even if it were practical to accomplish all this, the process of selecting the relevant and important information still remains. Selectivity, which is one of management's perennial problems, is vital when implementing a Porter-type industry and competitor analysis. The critical skill is deciding what information is crucial and what is merely nice to have.

The approach may, nevertheless, help to structure strategic thinking about competitive issues and act as a checklist against which to consider the factors that might be important in given circumstances.

5.4   Competitive strategies

Industry analysis, however imperfect, provides the information on which competitive strategies may be based. Competitive strategies specify the means by which a business will achieve its competitive advantage, i.e. achieve the most profitable long term position it can in the industry in which it operates.

The approach to long term profitability used by Porter is derived

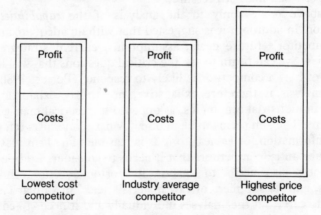

Figure 5.2   *Profitability and competitive strategies.*

from the theories of classical economics, rather than empirical analysis. In this simple model, profitability is seen as deriving from the relationship of costs and prices as shown in Figure 5.2. This is the theoretical reason why there are only two effective strategies available – least cost or highest price.

Highest profitability can be achieved by accepting the average market price and achieving the lowest costs, or by accepting industry average costs and achieving the highest product price. Any other strategy will fall between these two stools and be likely only to result in industry average profitability. Porter labelled these two strategies 'cost leadership' and 'differentiation', having a product that is differentiated from the industry average being the only way that a higher price could be sustained.

Both strategies can be applied either across a broad front, or by focusing on a limited segment of the market rather than the market as a whole as shown in Figure 5.3. Cost leadership and differentiation, focused and unfocused, in this model are the only competitive strategy options available. Consequently they are often referred to as 'generic' strategies – all strategies must stem from one or other. Moreover, any attempt to pursue more than one such strategy only leads to the firm being 'stuck in the middle', i.e. without any coherent strategy, lacking direction with no prospect of concentration and consistency and achieving only industry average profitability.

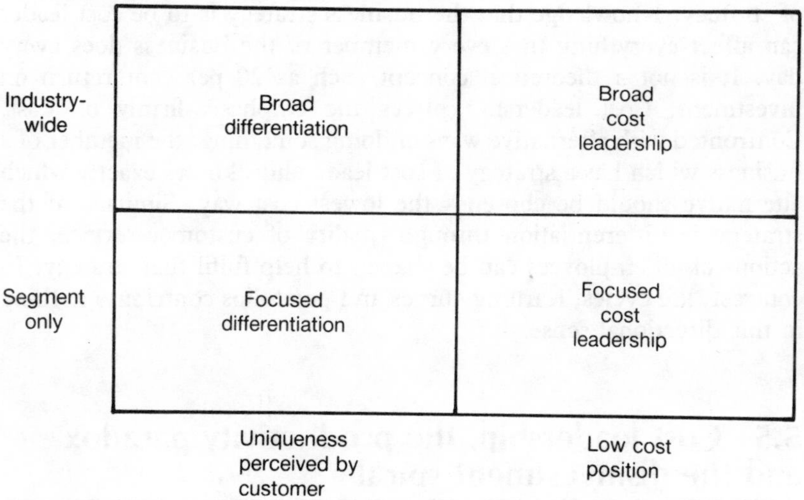

Figure 5.3 *Four competitive strategies.*
Source: Porter (1980).

Each strategy is dependent on the industry's structure and the firm's ability to cope with the five competitive forces better than its rivals. Again this contrasts with Boston's assertion that cumulative market share is the sole determinant of a firm's business strength.

The four strategies have created a great deal of interest. They accord with much accepted management theory and there is also considerable empirical support for the suggestion that many effective strategies tend to be either concentrated on achieving low costs or product differentiation.

However, objections are sometimes raised. If the economic model from which they are derived is rejected, the two strategies may not be seen as the only, and mutually exclusive, options. In the strategic marketing approach, for example, competitive strategy focuses on how the company satisfies the customer's needs, which may be any combination of product attributes including cost and any number of qualitative factors. Cost leadership is not necessarily related in any way to customer needs, but often tends to be related to internal factors such as production strategy. There may indeed be room for defining other competitive strategies, with other orientations, which may or may not make equivalent contributions to competitive advantage.

Above all else, however, cost leadership and differentiation identify the strategic direction of a business in a way that no other approach discussed so far does. They therefore have the possibility of achieving concentration and consistency, thereby achieving much of the purpose of strategy. Knowledge that the business strategy is to be cost leader can affect everything that every member of the business does every day. It is not a theoretical concept such as 20 per cent return on investment. Cost leadership places the emphasis firmly on cost. Confronted with alternative ways of doing something, the member of a business which has a strategy of cost leadership, knows exactly which alternative should be chosen – the lowest cost way. Similarly if the strategy is differentiation through quality of customer service, the actions of all employees can be shaped to help fulfil that strategy. In contrast, life cycles, learning curves and portfolios contribute nothing in this directional sense.

5.5 Cost leadership, the productivity paradox and the disinvestment spiral

Cost leadership is a term that has come to mean many different things. A firm which is accounting dominated and constantly emphasizes efficiency is frequently referred to as having adopted a cost leadership strategy. This is not necessarily correct. One of management's jobs, no matter what the business strategy, is to try and operate efficiently, but this does not imply they are necessarily seeking to be cost leaders.

The strategy of cost leadership applies to businesses which attempt to become the lowest cost producer in an industry. If competing products are more or less undifferentiated and therefore sell at a standard market price, the competitor with the lowest costs will earn the highest profits. This will put that competitor in the strongest competitive position, which is important where products are undifferentiated and competition is direct.

However, in any industry there can only be one cost leader. All other competitors following a cost leadership strategy cannot by definition succeed. The degree to which their costs exceed those of the cost leader is some measure of their vulnerability. In the event of direct price competition the would-be cost leaders who came second best will almost inevitably be forced to reduce market share or stand making losses, and in the extreme may be driven out of the industry altogether. Following a cost leadership strategy without success frequently leads managements to redouble their efforts to reduce costs. Their focus on cost reduction and efficiency, at the expense of all other factors, may become totally dominant and an end in itself. Such a firm would tend to become accounting dominated and place the greatest attention on production costs, rather than any business strategic factors.

A cost leadership strategy is widely followed by firms in Britain and America in the interests of short term profits, often with disastrous results. In an award winning article, Wickham Skinner (1986) wrote about what he called the productivity paradox.

> Efforts to improve productivity actually driv[ing] competitive success further out of reach . . . breaking loose from [so long established a] mind-set is not easy. It requires a change in culture, in habits, instincts and ways of thinking and reasoning. (Skinner, 1986, p. 58)

This phenomenon had been previously identified in two articles in the *Harvard Business Review* (Hayes and Abernathy, 1980; Hayes and Garvin, 1982). It was noted that American industry was starting to lose ground to Japanese and European competitors.

> In the past, American managers earned worldwide respect for their carefully planned yet highly aggressive action across three different time frames:

Short term – using existing assets as efficiently as possible.

Medium term – replacing labour and other scarce resources with capital equipment.

Long term – developing new products and processes that open new markets or restructure old ones. (Hayes and Abernathy, 1980, p. 68)

Whilst American managers were credited with continuing to achieve with the short term actions, they were no longer effective in the medium and long term requirements. Hayes and Abernathy illustrated the point with a number of quotations from American managers:

> To undertake such (medium and long term) commitments is hardly in the interests of a manager who is concerned with his or her next quarterly earnings reports. (Quoting from Suzuki, 1979, p. 1)

> We understand how to market, we know the technology, and production problems are not extreme. Why risk money on new businesses when good profitable low risk opportunities are on every side? (Quoting from *Business Week*, 16 February 1976, p. 57)

The short term cost focus inhibits investment in new plant and new technology which in due course results in firms losing the ability to compete effectively. In the face of price competition such firms inevitably lose both in terms of profit and market share. Consequently

> morale sags, performance suffers, and employees – generally the best ones – begin to leave. Faced with these circumstances, top management often concludes that a division or product line is unsalvageable and purposely continues the process of disinvestment. (Hayes and Garvin, 1982, p. 79)

Once started, this disinvestment spiral is extremely difficult to reverse.

Thus, at the very least, a strategy of cost leadership may be regarded as extremely dangerous. In practice the actions taken by would-be cost leaders often prove counter-productive.

Moreover, cost leadership is an essentially inward looking strategy that has no immediate implications for the customer. At best cost leadership can only facilitate a customer-oriented strategy of old-fashioned price leadership. Some writers see cost leadership as an inconsistency in the model, having little *per se* to do with competitive advantage unless accompanied by price leadership (Coyne, 1986).

The Japanese, and to a lesser extent the Germans, achieve cost leadership only in order to implement a customer-oriented strategy aimed at achieving long term growth and profitability. This is done using the cost advantage to satisfy some additional perceived need of the customer, such as quality or some other differentiated product attribute. By contrast, in Britain and America, cost leadership is often pursued for its own sake the motivation coming from the adoption of purely accounting norms and objectives. In this case the pursual of cost leadership, even if it is not directly counter-productive, actually has little relevance for strategy of any kind.

5.6   Differentiation

There is a great deal of empirical support for the strategy of differentiation, that is, providing a product or service that is in some way differentiated from competitive products. For example, Hall (1980) investigated sixty-four American companies and found that businesses that followed generic strategies performed better than the rest. All the high performers in Hall's sample

> used careful strategic analysis to guide their investments, avoiding simplistic adherence to doctrinaire approaches towards strategy formulation which come from naive application of tools like: share/growth matrices . . . experience curves and PIMS. (Hall, 1980)

The basis of the differentiation does not appear to matter. It may be to do with the product, its quality or with customer service. It may also be combined with aspects of cost leadership as when, for example, Philip Morris were found to combine 'lowest cost, fully automated cigarette manufacturing with high cost focused branding and promotion to gain industry profit leadership without the benefit of either largest unit volume or segment market share'. This seems to contradict one of Porter's main assertions about being 'stuck in the middle' which arises from the simple economic theory on which his model is based. The case of Philip Morris suggests that a viable strategy can be based on a combination of cost leadership and differentiation. There are many other examples, some of which Porter himself quotes, such as Proctor & Gamble's Ivory soap which is to its managers a fully-dimensioned brand rather than a one-dimensional cost leader or differentiator. The strategic marketing model discussed in the next chapter explains further how the notion of combining aspects of cost leadership and differentiation does not necessarily lead to being 'stuck in the middle'.

To be strategically valid the point of differentiation must be one for which there is a need, i.e. customers perceive it as being worth a premium price. Differentiation for its own sake has no strategic value whatsoever. If it is not worth a premium then the product will only command a basic, general market price and the business, unless it is the cost leader, will be unable to earn an economic return.

This point is worth emphasizing since there have been some misconceptions about the nature of differentiation in the context of competitive strategy. Some have suggested that the idea is simply to maximize the differentiation from competitors. Thus, the product might be differentiated by virtue of the degree of automation involved in its production. The leader in such a form of differentiation may consider, therefore, that further investment in automation will serve to reinforce and strengthen the differentiation strategy. However, the critical point is whether the customer perceives and values the differentiation, not whether or not the degree of differentiation from competitors is maximized.

The most successful differentiation strategies are those where the point of differentiation perceived and valued by customers, coincides with the organization's distinctive competence. This may be some skill or knowledge, often embodied in some unique or patented plant or process. It could also be in some organizational characteristic which, for example, enables the organization to deliver products of uniquely high quality. Distinctive competence is the key to effective competition in specific market areas or niches.

5.7   Implementing competitive strategies

The aim of competitive strategies is the achievement of long term competitive advantage. This is not simply a matter of which businesses to invest in, as is the case with portfolio strategies, but much more to do with how to manage the business strategically. Unlike the other approaches to strategy that have been discussed so far, competitive strategy does contribute to the concept of strategic direction.

Knowing that the direction is 'customer service', or 'product quality' can help people in the organization to know how they should allocate their efforts and enthusiasm, in a way that '20 per cent return on capital employed' or '30 per cent market share' do not. Such a directional strategy can then form the basis of concentration and consistency.

An effective business strategy should pervade every aspect of the business so that every member knows what the strategy is and every decision and action is consistent with it and serves to reinforce it. Porter uses the concept of the value chain to identify these various strategic impacts (Porter, 1984).

In a manufacturing business the value chain follows the route of the entry of raw materials through the production process and on to the despatch of finished product and beyond. The value chain, however, includes the related environments so that, for example, the raw material suppliers are seen as an essential part of the chain.

Variations on this approach to business analysis have been widely used in the past. Delay centre analysis and cost chains, for example, have been widely used in cost and management accounting, while the inclusion of the relationship with external environments is an idea from systems theory. Usually such approaches divide the business into direct and indirect activities which are analysed separately.

The competitive strategy approach analyses the following direct activities:

1. Purchasing and stock control.
2. Production.
3. Order processing and distribution.
4. Marketing and selling.
5. After sales support.

Potentially of equal importance in terms of external relationships, even though they may not be major costs in their own right, are the indirect activities:

6. General management.
7. Technological development.
8. Administration.

Analysis for competitive strategy does not simply identify those activities and costs which are not on the chain and could therefore be reduced or eliminated. This would hardly be strategic. Analysis of the value chain for the purposes of achieving competitive advantage is more detailed and more qualitative. The potential application of information technology will serve as an example.

The aim of the exercise is to establish the extent to which, in this case, information technology could impact on each activity of the business, and in particular on how each activity of the business contributes to the generic strategy of the business, be it differentiation or cost leadership.

Purchasing and stock control might be subject to a number of potential impacts. For example, the harmonization and compatibility of both computer hardware and software are making it increasingly more feasible and efficient to be directly connected with major suppliers' computer systems. This could be beneficial in terms of reducing essential inventory levels and providing instant supplies information. Moreover, the benefits to the supplier are likely to be realizable in some form of price reduction.

Similarly, automated warehousing might produce easily realizable and critical reductions in costs and increases in performance. Or it might be worth while in some cases linking up directly with raw materials/commodities data base systems giving instant information on availability and price movements.

The applicability and economic worth of these various facilities will vary from situation to situation. In some cases they might be an unnecessary and expensive sophistication, while in others they might represent the key to the achievement of an additional price premium, or unlocking the competitive situation and taking a major additional share of the market.

In this approach, each business activity is analysed in depth. For brevity some potential information technology applications in each value chain activity are simply listed below:

Production:
- Computer-aided manufacturing
- Flexible manufacturing systems
- Microprocessor control, robotization, etc.

Order processing and distribution:
- Automated order processing
- Direct computer connection with customers
- Software harmonization with customers

Marketing and selling:
- Use of videotext for instant information transfer
- New selling media: teletext, fax, etc.

After sales support:
- Computer scheduling/routeing of maintenance vehicles

- Remote/local access to service advice/facilities
- Computerized after sales follow-up of customers

General management:
- Internal information systems for fast feedback
- Access to strategic information databases, indices, etc.

Technology development:
- Computer-aided design
- Electronic market/technology research

Administration:
- Financial and planning models
- Computerized personnel records

The above is only a summary listing of some of the ways in which information technology might contribute to the achievement of competitive advantage. There are of course many others. Moreover there are many other potential applications and innovations outside the field of information technology.

The value chain concept serves to make the implementation of competitive strategies more systematic. In pursual of a cost leadership strategy, the approach leads to a more or less traditional cost accounting analysis of the business in terms of cost chains or delay centres. In pursual of a strategy of differentiation the approach is more interesting and may provide useful new insights. For example, take a business which differentiates its product from competitors by a high quality of customer service. Using the analysis of value chains, the possible contributions to that strategy could be identified for each business activity. Clearly many of the information technology items listed above might be relevant to the improvement of customer service. By comparison with competitors it would be relatively straightforward to identify the competitive performance on 'quality of customer service' in each activity and thus decide which applications to invest in and which to let pass. These directional decisions are the essential outcomes of competitive strategy.

5.8 Summary

The competitive strategy framework was developed for a period of low growth when efforts were concentrated on how markets were divided up between competitors rather than on how to make them grow faster.

The approach focuses on the factors which determine the long term profitability of an industry and the factors that determine a firm's competitive position in the industry.

The approach, based on classical economic theory, is information intensive – information is the essential foundation of competitive strategy. The information requirements identified as necessary by Porter are so extensive as to be impractical for most businesses and it is therefore essential to be selective, collecting data which is crucial to the strategy concerned, ignoring data which is not relevant.

Competitive strategy is concerned with how to beat competitors, or avoid them. Unless victory is assured, head-on competition is futile.

The strategy of beating competitors is achieved through cost leadership. In any industry there can only be one cost leader. Thus, all but one of the firms attempting to be cost leaders are doomed to mediocrity or failure.

In practice it has often been found that the strategy of cost leadership is counter-productive and results in the business progressively cutting away its ability to compete – the disinvestment spiral.

The strategy of avoiding competitors can be achieved by differentiating the product from the others on the market, or by focusing on a small niche of the market away from the competition. Differentiation and focus appear to be more successful strategies than cost leadership.

To be successful, differentiation must provide a product which is differentiated in a way which buyers perceive as worth a premium price. Without this premium the strategy of differentiation will not be rewarded by economic success.

To be effective competitive strategies must pervade and shape all activities of the business and including its relationships with its various environments.

Implementation is therefore achieved through a methodical analysis of all business activities, both direct and indirect, on the value chain.

Financial and psychological investment decisions are then taken in accordance with the need to achieve a sustainable competitive advantage.

DISCUSSION CASE:
OXDEN HORTICULTURAL PRODUCTS LTD

Oxden is a medium-sized producer of bagged horticultural products, composts, fertilizers, etc. One of its main product lines is John Innes compost made in four formulations for sowing, potting on, etc., the major difference being the strength of the nutrients included. (John Innes is the name of agreed formulations of soil-based compost.)

The production process is one of simply mixing soil, sand and gravel and nutrients together and then putting measured quantities into polythene bags. Bulk raw materials are purchased or extracted, sterilized where necessary, moisture content corrected, mixed and bagged. Strict quality control is crucial. Oxden had in the past suffered a number of claims from trade customers attributing the loss of thousands of seedlings with a consequential profit loss into several hundred thousand pounds.

Production costs are predominantly related to the bagging process. Oxden had three bagging lines, each handling different bag size ranges. The machines on all three lines are new and incorporate the latest technology. Utilization of this plant is the key to profitability. At present it works on a two-shift basis for about nine months of the year and single shift the other three months. Demand for product is highly seasonal and it is necessary to build substantial stocks for the spring and autumn sales seasons. They have not attempted to run a three-shift 24-hour-a-day operation.

Oxden are a leading soil-based compost producer with around 30 per cent of its served markets. These are divided into three sectors. Firstly, Oxden make substantial sales of bulk (i.e. unbagged) product to the nursery trade. Secondly, they also make substantial sales of bagged product to garden centres and other specialist horticultural outlets. Thirdly, they also make substantial sales to five national chains of stores (supermarkets and variety stores).

Sales to garden centres are made under the Oxden label, while the sales to retail chains are all made under the chains' own labels.

Bulk sales to the trade are slowly declining; garden centre sales are stable; and retail chain sales have been increasing rapidly. Oxden have succeeded in adding a new national customer each season for the previous four years and hope to continue this policy.

Last year, after printing the bags for Astoreco, their biggest retail chain customer, Oxden were instructed to overprint a bar code onto all the bags. This had been achieved, at considerable expense, by printing self-adhesive labels and then manually applying one to every bag as it left the bagging line. The bar codes were required by the customer to facilitate the rapid collection of sales data. This would be automatically input to a new sales order processing and stock control system and would result in automatic replenishment of stocks at each store and reordering of suppliers as necessary.

Discussion points
You are the Marketing Director of Oxden and just before visiting Astoreco to discuss next season's requirements you hear a rumour that they may require all major suppliers to invest in a new microcomputer system capable of running their order processing software and therefore being linked directly to Astoreco.

- How do you feel about this proposal if it proves to be so?
- What information would you require before meeting Astoreco?
- How will you ensure that Oxden obtain the required order from Astoreco?

One of Oxden's competitors is a small family business called ABC who have around 3 per cent of the market and are known to have very old obsolete plant. It has recently become known that the proprietor of ABC has handed over management of the business to his son. Aso that they have bought two new high putput bagging machines of similar type to Oxden's. It is also known that ABC have been very actively involved during the close season with all the retail chains, presumably trying to get new business in order to utilize the new plant. ABC have previously only sold to garden centres and a small amount through direct mail.

Discussion points
- As Marketing Director of Oxden, what is your attitude to ABC's activities?
- How seriously do you regard them as a threat?
- How can Oxden best combat the threat from ABC?

ABC have been preparing their ground carefully. They have been in close discussion with Astoreco for the past two years and, using a third party software development house, have produced Astoreco's new computerized order processing system which was designed from the start as an integrated customer–supplier system. This represented a substantial investment for ABC who possess the copyright and intend to sell the system as a product in its own right in order to recoup the development costs. It will be made available free to Astoreco who have the licence to make it also available to their various suppliers.

Astoreco are well satisfied with the new computer system and propose to use it as extensively as possible.

Discussion points
You are the Senior Sourcing Executive at Astoreco with responsibility for

all DIY and gardening supplies. In the past you have ordered all Astoreco's compost from Oxden and another leading supplier called JI Products in ratio of 60 : 40. This year you want to give some business to ABC who have developed the new computer system and are already connected to it and consequently very easy to deal with.

- How will you divide your order up this year?
- What assurances would you require from ABC before placing your order?
- What evidence is there that ABC have the capability to a substantial supplier?

Now put yourself in the position of the son of the proprietor of ABC. Although the horticultural products market is mature it nevertheless looks set for continuous if unspectacular growth. You have decided that it is worth trying to take a much bigger slice of the market than your father was happy with and the retail chains, particularly hyper- and super-markets look most attractive because distribution is much simpler for the supplier than distribution to garden centres.

- What will be your main problems in breaking into this new market?
- What will your best strategy be for extending business to other customers as well as Astoreco?
- How do you expect Oxden will respond to your moves?

Note
In the new season ABC took 13 per cent of the retail chain market, mainly with Astoreco, but also adding another store customer. This was only sufficient to achieve around 45 per cent utilization of ABC's plant. Nevertheless, ABC had become Astoreco's easiest supplier to deal with and in addition had forged strong personal links during the course of developing the computer system. Whereas competitors were left out in the cold – in most cases even their computer hardware did not fit the new system.

This case should prompt consideration of competitive forces and competitive advantage, as well as the value chain and the interrelationship with customers. Also consider the relevance of cost leadership and differentiation strategies, remembering that the product was a pure commodity of a formulation precisely prescribed for the companies. Consider what other aspects of differentiation might be relevant to these competitors.

CHAPTER SIX
Strategic thinking frameworks: strategic marketing

6.1 Introduction

The strategic thinking models considered so far represent a more or less chronological progression. The approaches described in Chapter 3 were introduced in the 1950s and widely adopted in the 1960s. Boston's empirical work on experience curves and portfolios was published in 1964 and they were very widely used throughout the 1970s. Porter's *Competitive Strategy* was first published in 1980 and that approach has been increasingly popular throughout the decade.

They also represent a progression in terms of the degree to which they appear to come to terms with the purpose of strategy. The life cycle model is a deliberate attempt to stand back from an industry or market and take a holistic view of its evolution. The analysis is objective and dispassionate, even to the point of assuming management is impotent to change the strategic development of the business. Experience curves and portfolio analysis move in a little closer and analyse the position of the individual business, but only to a limited extent. The strategic options are limited to buy, invest and sell decisions. As with life cycles, the analysis contributes little to the identification of strategic direction, concentration or consistency.

Competitive strategy takes a much closer look at the characteristics of the industry and the strategic position of the individual business in that industry. The identification of the generic strategies of cost leadership and differentiation, whether they are focused or on a broad front, is a way of defining direction and achieving concentration and consistency. In addition, the requirements for continuous industry analysis are also prerequisite for flexibility since it involves the definition of critical trends which may have impact on the firm's effectiveness as cost leader or differentiated producer, and thus identify the necessity to make strategic changes.

However, competitive strategy does not go as far into the detail of defining differentiation or cost leadership as does the strategic marketing approach described in this chapter. The philosophy that the 'customer is king' is made very explicit in strategic marketing. In competitive strategy there is a risk that the emphasis may be placed on differentiating the business from competitors, whereas in strategic marketing the emphasis is firmly on identifying and uniquely satisfying the perceived needs of the customer. The difference is not one simply of nuance, but extends into the methodology of how those needs, and thus the direction of a viable differentiation, are identified.

Each strategic thinking framework has its own validity and relevance to particular situations; none is universally applicable and none wholly wrong. Strategic marketing may be used as a complement to competitive strategy, as a means of thinking at a more detailed and operational level about the key issues raised in the competitive strategy context.

Strategic marketing concerns not simply the strategy for the marketing function, but the strategy for the whole business, based on the marketing philosophy. By marketing philosophy is meant a management orientation to determining the needs of target markets and to satisfying those needs more effectively and efficiently than competitors.

The tools for implementing a marketing strategy are those often referred to as the marketing mix, i.e. product, price, promotion and distribution. The other management tools used to implement strategy become subservient to these four. Thus, under this strategic thinking framework, production may be the most costly link in the value chain but nevertheless exists simply as a contributor to the satisfaction of customer needs. It would have no independent strategic validity of its own as it might, for example, if a competitive strategy of cost leadership were adopted.

It should be emphasized that the framework description in this chapter is not intended as a comprehensive explanation of strategic marketing, but merely to identify the approach in as much as it can guide the definition of strategy. The importance of strategic marketing as a strategic thinking framework is that it provides a means of deciding the focus of an effective differentiation strategy, based on what customers want. In this chapter attention is focused on a particular technique, which while practically useful in its own right, is also representative of the strategic marketing philosophy.

6.2   Customer orientation

Customer orientation is the essence of the strategic marketing frame-work. The concept is familiar enough to contemporary management and is invariably espoused by marketing specialists. However, if it is to have any real power in a business, it must be all-pervasive. Everyone in the firm must be customer oriented. It only takes one employee who 'can't be bothered' with the customer to undo months, even years, of painstaking reputation building.

Peters and Waterman (1982) found that the excellent companies were invariably customer oriented – they accorded a far higher priority to giving the customer value, quality and service, than they did to operating efficiently in cost terms, or being technological leaders.

Customer orientation may be vital to 'excellence'; this is no different from what marketing text books have been saying for years. The fact that customer orientation is not widely practised hardly makes the message more stimulating. The point about customer orientation is that it has to be focused and strategy driven. IBM's customer orientation is focused on providing service, because that is the cornerstone of its strategy. However, service is not the cornerstone of every business. Some thoroughly successful firms have prospered through the simple and valid strategy of 'pile it high and sell it cheap', or 'any colour so long as it's black'. Such cornerstones are intrinsically no less customer oriented than 'service'. It all depends on what customer need the product is satisfying.

Customer orientation implies that a business concentrates its efforts on satisfying the customer need. Peters and Waterman's 'excellent' businesses were excellent because they developed this orientation into their greatest strength. Thus, excellence appears to result from the co-incidence of a firm's greatest strength, or distinctive competence, with the satisfaction of the customer's perceived need. This coincidence is not accidental.

6.3   Leadership

Every viable business has some 'distinctive competence', something at which it is peculiarly effective. It may not be unique and the firm may not be the best, but at least in some aspect it must be better than the common herd. If it were not so, the firm would go out of business.

For the distinctive competence to be of any strategic value it must be embodied in the product the customer buys. For example, a firm may be peculiarly effective in R&D, but if the fruits of its research are not incorporated in a firm's product this competence will avail it nothing. Similarly the distinctive competence might relate to some aspect of cost, but if that strength is not embodied in the product either in the form of reduced price or increased quality, etc., it will have no strategic impact.

If the distinctive competence accords with the customer need and is embodied in the product, it creates a leadership position. The idea that 'economic results are only earned by leadership, not by mere competence' has been a central Drucker concept over the years (Drucker, 1964). While he is sometimes accused of making things seem too simple, his concept of leadership is in fact much more subtle than some of the later contributions, such as Boston's.

Leadership for Drucker did not mean that a business had to have the dominant share of the market, or that it had to be first in every product line, or the most technologically advanced. Leadership had merely to relate to 'something of value to the customer'. It might be in service, or distribution, or some quite narrow aspect of the product, it might even relate to the firm's 'ability to convert ideas into saleable products'.

Potentially then a leadership position attaching to anything which the customer values provides the business with economic results. With no leadership position, even if the firm has the major share of the market, the business will at best be 'marginal'.

The problem with this concept of leadership has been how to make it operational. The generality of the concept makes it difficult to measure. If it cannot be measured, it can only remain a generality. Within the main strands of strategic management literature there is no definitive method for how a firm might identify a worthwhile leadership position, much less how it might achieve one. But the idea that it has to be of value to the customer, and therefore embodied in what the customer buys, leads to consideration of the product.

6.4 Product attributes and customer perceptions

An expensive bottle of wine is not usually purchased simply to satisfy a thirst. Similarly, an automobile is not bought solely as a means of transportation. Products are loaded, both physically and psychologically,

Table 6.1 *Product attributes.*

Physical attributes	Implied attributes	Psychological attributes
Price	Distribution	Corporate image
Quality	Delivery	Brand image
Performance	Reliability	Product image
Design	Warranty	Need image
Packaging	After sales support	
	Advertising	
	Service	

with many extras that may be important determinants of sales success. Marketing literature is replete with descriptions of the many and various components that comprise the modern conception of a product.

One widely held view sees the product as having three layers: the core benefit or service, the formal product and the outer, augmented product layer which includes such things as warranty, service support and so on (Kotler, 1984). This onion-like model implies that the product can be unpeeled to reveal hidden depths. The analogy only partially stands up to scrutiny.

The various attributes of a product are not necessarily related in any predictable fashion, onion-like or otherwise. All that can be said is that there are many and various attributes that could be categorized for convenience as physical, implied and psychological as shown in Table 6.1.

What matters about this complex product is the customer's perceptions of its various attributes. Producing the best mousetrap is of no avail if it is not perceived as such by potential customers. The customer's perception of the product is an amalgam of their perception of the various product attributes, *any* of which may be critical. The product may be bought because the price is right – it satisfies an economic need; or its performance may be what is attractive; or its quality; or it might be some deep-seated psychological need which is satisfied by the product's sexy design, or image.

The customer's perception of products is not necessarily compatible with a common sense notion of reality. Too great a divide between perception and reality is likely to be only short-lived, but there will nevertheless be differences, and some of them may be important. Even an attribute as apparently unambiguous as price may be affected by this dichotomy between customer perception and reality. A product which is actually cheap relative to its competitors, may, in fact, be perceived as being relatively expensive. If the customer regards price as the critical attribute, then their perception of the product's price will dictate the buying decision. If Brand A is perceived as cheaper than Brand B then the customer will buy Brand A, even if the reality is that Brand B has the lower price.

Customers may have perceptions about every product attribute, though many of them may not be sufficiently strong to affect the buying decision. However, an attribute as potentially woolly and complicated as brand image can be a powerful determinant of customer behaviour. This has frequently been shown with 'blind' product tests, a standard way of assessing brand image (King, 1967).

In such tests, typically, a panel of consumers is given two or more brands to test and compare, the brands being presented in plain packs so that their identity is unknown. The consumers may prefer Brand A to Brand B when they are anonymous, but when the real brand names are attached the results may be reversed. This suggests the existence of a brand image consisting of a set of associations that may be set off by the brand name. This image can be sufficiently strong to overwhelm previous experience and perceptions of the product tests and impacts directly on the buying decision. Image leads to the purchase of items which would not otherwise have been chosen. It applies to all product types, industrial as well as consumer, the main difference being that advertising, which is the prime image-building tool, is a higher proportion of the promotion expense in consumer products than it is in industrial products. Thus image may be more easily adjusted for consumer products.

The process of identifying what need the customer satisfies in buying a product can be approached quite systematically. Firstly, it is necessary to know which product attributes the customer perceives as important. Secondly, it is important to know what the customer perceives as being ideal performance on these important attributes. Thirdly, it is important to establish how the customer perceives the firm's product as performing on the same attributes. Finally, it is important to know how the customer perceives competing products in the same way.

Customer and potential customer perceptions are a crucial ingredient of strategic marketing and their identification is a key step in defining an effective competitive strategy. A differentiation strategy can be avowed simply by managerial decision without any recourse to customer perceptions. Such differentiation may fail because it is quite irrelevant to the customer who is not particularly concerned with the attribute being differentiated. Effective differentiation must therefore be based on a sound knowledge of customer perceptions.

Such precise information is unlikely to be achieved simply by being 'close to the customer'. Obsessions with service and quality, effective nichemanship and listening to the customer are what Peters and Waterman (1982) identify as 'close to the customer', but understanding their real needs and perceptions implies a more systematic form of customer orientation which has to include a technically reliable form of enquiry. Such methods are available and are fairly straightforward. One such approach is preference mapping, described below, which enables the customer's perceptions about the product and its competitors to be identified.

Preference mapping is an operational marketing technique and it may seem inappropriate to discuss it in any detail in a text on strategic thinking. However, the idea of overtly discovering how potential and existing customers perceive and value the various attributes of the product and its competitors is fundamental to defining direction, which is the basis of strategy. An operational means of achieving this is perhaps one missing ingredient in the competitive strategy described in the previous chapter.

6.5 Preference mapping and product positioning

Preference mapping and product positioning are techniques of marketing research which embody the marketing philosophy so fundamentally that they capture the essence of strategic marketing itself.

Preference mapping is a technique for identifying and presenting consumer preferences for the product attributes which they perceive as important in satisfying their needs. The technique has been described in operational detail in many other texts (e.g. Green and Tull, 1970), so a simplified explanation is sufficient for the present purpose. A common consumer product such as instant coffee is ideal for illustrating the process.

Firstly, orthodox qualitative methods such as unstructured and semistructured interviews and consumer panel tests are used to establish a list of potentially significant attributes of instant coffee. As far as possible these attributes are generated without prompting or leading in any way by the researcher. Possible attributes of instant coffee might include price, strength, flavour, aroma, country of origin, brand image, etc.

Secondly, the list of potentially significant product attributes are then tested with selected samples of consumers to establish which appear to be regarded as important. The apparently unimportant attributes can then be disregarded. In our instant coffee example we can assume just two attributes are found to be perceived as important, for example, price and strength. Thus a 'map' could be constructed as in Figure 6.1. In practice the number of important attributes is unlikely to be restricted to just two – this example is limited simply for ease of illustration. As the process of graphical presentation of the map, which may have any number of independent dimensions, has been computerized, mapping presents no difficulty.

Thirdly, a selected sample of consumers are tested or questioned as to the nature of their 'ideal' instant coffee in terms of the important attributes of strength and price. This is done using methods which result in some sort of scaled response, for example, placing responses along a seven-point scale from 'very strong' to 'very mild'. In this way the response can be scored and the respondent's position plotted on the map if similarly scaled (e.g. from +3 to −3). In this way the aggregate 'ideal' instant coffee can be positioned on the map, being simply the aggregate of all responses.

Similarly, other 'ideal' instant coffees can be positioned relating to various subsets of the sample of respondents. The 'ideal' coffee of people living in Greater London may differ substantially from that of people in, say, Scotland or Wales. The samples used for testing may be selected on any basis (geographic, demographic, psychographic, etc.) so long as the market segments they represent are actually measurable, accessible (i.e. capable of being focused on) and of sufficient volume to be economically worth while.

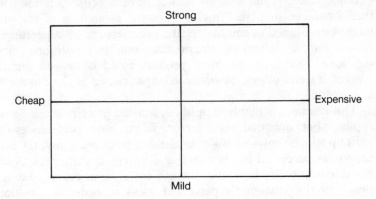

Figure 6.1 *A preference map for instant coffee.*

Having established 'ideal' positions, research is then conducted to establish the position of actual brands of instant coffee. Again this can be done by either testing or by direct questioning or a combination of the two. Thus positions on the map may be identified as in Figure 6.2.

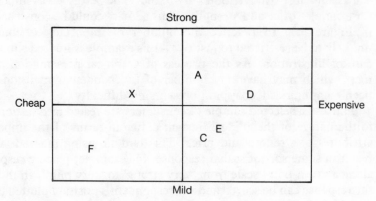

Figure 6.2 *Brand positions on instant coffee preference map.*

Position X marks the 'ideal' position of the relevant sample of respondents, while Positions A to F represent the various competing brands. Brands C and E appear to be perceived as in close competition, whilst brands A, D and F are perceived as distinctive in terms of the two attributes perceived as important.

The implications for the manufacturer of Brand F, for example, are that the product is perceived as being cheaper and milder than the ideal. Blind testing could be carried out to see if the consumer's perceptions of its attributes differ significantly from its reality. For example, the test might show that the brand actually tastes stronger than its image suggests. In this case, the promotion of the product might be designed to emphasize strength, perhaps by suggesting some new ingredient. In this way the product could be repositioned closer to the 'ideal'. Similarly the 'new' product could be moved slightly up market in terms of price in order to be positioned as close to the 'ideal' as possible.

This example is highly simplified, but the principles can be widely applied. For any product, a picture of customer preferences can be built up which shows what key leadership position, if any, the product enjoys, as perceived by its actual and potential customers. And it is possible to identify how this strength could be improved, i.e. moved closer to the customer's perceived ideal in order to position, or reposition, the product on the customer's preference map.

Preference mapping gives real focus to customer orientation and, if used regularly, makes it possible to detect changes in customer perceptions and needs, and in the position of competing products, before they make themselves apparent in reduced product sales. The concept of leadership is thus made more specific and identifiable as the firm's competitive specialism on which its competitive advantage rests.

The idea of competitive specialism combines the concept of leadership with that of differentiation. For the specialism to have any significance it has to be of value to the customer or else the customer will not pay an economic price. For it to be of value to the customer it must be embodied in the product, in at least one of its attributes. Moreover, the customer must actually perceive the specialism as being both present in the product and of value. Thus competitive specialism is a rather more precise term than either leadership or differentiation. It refers to the distinctive way in which a business satisfies the needs of its customers, distinctively in that it focuses on those aspects of need satisfaction which the business achieves better than its competitors.

Product positioning is one way of achieving a coherent strategic direction. This is prerequisite to achieving concentration and consistency, some aspects of which are implicit in the application of positioning across the whole business.

6.6   Business positioning

The discussion of product positioning and the competitive specialism appears to have assumed that businesses only have one product. This is patently absurd. Even the smallest firms have multiple products and multiple product lines. And each product may have different attributes which are perceived as being the reason why customers buy. Thus a firm with, say, three product lines could find that customers value different attributes of each product. They might value one for its price, one for its quality and one for its brand image.

This is a genuine problem which managements must confront. Using the methods proposed here the firm will be fully aware of this problem. Many businesses are not. Would a firm such as Porsche sell a product on price? If Porsche were to move into writing instruments would they be more successful selling a cheap throw-away rolling ball or an expensive piece of designer jewellery with a writing head? There is a need for the firm to adopt a consistent approach, exploiting the same or compatible specialisms on every product. If this is not achieved customer perceptions will tend to be incoherent and confused, and the image of no value. Moreover, the resultant confusion will be at least as apparent within the firm as among its customers.

Minor incompatibilities in the competitive specialisms of different products can be corrected by repositioning the product in question. However, a complete lack of consistency, such as arises from repeated diversification, defeats any coherent business strategy. Such diverse specialisms are only supportable as the more or less random result of an investment portfolio put together on the basis of purely short term financial criteria.

Acquisitions require consistency of specialism, if they are to be successful in business terms. The acquisition of businesses with different specialisms is frequently the cause of failure to integrate satisfactorily. A firm whose specialism centres around its competitive pricing might acquire a competitor whose business is based on technological leadership. Not only would both sets of customers obtain conflicting messages, but both sets of employees can suffer similar confusion. The answer is to make the new position very clear both internally and externally. If the strategy is to integrate the two businesses, the value of one specialism will be eliminated and this may well off-set the value of any apparently more tangible synergy which may have justified the acquisition in the first place.

6.7 Summary

The strategic marketing framework is concerned with business strategy based on the marketing philosophy of orienting the whole business to identify and satisfy customer needs.

To be effective customer orientation must involve every member of the business and result in the concentration of all efforts and resources on satisfying the customer needs that are identified.

Every viable business has some distinctive competence which sets it apart from other businesses. This may be limited and focused, or it might be quite broad and general. For the distinctive competence to provide the basis of a leadership position it must be embodied in the product or service the customer buys, and it must be perceived by the customer and be of value to the customer.

This leadership position and its exploitation is the basis of an effective competitive strategy. But for it to be of operational use it must be clearly identifiable and measurable. This is the key to defining strategic direction.

The first stage in this process is to analyse the product and its various attributes, physical, implied and psychological. It is then necessary to research customer perceptions of product attributes, as to their ideal product, the actual product and its competitors.

This analysis is the basis of a preference map which can show the positions of the various competitive products and identify the action required to reposition the product to give it a greater competitive advantage.

The product's position identifies the way customers perceive it in terms of its most critical attributes. The competitive strengths the customers thus identify represent the results of the firm's distinctive competence.

The strategic marketing framework suggests that the business should be focused on exploiting its distinctive competence in the satisfaction of customer needs. Thus, for a multiproduct business the satisfaction of customer needs implies there should be a consistency and compatibility across all product lines. Otherwise the distinctive competence will be lost and the business will tend to drift. For a diversified business where strategy is controlled from the centre, this is a highly probable outcome.

DISCUSSION CASE: FLETTON BRICK CO. PLC

Fletton Brick was a major producer of clay building bricks, the cost leader in its industry by a considerable margin. Its leadership arose from two main factors. Firstly, the fletton brick was made from clay which came from a deposit which uniquely contained a considerable amount of carbon material distributed as small particles throughout the clay. These carbon particles ignited during the kiln firing process thus significantly reducing the energy costs involved. Of all the brick manufacturers having access to the fletton clay deposit, Fletton Brick was much the largest and was thus able to exploit the latest and most automated manufacturing, handling and distribution equipment.

Fletton clay, however, also had some disadvantages. During firing fletton bricks developed mottles and discoloration which meant that they could only be sold as 'commons', i.e. for applications where their appearance was not regarded as important. They were unsuitable for sale as decorative facing bricks. The price of facing bricks was at least double the price of commons and for any non-fletton producer the key to profitability was to maximize the sales of facing bricks and minimize sales of commons.

In addition common brick sales were anticipated to reduce in the face of ever-increasing competition from concrete blocks and in particular from foamed concrete which had substantial benefits in terms of thermal insulation properties.

Discussion points
You are Marketing Director of Fletton Brick and have to produce a five-year marketing plan.

- What additional data do you require in order to identify the major proposed actions?

A board subcommittee comprising yourself, the R&D Director and the Finance Director is formed to consider the strategic options facing Fletton. The unanimous recommendation of this group is that Fletton Brick Co. must substantially reduce its reliance on its traditional main product, the common clay brick.

- Consider the ways in which such a change might be achieved and suggest the probable recommendations of each member of the subcommittee.

A new way of putting a decorative face on the fletton brick is successfully developed, permitting flettons to be sold as facing bricks. The pricing of this new product was crucial – too high a price would limit and slow down market penetration, too low a price would reduce profitability and also risk giving the new brick a cheap image.

Discussion point
- How would you, as Marketing Director, recommend the most appropriate pricing strategy to be adopted?

It was also proposed to acquire an existing high quality clay facing brick manufacturer. Acquisition candidates were all very much smaller than Fletton – the largest had less then 10 per cent of Fletton's production capacity.

Discussion points
- List the three main potential strategic benefits to be gained for Fletton from such an acquisition. Consider the different product positions of Fletton and its potential acquisition.
- What product repositioning should be considered?

- How would it be achieved?
- In the light of this, how would any synergy from the acquisition be likely to arise?

The full board of directors discussed the Fletton's business strategy and concentrated their attention on whether reduced reliance on common bricks should be achieved through the acquisition of a facing brickmaker or through purely diversificationary acquisitions.

In consideration of the facing brick proposal, one of the non-executive directors argued strongly that:

(a) the only way any benefit from the acquisition would accrue to Fletton Brick Co. was if fletton facing bricks were sold under the name of the acquired company, and
(b) to do that would raise considerable ethical problems.

Discussion points
- As Chief Executive of Fletton Brick would you agree with the non-executive's two points?
- Do the ethical issues, raising questions about corporate integrity, have any implications for strategy?
- What are the pros and cons of diversification?
- What more information would be needed in order to decide on the relative attractions of diversification?
- Who, or which body, should take decisions about diversification?

CHAPTER SEVEN

Strategic thinking frameworks: technology and innovation

7.1 Introduction

During the course of a technological revolution, technology itself and the progress of technological innovations may become all important. Through innovation companies can, at a stroke, make radical changes in the competitive structure of markets. The Oxden Horticultural Products case (see Chapter 5) illustrates how this can apply even to quite small businesses. Innovation can completely change the rules of competition and competitive strategies.

Looking at industries and competitive structures from the perspective of technology and innovation represents a further distinctive framework for strategic thinking. This framework is concerned with how technology develops and innovation can be predicted, and how businesses can exploit this knowledge for their own strategic benefit.

If the key to defining strategic direction lies in the strategic marketing framework, technology and innovation not only provide a powerful means of putting that direction into effect, but also suggest some of the crucial ingredients of flexibility.

7.2 The shape of technological progress

At the heart of any innovation is some creative idea or invention, which is increasingly knowledge and information intensive. The days of the fundamental breakthrough by the inspired amateur are long gone, if they ever existed. The story of Watt visualizing the steam engine prompted only by a boiling kettle is a useful memory aid but bears little relation to fact. Fleming's discovery of penicillin is similarly apocryphal, if only because of what is left out. Watt and Fleming and all their illustrious soulmates shared this one thing in common: they were all at or near the boundaries of knowledge in their particular fields, and already prepared to make the next small step forward into the unknown.

Innovation comprises both revolutionary and evolutionary developments. Whilst the revolutionary, fundamental items may be the stuff revolutions are made of, the vast bulk of innovations are clearly evolutionary. On closer examination, even the fundamental innovations appear really to comprise a multiplicity of lesser innovations. Watt didn't invent the steam engine but merely improved it, in 1769 with the external condenser and in 1781 with rotational power. Newcomen's steam engines had been pumping water since 1712 and even before that a primitive engine had been built by Savery in 1698 and there is evidence of ideas about steam power as early as the renaissance. Just what exactly it was that prompted the explosion of growth which depended in great part on the improved steam engine remains illusive. The same indeterminacy applies to all the so-called revolutionary innovations. On detailed inspection they appear, almost without exception, to comprise a large number of lesser innovations.

The innovation process, though not always a strictly rational progression, does exhibit some identifiable pattern. It is long and slow. Typically new technology emerges only gradually because in the stages of research and development only a few people are generally involved. Basic scientific knowledge must be won and engineering problems solved. It may take time to overcome the orthodox wisdom and correct wrong assumptions. Moreover, funding may at first be limited and experimental equipment in scarce supply. All these factors may delay early progress.

However, a promising project that wins through this phase to commercial development will attract the needed support and backing and start to grow fast. Efforts are typically then focused on both developing the key concept and on refining all facets of the technological execution by incorporating the very best of existing practice. Competition during this rapid growth phase would also act as a spur to further rapid improvement.

Finally, progress slows, or ceases altogether, possibly because of diminishing returns from further development effort, or because of some natural block or limit on further improvements in performance, or possibly because of some legal or societal limit.

This model of technological progress, when shown as a graph over

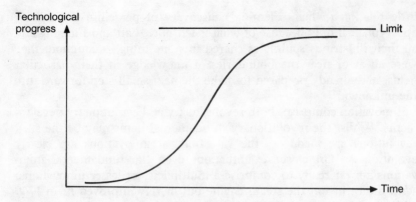

Figure 7.1   *The shape of technological progress: the S curve.*

time, seems to adopt an S-shaped curve as shown in Figure 7.1. The slow start, followed by rapid growth, which levels off against some limit imposed by nature or man, seems a plausible explanation of how technology might be expected to develop. Furthermore it appears to line up with reality in many different situations.

The S curve has been used to model technological progress for many

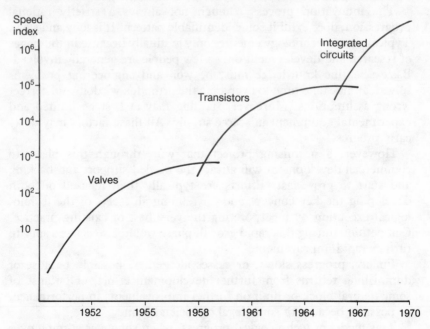

Figure 7.2   *The development of computer technologies.*
Source: Hall (1969).

years (see Twiss, 1986, p. 213), being one of the early tools of operational research developed during the Second World War. Even after so long it remains probably the most practical approach to forecasting technology development. The vertical axis can be measured in various terms without fundamentally altering the shape of the curve. For example, the following measures have been used: technical performance, cost per unit, return (i.e. performance increase) per unit of R&D (in £, or man years, or calendar months) and many others. All appear to generate an S-shaped curve.

The most striking thing about the S curve is its apparent broad applicability. However, this can also be its biggest danger.

The development of computer technologies is frequently instanced as a typical pattern of technological progress. Figure 7.2 shows the progression through three separate technologies, valves, transistors and integrated circuits. Each of the three technologies is shown as having a rapid growth phase which in due course slows down and flattens out and is then overtaken by the succeeding technology. There appears to be a regularity about this pattern. When performance ceases to rise with one technology, in due course another technology takes over.

Figure 7.3 shows a similar progress in tyre cord with cotton being replaced by rayon, then nylon and then polyester. In this case the vertical axis shows total sales instead of technical performance, but the pattern is just the same with each technology developing along an S-shaped curve, and the envelope curve also having a similar shape.

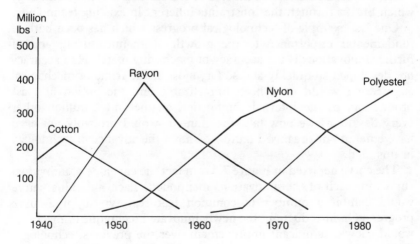

Figure 7.3 *Tyre cord projections.*
Source: Dewhurst (1970).

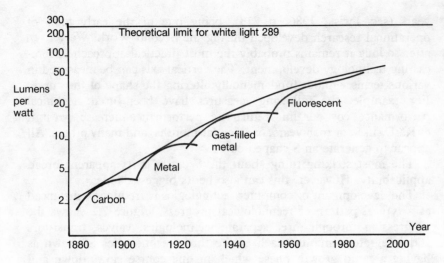

Figure 7.4   *Electric lamp performance trends.*
Source: Lenz (1983).

Figure 7.4 shows the envelope of different technologies in electric lighting and in this case the theoretical limit to technological development has also been shown. In this particular case the limit is simply a matter of physics: white light is 289 lumens per watt. Such limits apply to all technologies though they are by no means always so simple to specify. Each individual technological solution has its own limits, which may in themselves be the spur to establishing the new technology which breaks through the constraints inherent in existing technology.

One last example of technological progress which has been both of fundamental importance to the growth of manufacturing and of further innovations is the accuracy of machining metal. Had accuracy not developed so quickly and so far, most of the fruits of mechanical engineering would have been unrealizable and the notion of mass production, of the internal combustion engine and a million other every day items we now take for granted, would probably not even have entered our dreams. Figure 7.5 shows the advance of technology in this field.

The curve depicted in Figure 7.5 is in fact the envelope of individual curves for each of the innovations mentioned. Each individual curve would exhibit a number of common features, typical of S-curve progress. On introduction, the newly innovated technique or machine, would show a significant improvement over the previous technology. Typically the new technology will have been prompted by the previous

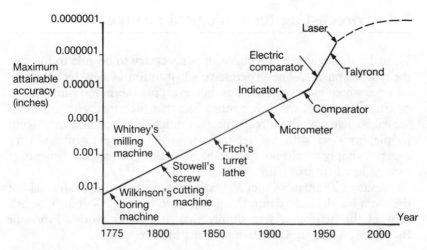

Figure 7.5   *Progress in accuracy of metal removal.*
Based on Bright (1983).

one reaching the limits of its potential, the new technology not being subject to those same limits. After introduction there would be further rapid improvement as problems were eliminated and potential benefits realized. Then, after a period, the rate of improvement would progressively slow down as the new limits were approached. Thus the development of these individual technologies appear to follow the S-curve shape. Moreover, the envelope curve describing the overall technological progress, may also approximate to the same shape: progress starting slowly, followed by rapid improvements, which gradually approach the limit of absolute accuracy.

The development of industrial revolutions, as described in the prologue, also exhibit S-curve progression, with the revolution curve being the envelope resulting from the coincidence of many fundamental new technologies, each exhibiting S-shaped progression. The economic growth curve of the current technological revolution being the envelope of the individual curves of electronics, information technology, new forms of energy or energy substitute, biotechnology, molecular engineering, genetic engineering, ocean development and new forms of transport or transport substitute.

Many, but not all technologies, progress along the lines of an S curve, as can be seen with hindsight. The problem with such analysis is that it is not always possible to tell where the current technology is on its S curve, where its limit lies and what alternative technologies might succeed and when.

7.3 Forecasting technological change

To make strategic use of S curves it is necessary to be able to forecast their development. The progressive substitution of new technologies for ones which have flattened out, however, may seem too simplistic to be true. If the real world happened like that then forecasting techno-logical change would not really present much of a problem. Intelligent people involved with the technologies, the most eminent industry experts, simply would not be capable of making wrong assessments of technological futures. But they do!

President Truman's Chief Military Adviser, Admiral Leahy, said of the atom bomb, 'that damn thing will never go off'. Wilbur Wright's view of the helicopter was simply that 'it'll never work'. Professor Bickerton, a leading Canadian scientist in 1926 said,

> this foolish idea of shooting at the moon is an example of the absurd length to which vicious specialization will carry scientists working in thought-time compartments. Let us critically examine the proposal. For a projectile entirely to escape the gravitation of the earth, it needs a velocity of 7 miles a second. The thermal energy of a gram at this speed is 15,180 calories. The energy of our most violent explosive, nitro glycerine, is less than 1,500 calories per gram. Consequently, even had the explosive nothing to carry, it has only one tenth of the energy necessary to escape the earth. Hence the proposition appears to be basically impossible. (Bright, 1983, p. 7)

Clearly the possibilities presented by technological innovation can far outstrip the expectations of experts. Professor Bickerton stands accused of being trapped in his own 'thought-time compartment', having his own mindset and being unable to open up to new possibilities. But he was a leading expert of his time, not a fool. The vast majority of us continuously and substantially underestimate the technological possibilities and what innovations can achieve. We may be able to envisage the development of existing technologies, but we either wrongly assess its limits, or completely overlook the possibility of new replacement technologies, or other extraneous events.

Detecting where a particular technology is on its S curve is one of the key issues in technological innovation. The limit itself may be a factor of some natural 'law' of physics, or it may be a matter of economics – further improvements using existing technology would cost more than the customer is prepared to pay. Or it may be a combination of the two: as natural limits are approached the law of diminishing returns applies to investment in R&D and the only option is to try alternative technologies, or await their development. During the course of a technological revolution, many technologies which have been in this moribund state for years or even generations, may suddenly be replaceable thus providing once-in-a-lifetime opportunities for new participants. Such a wholesale step change has occurred, for example, with the replacement of electromechanical controls by electronics.

Technological forecasting seeks to establish the position of a technology on its S curve and assess the possibility of new substitute technologies taking over. Developing a picture of the S curve itself involves both factual analysis and experiential judgement. One without the other may be highly unreliable.

The historical development of the curve can normally be identified without too much difficulty. In the long term the most important thing to understand is the envelope S curve, which represents the overall technological progress of the industry. Management should concentrate on three main questions:

1. How rapidly has technology evolved in the long term past?
2. How rapidly is the technology advancing now?
3. What will the limit of the technology be and how will it be approached?

These questions provide a structure for investigating technological progress in a particular industry. They do not in themselves provide a technological forecast, but reliable answers to all three questions would provide a sound basis for forecasting.

Technological forecasting simply provides a structured way of looking at an industry and it can help management detect the shape of innovations and the breaks and limits to technology. But it is a limited approach. It will not tell managements what business they should be in by the year 2000; nor will it forecast the profitability of great new innovations; nor predict scientific breakthroughs; nor the point at which chaos will take over. However, it can contribute to all these things and help give management some indications of when a technology is running out of steam and is ripe for replacement.

7.4 Changing the technology

Any leadership position is transitory and likely to be short-lived; 'what exists is getting old' (Drucker, 1964). Defending the old, rather than grasping the new, is a natural, almost automatic response, but it is likely to fail.

The replacement of vacuum tube manufacture by solid-state electronics is a good example. When transistors first came on the scene National Video, Rawland, Eimac and Lansdale Tube decided not to invest in the new technology. This effectively sealed their fate. Hughes, Transitron and Clevite decided to invest in the new, but chose the wrong technology (germanium) and consequently also lost. Of the successful American vacuum tube manufacturers of the 1950s only RCA and Philips successfully made the switch to semiconductors. However, deciding to invest in the right new technology is the easy part.

As a technology approaches the flat part of its S curve and the returns from R&D start to diminish, it would seem sensible to concentrate on seeking out potential substitute technologies which might take over. Typically this would be done using the expert knowledge within the firm, by making full use of the rapidly growing external data base of published technological information and perhaps by some form of Delphi-type enquiry among industry experts. Using any or all these approaches it should be possible to identify the new technologies which might take over. Once identified, it is relatively simple to monitor their progress and even to climb aboard and participate in the development.

What is much more difficult, especially for the industry leaders, is the decision to ditch the existing technology. This is where organizational conservatism really bites. The decision might simply mean prematurely writing off some plant which, though it has a one-off impact in the accounts, is not of any substantive importance. Or it might mean ditching an established leadership position and fighting on more or less equal terms with competitors to re-establish leadership in the new technology. This is a much more difficult decision. The leadership position may be long-standing. The existing technology may have lasted for a generation. The decision to change may confront all the existing industry recipes. It may render inhouse expertise valueless; destroy the power base of the existing top management, overturn the implied meaning of major organizational symbols and break every cultural norm in the firm.

Transitions from one technology to another present great difficulties to firms with heavy psychological investment in the existing technology. By psychological investment is meant not simply money and machinery, but expertise, history, marketing strength and the strategic position and culture of the business. Such firms almost inevitably find themselves defending this investment when the time comes for a technological transfer. If the existing technology has run out of steam and the replacement technology is not constrained by the same limits, then the old technology will prove ultimately indefensible. But the existing leaders will almost always defend it nevertheless. This is what provides the attacking firms with great opportunities to change competitive structures and achieve once and for all competitive advantages (Foster, 1986).

At a time when technological change is beginning to gain momentum, the most and greatest opportunities are being presented. But for industry leaders who are bogged down in the existing ways of doing things, the new technologies may only spell disaster. Too many firms, across a very broad front, are casting themselves in this role. For instance, although only two of the original American vacuum tube manufacturers are involved in semiconductors, the Japanese have attacked and the present list of participants includes NEC, Fujitsu, Toshiba and Hitachi. Thus, while the defender faces a dilemma, the attacker has the advantage.

7.5   Innovation and competition

As technological innovations mature and industries settle down, so companies became accustomed to continually growing markets and established steady-state systems of coping with the world as it then is. For a limited period, perhaps even a few decades, technology is on the back burner and marketing becomes the leading business discipline. This pattern can be seen in the second industrial revolution. During the 1950s and 1960s, purely cosmetic change was all that was needed in the way of innovation in order to maintain a buoyant market. Drucker himself advocated product standardization as the key then to business success (Drucker, 1964).

However, in the early 1970s the oil price crisis brought that period of stable growth to a shuddering halt. Since then technology has emerged once again as the trigger for future prosperity. Standardization is no longer sufficient, except in some service sectors. Some distinctive feature which provides a competitive advantage is what is now required and it is primarily through innovation that such competitive differentiation is created.

Until recently America was the clear technological leader of the world. However, as Simon Ramo pointed out this position is being lost: 'indications are all about us in the form of European and Japanese cars on our streets and foreign-made television sets and tape recorders in our homes' (Ramo, 1980 p. 8). By the mid 1970s America's technological pre-eminence was being attacked on a wide front just as Britain's had been generations previously. Whilst still well in the lead in terms of numbers of patented innovations, America remained static while other countries including Japan, France and Germany were growing steadily (Chakrabarti *et al.*, 1978). This apparent relative loss of innovativeness is likely to have a devastating long term effect.

The reasons why some countries become less innovative and therefore less competitive and others more so is not completely clear. In Britain and America, the fact that the great majority of government financed R&D is focused on military and defence projects means that commercial industry does not have the advantages enjoyed in, say, Japan or West Germany. However, this is by no means the whole story. There appears to be something more culturally-based which results in the national focus moving away from the creation of wealth on to the question of its ownership through financial institutions. Additionally, and possibly resulting from this cultural factor, there may be a shortfall in the quantity and quality of scientific and technological training and education when compared with major competitors.

Whatever the explanations at a national level, the success of the individual business will remain critically dependent on its ability to compete. Increasingly competition is international, if not global. Firms which make full use of innovation as a competitive weapon are those which in the end will win. One of the prime responsibilities of management is therefore to understand and control the process of innovation in their business.

The orthodox wisdom that mature business should concentrate simply on cutting costs no longer holds true, as managements in so many mature businesses are demonstrating. New technologies are creating completely new rules even in the oldest industries where the application of computers to machinery frequently results in the development of completely new products.

7.6 The innovation process

The process of innovation has been identified as comprising the following stages (Rogers, 1983):

1. Recognition of a problem or need.
2. Preliminary evaluation.
3. Invention.
4. Research and development.
5. Evaluation.
6. Commercial development.
7. Adoption.
8. Post-adoption consequences.

The point has often been made that this apparently logical sequence of events does not apply in every case. Nevertheless, the model does serve to highlight some of the key issues.

There has long been a debate as to whether successful innovation results from the push of technology or the pull of market need. This could be an important issue when deciding how to organize for innovation in any particular business. Should the marketing function have the most influential role, or engineering and R&D? The point has been made that 'we have got to stop marketing makeable products and learn to make marketable products' (Hayes and Abernathy, 1980). Empirical research (Utterback, 1976) indicates that around 70–80 per cent of innovations result from 'demand pull' and 20–30 per cent from 'technology push'. However, this may not be an ideal situation. Some R&D engineers argue that 'demand pull' provides plenty of 'slight product modifications' (e.g. annual model changeovers) and 'new improved' formulations, etc., but few truly innovative products and major breakthroughs (Shanklin, 1983). This assertion would be difficult to prove or disprove. The most important question to be asked about this debate is whether the two, 'demand pull' and 'technology push' are actually mutually exclusive. In the concluding chapter of this book it is suggested that an effective innovating business combines both the power of 'technology push' with the direction and vision provided by a market-oriented strategy. Thus the two can be mutually supportive.

Stages 1 to 4 of the innovation process comprise what is often termed *initiation*, which is discussed in Section 7.7.

Stage 5, *evaluation*, almost invariably involving a form of financial appraisal and in some cases a form of qualitative assessment of the innovation's contribution to the strategy of the business is discussed in Section 7.8.

Stages 6 to 8, *implementation*, are often disregarded as an essential part of innovation; these would include the management of change resulting from innovation as well as the innovation itself.

The simple initiation–evaluation–implementation model is sometimes accompanied by equally simple prescriptions such as 'creative freedom' being the essential prerequisite for initiating innovations, while management control is essential to effective implementation. This dichotomy between freedom and control is one of the fundamental dilemmas implicit in all management situations, but especially so in innovation. The difference is both philosophical and practical.

The initiation phase comprises the generation of ideas, the screening out of unsuitable ones, and some form of preliminary testing and development of the suitable ideas in concept prior to their financial evaluation. *Prima facie*, idea generation seems to be the really innovative part of the whole process, the part that demands some spark of creativity, the essence of innovation.

The whole process of innovation, including evaluation and implementation is fraught with difficulty, but it is often thought that firms which fail to be innovative, fail because they lack the ability to be creative. They are too set in their ways, too committed to existing ways of doing things and too inflexible, to be able to adopt new ideas, much less generate them.

There has been a lot of research into how innovative firms differ from the less innovative. To a great extent the differences centre around the way firms approach the apparently creative processes involved in initiation. The following section therefore looks into these processes in some detail and identifies the conditions that appear to be necessary for the creative generation of ideas.

7.7   Initiating innovations

7.7.1   Creativity and the generation of ideas

The Boston Consulting Group's simple concept, the experience curve, demonstrated the increasing efficiency with which operations are carried out the more often they are done. The establishment of repetitive routine was, for Boston, a crucial determinant of economic success. Consequently firms were encouraged to achieve a high market share of growing markets, in order to increase their experience and efficiency as rapidly as possible. Market share was thus seen as both the source and the result of success.

The successful firms established, possibly unwritten, industry recipes: ways of doing things which were regarded as good practice and which became widely adopted routine. Businesses were organized in order to perform these routines efficiently. The more successful the business and the more proscribed its routines, the less able it was to cope with change. The most successful, thus blinded by their success, might not even recognize change when it occurred.

We all develop a perceptual bias, based on our values and experience, which results in a routinized selection of perceived factors. We reject those which appear not to fit our value and experience set, and we accept those that do fit, as confirmation of the continuing validity of our perceptions. Darwin apparently disciplined himself to write down every observation which did not fit his theories because, like the rest of us, he always forgot them otherwise and disregarded their consequences.

Businesses do the same. The American tyre manufacturers disregarded the benefits of the radial-ply tyre because it did not fit the industry's accepted norms for cost, wear and performance characteristics. Instead, they stuck to the old cross-ply technology too long and let Michelin into the market with the radial, which proved to be the next technology. The new idea did not fit the old recipe so it tended to be disregarded. This is not simply because of the huge capital investment sunk in the existing technology, but the even greater psychological investment of all the key individuals in the existing recipe.

There is therefore within any successful business, the seeds of a mindset which represses creativity and blocks off openness to new ideas. Mindset is the opposite of creativity, a fixed point of view which derives from experience and is reinforced every time that experience is successfully repeated and forces thinking along tightly proscribed lines.

Some advocate lateral thinking as an adequate response to the mindset problem (De Bono, 1978). We all have the facility to think along straight lines or to think laterally. Lateral thinking, as a creativity technique, is a generic term covering a number of approaches which try to open up new ways of looking at problems. It seeks to change the way individuals are able to perceive problems and potential solutions. However, innovation is today essentially a group problem. The knowledge and skills necessary to initiate innovation generally lie beyond the scope of the single individual no matter how gifted. Thus, lateral thinking though stimulating does not address the problem of corporate mindset which shows itself in the form of 'yes but' thinking (Rickards, 1985) which signals a closed, unreceptive outlook which can kill creativity.

Creativity is not dependent on 'sparks of genius' and is not an essentially random process. Newton and Leibnitz both invented calculus, not by chance or inspiration, but on the back of ten years' relevant experience and 50,000 bits of pertinent information (Simon, 1986). With the relevant experience and information absorbed it becomes possible to respond with speed, as though untuitively, and successfully. However, if the conditions are repressive and ways of thinking proscribed, innate creativity is frustrated.

Most approaches to creativity are therefore deliberate attempts to set up circumstances and processes which break out of this repressive regime, breakdown mindset and eliminate barriers to imaginative ways of thinking. Probably the best known such technique is brainstorming. The essential idea of brainstorming is to breakdown mindset simply by postponing judgement among the brainstorming group for the duration of the session. The intention is to generate a large quantity of potential 'solutions' which are only sifted later.

The 'freedom to be creative' is far from total even in brainstorming. As with all creativity techniques, there is first and foremost a need to be goal-oriented. If there is no goal orientation the techniques cannot achieve results. Generally the goal is the solution to some stated problem. Goal orientation is itself one limit on freedom. But freedom is further constrained because the normal barriers to creativity still have influence. For example, the belief that there is one right answer inhibits the examination of possibilities which clearly do not relate to that single track. Similarly, every member of the brainstorming group will have their own set of self-imposed barriers which arise out of the individual's own experience and values.

Moreover the nuances of rank and status among different members of the group which attach in the ordinary working situation are not completely divested for the duration of a brainstorming session. Consequently, the fear of looking stupid or of challenging the obvious, will remain potent, and the desire to conform, or the equally inhibiting desire not to conform, will still affect creative performance. Thus even in brainstorming where the rules of the game are reasonably well understood, and the reason behind those rules generally supported, the inhibitions to creativity are rarely dropped completely.

7.7.2   Structured creativity

Initiating innovations involves both the generation of ideas and the screening out of unsuitable ones. The process of screening is deliberately separated from idea generation in brainstorming because it is so inhibiting to creativity. In other approaches the creative process itself is given rather more structure so that idea generation and screening go almost hand in hand.

Synectics, a more structured development of brainstorming, is one such technique which has achieved success in creative problem-solving (Gordon, 1961). The technique involves a multistage process, using a brainstorming style forum, firstly to agree appropriate definitions of the problem and then to identify potential solutions. The barriers to creativity in many cases are implicit in the way the problem is defined. Its redefinition by a synectics group may itself suggest new potential solutions.

Synectics sessions can be run in a variety of ways, with varying degrees of formality (Rickards, 1985). However, a typical group might operate as follows:

1. Problem owner states the problem to the group.
2. Group, in brainstorming mode, identifies potential alternative statements.
3. Problem owner selects a small number of problem definitions for further examination.
4. Group, again in brainstorming mode, identifies potential solutions to one or more of the defined problems.
5. Problem owner selects from potential solutions for either further development by the group or technical analysis, etc.

The above is not intended as an operational explanation of synectics, but serves to highlight again the compromise that has to be made between the 'freedom to be creative' and the necessity to ensure that the work done is relevant. In brainstorming, the relevance is intended to be established at the outset, after which the group works in as open and unproscribed a way as possible. In synectics the intervention of the problem owner with continued participation in the group, either actively or passively, helps to maintain some form of relevance throughout the process. Other aspects of synectics act to reinforce the creative aspect of the process and counteract the imposition of structure, e.g. the advocated use of metaphor in problem definition and solution proposal.

Initiation of innovation requires a positive breaking down of barriers to imaginative thinking. On the other hand the common sense requirement to make innovation relevant to the individual business inevitably results in the re-erection of barriers and the restriction of thinking.

These same considerations are not only the determinants of

behaviour in specific circumstances such as brainstorming or synectics sessions, but also of behaviour in the wider organization. They appear to have implications for how those organizations should be managed in order to be creative in their application of technology for strategic ends.

7.8 Evaluating innovations

This second phase of the innovation process, though often regarded as a more or less mechanical process, may be just as crucial as the initiation phase. Moreover, from the standpoint of strategic thinking, evaluation is both important in its own right and, at the same time, illustrates other organizational issues which are crucial to strategic success. The contrast between Anglo–Saxon approaches to evaluation and the methods adopted by the Japanese is particularly suggestive.

7.8.1 The technology gap

A technological gap has been opened up between the United Kingdom and America on the one hand and Japan on the other and it is becoming increasingly difficult to close. As the Japanese rate of investment in innovation continues to increase so the gap widens. The quality of Japanese products continually improve, the real prices are reduced and the range of tastes they cater for broadens. The world demands more of their products and consequently less of their competitors.

Both America and Britain appear to be distinguished by declining competitiveness in markets that they have traditionally dominated. The United Kingdom is a particularly vivid example with a long, familiar and depressing list of failed industries, and the picture that is emerging in America has disturbing similarities. The Japanese seem to possess the secrets of success, whereas the older industrialized nations seem to be losing their way.

There has been a lot of research into the different management practices in the United States and Japan. The idea of organizational culture found many of its earliest applications in cross-cultural studies comparing how things are done in the two countries, and also including research of the successes and failures of Japanese management exports to the United States and the United Kingdom. From all this an interesting picture emerges. In the United Kingdom in particular, concern with rank status and pecking orders, for example, contrast starkly with the more democratic and consultative Japanese culture. There are many such contrasts, some well-documented, others more speculative. The case is interesting, but not entirely definitive.

So far as investment performance is concerned, the critical differences seem most probably to lie within the ambit of financial evaluation. The evaluation of innovations appears to play a vitally important role in the way technologically-based strategies are implemented and an awareness of this is consequently an important part of this particular strategic thinking framework.

7.8.2   Investment hurdle rates

Whereas American and British firms typically use some variation of discounted cash flow (DCF) to appraise the viability of a proposed investment, relatively few Japanese firms use the technique. The fact that Japanese investment performance has been so successful has raised the question whether DCF is not fundamentally flawed, producing an inevitable bias towards the short term (Hayes and Garvin, 1982). More recently Hodder has published a detailed comparison between Japanese and American investment appraisal practices (Hodder, 1986).

From Hodder's study it is apparent that though the appraisal methods vary, this is not the reason why investment performance is so different. Though Japanese accountants do not use DCF very widely, tending to use straight accounting rates of return rather than discounted rates, they nevertheless do make allowance for the time value of money. Thus, the calculations made in Japan are not, in fact, so very different from those made in the United States or the United Kingdom. It does not appear to be the different appraisal techniques they use which gives the Japanese an advantage.

However, a fundamental difference between the US and Japanese practices was the discount or hurdle rate. In the United States rates typically fall in the range 15–25 per cent, with the occasional high risk project being assessed at 30 per cent. These figures are probably fairly typical of the United Kingdom also. In Japan, Hodder found the typical hurdle rate was only around 10 per cent.

Clearly, as a result of this fact alone, Japanese firms will accept many more projects than their American and British competitors and thereby start to open up the technological gap. Put another way, the

American and British firms will reject many more projects, lose competitive position, turn increasingly to defensive cost-cutting investments and thus be forced into a short term focus.

The difference in hurdle rates clearly contributes to this difference in performance, which in turn justifies the different hurdle rates. But what causes the different hurdle rates to be used in the first place? There appear to be two prime reasons: firstly, the cost of capital and, secondly, the treatment of risk.

The cost of capital

Firms obtain their funds for investment from a mixture of sources such as overdraft, long term loans, share issues and cash generated by the existing business. The cost of such funds can be calculated, in theory by simply calculating the costs of the individual sources (e.g. in terms of interest, after tax cost of dividends, etc.), weighting them according to the overall mix of capital in the business and adding them to obtain the weighted average cost of capital. Again, in theory this cost of capital is used as the hurdle against which projects are assessed. If they are expected to earn more than they would cost then they should go ahead. If on the other hand they would cost more than they are expected to earn then they should be rejected.

In practice it is not clear to what extent a firm's hurdle rate depends on the weighted average cost of its capital. Even though most firms do not measure their cost of capital, the connection is often perceptible. When interest rates are high, hurdle rates may also rise, or alternatively capital rationing may be applied which has largely the same effect. When earnings decline and the share price follows suit, the cost of equity capital rises and again hurdle rates may overtly, or covertly, also be raised. In the end, the connection between the cost of capital and the return required from it will make itself apparent.

In Japan the cost of capital is lower. Not only are interest rates significantly lower than in America and Britain, but as earnings are higher the cost of equity capital is also lower. The lower cost of capital in the end enables lower hurdle rates to be used.

The high cost of capital – high hurdle rate – low rate of investment – low earnings – high cost of capital is a vicious cycle. Moreover, the reverse is equally true. A low cost of capital produces a low hurdle rate which enables a higher rate of investment in new plant and products. This in turn generates new business and improved earnings which results in a lower cost of capital. This latter cycle seems to be the one enjoyed by Japanese businesses.

The treatment of risk

The second cause of inequality between the Japanese hurdle rates and ours is the treatment of risk.

It is British and American practice, in accordance with risk-averse accounting philosophy, commonly to increase the hurdle rate of a risky project by means of a risk premium of between 5 and 10 per cent, and not infrequently 15 per cent. In contrast, the Japanese do not use a risk premium at all. Since all but the simplest of cost reduction investments contain risk, a premium is almost invariably applied. The use of a risk premium, even without the other two factors already discussed, very largely explains the differences between the returns required in Japan and those required in the United States and the United Kingdom.

Furthermore, the longer term the project, the greater the penalty. Thus innovation is a prime victim of this practice; the more exciting the innovation then the longer term its effects, hence the more risky it is likely to be assessed and the higher the premium it will be set.

However, the risk premium cannot be justified either in practice or in theory. It is simply a manifestation of the accountant's natural desire to avoid risk. But the fault does not seem to lie in accounting methods as such, but rather in the clinical logic of statistical decision theory. This asserts that if a firm has two courses of action, one with a pay-off of $100 and a probability of occurring of 0.8 and the other with a pay-off of $800 and a probability of 0.1, the 'expected' outcomes are the same, despite the fact that the riskiness of the two projects is very different. The expected outcome is simply the value of the outcome times the probability of its occurring. Thus a project with a probability of less than 1 needs to earn a higher return than a risk-free project if its 'expected' outcome is to be the same. This extra return is a risk premium and the higher the risk the greater the premium will have to be to equate the expected outcome with that of the risk-free project.

However, the application of this sort of thinking to investment appraisal is fallacious. In theory, the expected returns from a project can be compared with those from a group of competing projects, and, subject to achieving some preconceived risk profile, expected returns can be maximized by the choice of project. In practice, however, a firm appraises projects singly and compares the outcome for if the investment is made with that for if it is not made. Thus the risky element of the project will either occur or not occur. If it does occur, it will either damage the outcome or it will not.

In this context a risk premium is hardly relevant. It can only serve to change a firm's overall risk profile by rejecting risky projects. It can have no other effect. The application of a premium in no way increases the return from a project, it merely reduces the probability of it going ahead. If all projects are risky, then it only serves to limit investment.

Since almost by definition all innovations are risky, the risk premium in particular serves to restrict investment in innovation.

By contrast, the Japanese rarely use this mechanical application of a risk premium. Instead they follow through the details of a project analysis and identify precisely what it is that makes it risky. For example, in the case of a new product innovation, is it the probability of a punitive competitive reaction? If so, what can be done to limit or avoid that reaction? What marketing or production tactics might make the short term competitive advantage achieved by the innovation, sustainable in the long term? What will each of the main competitors do? What will the effect of their action be? What could be done about it?

This detailed analysis of what might inhibit the achievement of the innovation's potential return involves all members of the management team. The project is discussed in detail at all levels of the organization and risk is investigated in every aspect and programmes devised to circumvent it. If a credible programme for the circumvention of risk can be devised, then the project is likely to go ahead because its appraisal will not be clouded by the blind application of an arbitrary risk premium.

The Japanese approach thus increases understanding of the risk involved and identifies how it could best be handled. Moreover, the detailed analysis itself has a number of side benefits apart from the basic problem of investment appraisal. The process involves many members of the organization and thus itself becomes a means of communication among members. It also provides a genuine way for members to participate in organizational decisions. Both communication and participation are important aspects of organizational style and Japanese practice endeavours to establish, during the course of this project evaluation, a consensus among organizational members. If consensus is difficult to achieve, then the appraisal process takes longer. Achievement of consensus, after widespread communication and participation, means that organizational members all know and understand what the business is trying to achieve and which way it is headed.

7.8.3   The projection of returns

The hurdle rate is one side of the coin, but what do the investments actually achieve? There is very little information available on this simply because very few firms actually recalculate the internal rate of return (IRR) actually achieved after the project has completed its life. There is no published data on this at any level of abstraction. From published macroeconomic data one might tentatively suggest that the average return on investment in UK manufacturing has been around 7–9 per cent and a little higher in the United States. By comparison a similar figure for Japanese manufacturing might be around 12–15 per cent. Economists would probably disagree with the actual figures but would be unlikely to differ greatly on the relative position. The Japanese firms demand less and achieve more from their investments. In the United States and the United Kingdom we demand more and achieve less.

Different expectations of growth are a major cause of this difference in project returns. If a project is being evaluated on the basis of market growth assumed at 10 per cent p.a., then it will quite clearly earn a substantially higher IRR than a similar project which is based on an assumption of zero growth. It is common practice, when assessing new capital projects, to make growth forecasts that bear some relation to past performance. In most cases if the growth forecast far exceeded past experience most managers, not to mention accountants, would regard the forecasts as naively optimistic and would be unwilling to let them go unchallenged. Past growth performance in Japan has been over 10 per cent p.a. overall, in the United States around 4 per cent and the United Kingdom 2.5 per cent. Thus, if two similar projects were assessed simultaneously in Japan and the United States or the United Kingdom, as a result of this factor alone, the Japanese project might well go ahead and the other one be firmly rejected. In which case the Japanese investment would contribute to a further rise in earnings and a further consequent lowering in the cost of capital, and the US/UK rejection would become a further step on the disinvestment spiral. Growth expectations tend in this way to be self-fulfilling.

The self-fulfilling nature of expectations can be seen by considering, for example, the difficulties management of the state-owned British automobile group, Rover, might be expected to have in accepting a major investment proposal. As a result of the establishment and expansion of the Nissan plant in Britain, and in due course of Toyota's, the Rover Group's future market share assumptions must inevitably show *contraction*. Consequently, all other things being equal, Rover will find it ever more difficult to make sound investment proposals with any hope of success. Nissan, on the other hand, with the active support of the British government, make assumptions of market share *growth* which are realistic, if not conservative. Since the cost of Nissan's capital is substantially supported by the British government, they will have little difficulty in exceeding their hurdle rates with almost any investment. This is especially so when it is remembered that the whole investment is probably assessed as an insurance against protectionist barriers being raised against direct exports from the plants in Japan. Exactly parallel examples exist in America.

There might appear to be little that managements can do unilaterally to change expectations. To a great extent it might appear to be a matter for governments to resolve. However, government can only take limited action, for example, by acting in the interests of domestic industry rather than foreign competition. They can only affect the basic growth rate peripherally by removing constraints on growth. Real growth is down to management to achieve. Expectations of growth must be realistic, but they need not be so firmly based on the accounting principles of conservatism and prudence that they lead inexorably to disinvestment.

7.9 Summary

Innovation, the process of invention and its commercial exploitation, is a competitive tool available to all businesses. Being early with the new technology provides a substantial competitive advantage which can be used to make rapid and dramatic changes in long-standing competitive relationships.

The technological strategic thinking framework seeks to increase understanding of how technology develops and can be used effectively as a strategic competitive weapon.

The shape of innovation is surprisingly consistent and conveniently modelled by an S curve which tends to a limit of performance which may be either natural or man-made.

Technological forecasting is a knowledge and information intensive activity, and involves identifying the S curve and, as far as possible, the current position on it, the nature of the operational limits, the potential new replacement technologies and the likely timing of the transfer from the old technology to the new. This is the easier prerequisite of effective strategic innovation.

Deciding to transfer out of the existing technology is much more difficult. It involves changes in the psychological investment of the business, as well as its financial commitments. These will be particularly hard decisions for the leader businesses in the old technology.

The process of innovation comprises three main stages: initiation, evaluation and implementation.

Initiation comprises the generation, screening and developing of ideas. The fundamental prerequisite of successful initiation is the freedom to be creative.

Creativity is the essence of innovation and is marked by an openness to new thinking and an absence of mindsets and thinking along tramlines, which is the natural result of a successful business operation.

Nevertheless, the freedom to be creative appears to need some structure and bounds to ensure that the creativity is harnessed to relevant business needs.

The development of technology is also critically affected by the processes of innovation evaluation and the different approaches of Japan, on the one hand, and Britain and America on the other, appear to have resulted in the opening up of a continually widening technological gap. As a result of these practices, investments which would contribute positively to future wealth creation tend to get rejected in Britain and America whereas they may be accepted in Japan.

The main differences between Japanese and American practice relates primarily to the cost of capital and, most importantly, the treatment of risk.

The British and American assessment of risk simply uses an accounting risk premium as an additional hurdle for the project to overcome. This further limits the number of investments being evaluated positively. Innovation investments, being almost by definition more risky than others, tend to suffer particularly badly as a result of this approach to investment evaluation.

The Japanese approach uses a more behavioural indepth analysis designed to achieve consensus through a process of communication and participation. This results in the decision process itself being relatively slow, but once taken decisions tend to be rapidly and effectively implemented because the decision and its consequences have already been widely discussed throughout the organization.

DISCUSSION CASE:
THE NORTH EAST GENERAL HOSPITAL

At the North East General Hospital the routine system for carrying out blood and urine tests on ward patients was as follows:

1. Consultant's morning visit to patient results in request for blood or urine tests.
2. Ward nursing staff take sample from patient.
3. Sample bottle is dispatched to laboratory.
4. Laboratory staff carry out tests and complete analysis report.
5. Laboratory report is returned to the patient's ward and added to the patient's notes.
6. Consultant looks at report on next ward visit.

In more than 60 per cent of cases the report was returned to the ward on the following day *after* the Consultant's morning visit, there thus being a 48-hour delay from the time the Consultant requested the analysis and it being read by the Consultant. The remaining 40 per cent of cases, including all identified as urgent, were processed within twenty-four hours.

A recent technological innovation could provide instantaneous results from blood and urine tests. The new equipment carried out a full analysis completing all routine tests in a matter of seconds. Moreover, it could be operated by non-specialist staff after a very brief period of training. Thus, using the new technology it would be possible for ward nursing staff to provide the blood analyses while the Consultant was still with the patient on the ward.

This new instantaneous method had a number of advantages:

1. It was quicker, thus speeding up the process of returning the patient to full health.
2. It was cheaper to operate.
3. It freed the laboratory staff from a significant amount of routine work and allowed them to concentrate on more important jobs.

Discussion points
From the point of view of the patient and the Consultant the new system appears to be wholly beneficial with no apparent disadvantages.

● Are there any disadvantages or problems with the new system from the points of view of other parties involved?

- Which group is the most important in this situation?
- What, from a strategic point of view, would be the most satisfactory outcome?

The new technology would require a change in working practices and hospital staff, like the rest of us, prefer not to have to change the way they do things, unless they see it as being in their own interests, or, in some circumstances, as being for the greater good.

Discussion points
- Consider the implied changes in working practices firstly for the nursing staff and, secondly, for the laboratory staff.
- Which are likely to create the greatest problems? And why?

The purchase of such test equipment is in practice controlled by laboratory management. They initiate and evaluate all such equipment and make recommendations as to purchase. Their recommendations are invariably accepted, limitations on funding being the only reason why investment is sometimes delayed.

Discussion points
As a senior member of the laboratory staff you have been asked to make a recommendation as to whether the new equipment should be purchased.
- What additional information do you require before making a recommendation?
- What new working practices will be necessary if the new equipment is to be fully exploited and the patient be given the full benefits?
- Assuming that the cost of the equipment is not prohibitive what recommendation would you be likely to make?
- What problems do you foresee in using the new equipment?

The laboratory recommended the new equipment be purchased, but retained in the laboratory rather than being made available to the ward nursing staff. Thus the expense of the new technology was incurred but few of the benefits were enjoyed. The previous 24- or 48-hour service was retained, thereby eliminating the potential benefit to the patient.

Discussion questions
- Why do you think there was such an apparently irrational outcome?
- How could it have been avoided?
- Are these considerations likely to be relevant to other change situations?

- What are the particular characteristics which may make such 'irrational' and inefficient outcomes likely?

Note
This discussion case is loosely based on a case reported by Child *et al.* (1987).

CHAPTER EIGHT

Strategic thinking frameworks: structure, culture and symbolism

8.1 Introduction

The perspectives on strategic thinking discussed so far have been largely concerned with defining direction and, in the case of technology and innovation, also achieving some degree of flexibility. However, most approaches to strategy are not concerned with the fact that it is people who turn strategic thinking into strategic action. Strategic thinking will be worthless if people are not free to use their initiative and creativity in turning strategy into action. The most effective action will be taken by people who are not merely free to act but also motivated and dedicated to doing so.

This current cultural perspective is directly concerned with people and how they behave in organizations. This perspective seeks to provide a way of achieving concentration and consistency as well as flexibility in pursuing strategic direction.

Understanding and motivating people is a crucial part of the strategic thinking agenda. Never is this more obvious than in the service industries where the 'product' is very largely embodied in the interaction between people in the organization and the customer. Two contemporary changes are underlying the importance of this perspective. Firstly, the industrial revolution is changing the nature of work so that the emphasis is moving away from manually intensive, large scale production industries to knowledge intensive, small scale service industries where quality is totally dependent on individual personal behaviour (Hogg, 1986). Secondly, there has been a growing interest in, and understanding of, the way corporate culture can influence behaviour.

Concern for how various organizational characteristics impact on

153

the behaviour and performance of organization members is not new. It has been a recurrent topic of management research. Initially the focus of attention was on structural characteristics. The most effective structure was found to be influenced by production technology, whether process, mass production, or large or small batch production (Woodward, 1958) and a dominant characteristic of structure was thought to be the number of layers in the hierarchy of an organization from top to bottom. A tall, narrow organization (as depicted on a traditional organization chart) appeared to have a different impact on the behaviour of organization members from that of a wide, flat organization. Later researchers suggested that structure was influenced by the environment (Lawrence and Lorsch, 1967) and by market forces (Chandler, 1977).

In common sense terms it seems quite predictable that an organization with a lot of layers in it will tend to be bureaucratic and consequently either frustrate or facilitate certain behaviours. In addition there are various other structural characteristics, as well as configurations, which appear to have similar effects and there has been a lot of research into quite how these impact on organization member behaviour, organization effectiveness and organization strategy. There has long been a rather academic debate as to which is cause and which effect between strategy and structure (Chandler, 1962).

It has also been suggested that the concept of structure does not really encapsulate the most potent determinants of behaviour. Other less tangible influences, such as implied by the term climate, may be more powerful. But then structure and climate may even be different aspects of the same phenomenon.

> The relationship between structure and climate is totally interdependent. Together, they relate the structure of the organisation, its environment and behaviour and objectives of the individual member. (Kennedy, 1983, p. 40)

Closely allied to the concept of climate is that of organizational culture. Culture is more long lasting than climate and perhaps more influential, but, like climate, is difficult to measure in any reliable way.

Structure and culture are each aspects of organization, and at the same time, ways of looking at organization. Whereas structure may be defined in what appear at first sight to be precise and unambiguous terms in relation to such concepts as formalization, specialization, etc. (Pugh *et al.*, 1969), the extent to which such factual analysis explains how people in organizations behave remains uncertain. The cultural perspective, on the other hand, is not so amenable to unambiguous examination, but promises a fuller explanation of behaviour. Because of the difficulties in identifying and measuring culture, symbolic measures are sometimes adopted as proxies that can be measured. However, the compromise between measurability and richness of behavioural explanation remains.

Structure, culture and symbolism are behavioural influences which form a further framework for strategic thinking. Unlike the other frameworks discussed so far, this one is not concerned with the direction of the strategic thrust so much as the effectiveness of the process. In some circumstances strategic direction is not so important as the coherence and power of the focus achieved. Some businesses adopting this framework and achieving what has been referred to as 'strong culture' count among the most economically successful of the day.

8.2 Organizational structure

Businesses almost always start out with what might be called a simple structure where each member reports direct to the entrepreneur. As they grow firms progress through various evolutionary phases. Typically, when the firm has outgrown the simple structure, it adopts a functional organization, based on the primary tasks such as production, marketing, finance, etc. This enables the firm to accommodate functional professional specialists at senior levels of management and it also enables relatively short lines of communication to operate.

However, functional structures are not best suited to managing diversified activities. As firms grow and diversify into new product market areas there is an explosion of complexity which is generally contained by setting up an organization of more or less separate businesses, either as divisions or as separate subsidiaries under a holding company organization.

In the years after the Second World War there was a move towards divisional structure. Rumelt (1974) studied this evolutionary process in large American firms between 1949 and 1969 and identified a continuous trend to increased complexity from the single business firm to the diversified conglomerate. In the United Kingdom Channon (1973) found that between 1960 and 1970 the proportion of major British manufacturers using a divisional structure had increased from less than a third to more than two thirds. In the 1970s and 1980s this trend appears to have continued with an increasing emphasis on global businesses which, in many cases, operate divisional structures within an overall holding company organization.

A firm's organization structure results from specific management decisions based on certain structural concepts. The organization, as described on an organization chart, is only one side of the structural picture and gives only a limited idea of how it actually works in practice.

Pugh *et al.* (1968) developed a model of structure which others have since replicated. The research was originally based on a diverse sample of forty-six organizations whose formal structures were analysed in the following terms:

1. *Specialization of functions and roles.*
   Specialization refers to the extent to which different functions in an organization are carried out by specialist individuals or departments and the degree to which those individuals are required to have specialist knowledge as denoted by formal qualifications.

2. *Standardization of procedures.*
   Standardization refers specifically to employment practices such as recruitment and selection, disciplinary and grievance procedures, and the degree to which jobs are defined and governed by standard policies, rules and procedures.

3. *Formalization of documentation.*
   Formalization refers to the degree to which instructions, etc., are written down, for example, job descriptions, employee handbooks or rule books, agendas and minutes of management meetings.

4. *Centralization of authority.*
   Centralization refers to the extent to which the taking of decisions is centralized and is measured by instancing specific decisions (e.g. the pricing of output, the allocation of specific resources, etc.) and establishing at what level in the organization they are taken.

5. *Configuration of role structure.*
   Configuration refers to the shape of the organization in terms of hierarchical layers and spans of control, and is assessed by

		Low	High
Concentration of authority	High	Personnel bureaucracies	Full bureaucracies
	Low	Non-bureaucracies	Workflow bureaucracies
		Low	High
		Structuring of activities	

Figure 8.1   *The Aston taxonomy of structural forms.*
Source: Pugh *et al.* (1968).

establishing the spans of control of specific jobholders, and the proportions of employees in the various functional specialisms.

These factors are essentially measures of bureaucratic tendency producing a categorization of structures as shown in Figure 8.1.

Typically big businesses fall into the category of workflow bureaucracies, being highly structured but not as centralized as some organizations. Public service organizations (e.g. of government) were personnel bureaucracies, having highly concentrated authority with procedures focused on hiring, promoting and firing of personnel, but relatively unstructured activities. Smaller units within large private or public groups were the full bureaucracies, and smaller firms in personal ownership the non-bureaucracies.

The significance of these measures of structure and concentration of authority lies in the fact that they are proxies for factors that directly affect the way people are motivated, developed and led in the organization. The studies of Pugh's group suggested that such factors were measurable in a way that made it possible to compare organizations.

The apparent strength of the Aston studies lay in the precision of the research. The existence of an organizational chart, a written disciplinary procedure and other artefacts could be used as a measure of an organization's formalization. The research identified whether or not such items were in existence and thus measured formalization in the terms it set out to do. However, other researchers have found that these matters are not completely unambiguous. For example,

A number of formal documents were shown to the researcher in answer to questions about the structural characteristics of Company Y, including a rather scruffy hand written document produced by the personnel manager for the benefit of new employees, policy statements on health and safety and a grievance procedure that was agreed with the recognised trade union.

The evidence of the organisation charts was revealing. It might appear that Company X, with its exhaustive set of typed organisation charts had a rather formal structure compared with Company Y. However, during interviews it became apparent that the managers in Company X (and presumably all other members) were unaware of the existence of the organisation charts and assumed that none existed. By contrast, the initial response in Company Y was that the company did not have a formal organisation chart, and the hand written version was only produced with some reluctance. Yet its existence was widely known. It seems most probable that Company Y's chart had a greater impact on behaviour in its organisation that the Company X chart did. This possibility highlighted some of the potential problems with interpreting data from this type of enquiry. The existence or otherwise of such artefacts is not only ambiguous as to its impact on behaviour in the organisation, but even the facts themselves, as to their existence or otherwise, are not as straightforward as at first seemed probable. The answer to the question 'does your company have a formal organisation chart?' could be 'yes', 'no' or 'maybe'. This degree of uncertainty had not been foreseen. (Pearson, 1989a, p. 272)

From the point of view of the present, rather more pragmatic text, the Aston model might have some further shortcomings. For example, formalization, so defined, might or might not be an organizational characteristic which satisfactorily explains, or even affects, the behaviour of people in the organization.

The characteristics used by Pugh appear therefore to be only of limited use. Mintzberg (1981) added a number of other structural characteristics which appear even less readily measurable. These included, among other factors:

- Formalization of behaviour.
- Training and indoctrination.
- Planning and control systems.

Such measures relate more closely to the factors which actually determine how people in organizations behave and perform. Thus as ease of measurement declines, so usefulness of output seems to increase. The taxonomy of organizational structures resulting from Mintzberg's wider analysis is as follows:

- Simple structure.
- Machine bureaucracy.
- Professional bureaucracy.
- Divisionalized form.
- Adhocracy.

A simple structure has little standardized or formalized behaviour, minimal use is made of planning or training, there are few staff analysts and few middle managers because the business is run, more or less autocratically, by direct supervision from the top. The organization is flexible and able to outmanoeuvre the bureaucracies. It is effective in simple but dynamic environments and, *given the right chief executive*, is ideal for rapid, flexible innovation. Most firms start out as simple structures. Only a few retain simplicity as large organizations.

Machine bureaucracy, professional bureaucracy and divisionalized form have already been described in the Prologue (pp. 12–13). Machine bureaucracy is typical of the older industries with large scale production providing large numbers of highly specialized, low skill jobs, many staff analysts to maintain the systems of standardization, rigid departmentalization, and a large scale middle management hierarchy.

The professional bureaucracy relies on standardization of skills rather than organizational processes or products, ceding much of its power to trained professionals, but with an autocratic, non-participative structure for the substantial supporting administrative staff.

The divisionalized form, which almost inevitably results from a process of diversification, is a means of setting up market- or product-based subunits with a considerable degree of autonomy, but nevertheless subject to central control which in effect imposes a structure of machine bureaucracy at divisional level.

Adhocracy is the ill-defined structure that has no standard form but which may, in whatever form it takes, facilitate flexibility, independence, innovation, risk-taking and the ability to cope in environments which are both complex and dynamic.

Mintzberg distinguished two types of adhocracy. The operating adhocracy, such as a creative advertising agency, carries out innovative projects directly for its clients; and the administrative adhocracy such as a producer of electronic components, which carries out innovative projects for itself and consequently has both an administrative and an operating structure.

Within these five categories, Mintzberg identified certain distinctive trends. For example, the machine bureaucracy, fundamentally unsuited to innovation, is being seen increasingly as inappropriate to contemporary needs for flexibility and speed of response. Its dominance of large scale business is nevertheless more or less complete, not only within the older industries, but also in the new industries which large scale business has bought into. There is a natural tendency to seek out stability and set up an organizational form that would prosper in such conditions. Bureaucratization is therefore, for all its faults, an almost inevitable process, which will only be avoided or reversed as a result of great and deliberate effort. This natural tendency to bureaucratize over time and particularly in response to size, and the deliberate management initiatives required to counteract it, are fundamental to understanding the factors that inhibit and facilitate strategic action in an era of rapid change.

The predominance of bureaucracy at divisional level creates severe problems for the effective divisional manager at the business face. Innovation is necessary to achieve the strategic objective, but the bureaucratic organization inhibits this. Three options are available: the manager can become a bureaucrat; an attempt can be made to change the organization as a whole; or a small suborganization may be set up within the main business, where different rules apply and where individuals can be given the freedom to innovate.

Change can be adjusted to by more limited approaches to structural adjustment, either by concentrating on a subset of the whole structure (e.g. work design), or by setting up a separate structure within a structure which adopts different organizational rules and norms.

Work design has attracted much attention since the turn of the century with figures like Taylor and the Gilbreths who concentrated on the simplification, specialization and standardization of work so that the then new mass production technologies could be exploited. Much of the subsequent work on organizational development has aimed to reverse these tendencies to bureaucratize. However, as Leitko and Szczerbacki put it,

> Organisational development (OD) has yet to escape from its past – from its origins within humanistic psychology, in part as a reaction to the restrictive and authoritarian conditions characteristic of the machine bureaucracies found in many manufacturing organisations. However, the limitations that this past has created for OD are becoming more apparent as . . . machine bureaucracies give way to more open systems within the manufacturing sector, and as OD experts study organisations outside the manufacturing sector. (Leitko and Szczerbacki, 1987, p. 52)

Work design has thus tended to move organizations away from

bureaucratic structures through such processes as job enlargement, job rotation, job enrichment, various exercises in group technology, notably in the Swedish motor industry, and the Quality of Working Life movement which is currently experiencing a revival of interest (Heller, 1988).

Whilst these approaches address the problem of mechanistic structures which are difficult to change, they do so by changing the nature of *some* jobs in the organization, rather than all jobs. Moreover, these movements have tended to focus attention on non-managerial work. There has also been increasing interest in setting up an organization within the organization, specifically charged with the task of 'entrepreneuring'. The main organization continues to be managed on a more or less bureaucratic basis because this is believed to be the most efficient mode for the stable conditions assumed to exist, while separate structures are deliberately created to handle innovation.

These approaches all focus on the formal organization. But the distinction between formal and informal structure is critical to considerations of organization change. An organization chart, representing the formal structure, may exist which clearly delineates the chains of command, the spans of control and the hierarchical strata of the organization, but may have little to do with reality. It may be continually updated, but never used. The chart is a graphic representation of the formal organization, but it may shed little light on how the organization actually functions and how it affects the way people behave and the decisions they take. Structure alone cannot encompass all these aspects of organization.

Attention has more recently been focused rather more on 'the way we do things around here' and one way to understand *that* is through the wider cultural perspective which is the subject matter of the following chapter.

8.3 Organizational culture

Culture is of interest here because it may offer a richer description of both the openness and flexibility needed to convert strategic thinking into strategic action, and at the same time, contribute to the sense of direction and climate of success, far beyond what could be achieved through structure. The meaning that these phrases convey is essentially subjective. To one manager they may seem to get to the core of what a business is all about. To another, they may seem to be meaningless.

The concept of culture seems still to be riddled with such ambiguities.

To some, the distinction between structure and culture has been purely semantic; to others, culture is shorthand for every conceivable aspect of the organizational scene. It comprises both formal and informal structure: the structure that is overtly decided and the structure which develops apparently of its own accord and comprises social organization, shared or unshared beliefs and values, informal communication systems, stories, language, a hundred or more factors which become invested with symbolic meaning and which together determine to a large extent the effectiveness of an organization.

Kanter (1983) identified factors which she described as relating to organizational climate and which can be broadly grouped under the two headings communication and participation. Non-innovative 'segmentalist' firms are characterized by closed communications, hierarchical information flows up and down the line and by a lack of horizontal interdepartmental communication. Segmentalist firms are also characterized by non-participative systems. By participation Kanter means persuading rather than ordering, team-building, seeking input from others, showing political sensitivity, willingness to share rewards and recognition.

There is surprisingly little agreement as to what corporate culture actually is and still less about whether it can be managed. Clearly, if it is not a manageable commodity then it is not much use to managers. Alternatively, if it provides the means of changing mechanistic organizations into flexible, innovative organic ones, it would be an important management tool.

There appear to be two opposed views as to the nature of culture (Smircich, 1983). One school of thought holds that culture is one of the many variables which make up organization; this is the 'way we do things around here' brand of culture. It can be changed by management almost as simply as changing the pay system. The other school of thought holds that culture is not an organizational variable, but a way of looking at organizations; a metaphor for the organization itself; a perspective which provides new insights and fuller understanding as to how the organization might be managed, but which is not itself manageable.

The term 'culture' originates from anthropology, which according to Webster's dictionary is 'the study of mankind, especially its societies and customs'. The classic picture is of the nineteenth century researcher, in bush hat and khaki drill shorts, going off to some remote and primitive part of the world to study the customs and practices of some previously unknown native society. The anthropologist sought to identify the customs, rituals, hidden meanings, taken-for-granted assumptions and shared values of the community being studied, in such a way that the society could be understood as it really was.

The achievement frequently fell far short of this ideal. Early anthropologists were criticized for their inaccurate descriptions and lack of true understanding. Quite clearly their presence in a small community disturbed the setting – the community studied was not the same as it would have been had the researcher not been present. Also, the researchers were not able to avoid their own ideas and perceptions colouring the way they saw things. Even if their description was coldly factual, their selection of what things were important enough to describe, and subsequently their selection of what was important enough to report, was inevitably subjective. They would be unduly influenced by things which they found surprising and thus would give a biased account.

To overcome these problems, anthropologists tried to avoid taking anything for granted. They tried to avoid interpretation, concentrating on recording and explaining, as far as possible, in the native's own terms.

Modern researchers still take this same approach: they try above all else to prevent their own experience and personality from biasing their portrayal of the social group being studied, whether it is a tribe in Borneo or a modern public corporation. Organizational anthropology has a further particular cause of bias arising from the fact that, almost without exception, it is in reality undertaken from the standpoint of management, what Burrell and Morgan (1979) refer to as the functionalist paradigm. The traditional researcher might claim a straightforward desire to record the various components of a culture in the simple interests of expanding the store of knowledge. With such an open position it might be possible to approach the native's point of view. The organizational culture researcher is not usually operating in such an open-handed way. The research is usually carried out for the express benefit, either directly or indirectly, of one group of participants in the organization: management. A few studies have been undertaken on behalf of other groups such as shop-floor operatives and trade unions, but the overwhelming majority of research has been done, like this particular project, for the benefit of management. So far as is known, no modern organizational anthropology has been carried out with the sort of disinterest that, say a village elder from Borneo might bring to the task.

Consequently there tends to be two fundamentally opposed views as to the nature of organizational culture. The one accepts that it is simply seeking out what there is in the concept that can be manipulated for management's benefit. The other tries, however imperfectly, to use the cultural perspective to increase understanding of organizations for any purpose, including that of management. The former approach appears on the face of it to be the most practical and effective, while the latter approach seeks to achieve a more objective analysis.

The early anthropologists sought out their primitive and isolated societies because they represented, in some sense, virgin territory. They were essentially small, enclosed groups, as yet unpolluted by contact with other cultures. This not only heightened their potential value as objects of study, but also made that study very much simpler. Every member of the tribe shared much the same experience. They were born in the tribal village, grew up in it, lived in it and eventually died in it. Consequently they shared the same experience, beliefs and understandings, made the same assumptions about their lives and understood the same symbolic meanings which they attached to their various sayings, rituals and artefacts. In their isolation from other societies they uniquely represented what might be called a monolithic culture.

No group of people in the modern world could achieve a comparable separation, no matter how hard they tried. Modern society is highly cosmopolitan and complex in its intercultural relations and a business is possibly more multicultural than most contemporary social organizations. People at work originate from different geographical locations, have different racial backgrounds, differentiated educational experiences and differing economic and social standings. For two thirds of their lives these factors are dominant. For the other third, they form into groups at work which are themselves further differentiated according to which side of the management/worker divide they occupy, the industry they work in, the function they fulfil, the product divisions to which they owe allegiance and in some cases the geographical location of their particular unit. Moreover, they are further subdivided by the professional allegiances they owe outside the business, e.g. their accounting association, engineering institute or trade union. All these various pressures affect the individual's values and understandings, the symbolic meanings attached to actions, objects and words, even the language which is used.

Language is sometimes made deliberately obscure to exclude members of other subgroupings with the deliberate intention of creating a mystique, or a 'closed shop'. Newly emergent specialisms typically use this approach as a means of establishing their professional status, as, for example, computer specialists did in the 1950s and

1960s. Even without the explicit use of such competitive measures, language frequently acts as a barrier between subcultures. For example, accounting has increasingly become the language of management and some of the jargon has spilled over into the everyday language. The term 'bottom line', for example, is widely used and it has a nuance of tough unflinching realism. But the real 'bottom line' actually comprises tough, unflinching realities plus value judgements plus guesses. Accounting jargon, like all specialist language, is a barrier to communication across the organization, even though it may be an efficient shorthand within its specialism.

In such complexity it is clear that organizational culture is not simply homogeneous, but the sum of many subcultures, each of which contributes its own nuances of meaning and its own rituals and images. Although there is a popular view that culture is 'the glue that binds organization together' (Deal and Kennedy, 1982), it is clear that culture can in fact be divisive, just as easily as cohesive. In the absence of any dominant superculture, the various subcultures may well be in conflict with each other. On occasion this conflict may become overt and sometimes highly dysfunctional, but more usually the conflict will be bubbling below the surface. Culture has thus been described as a 'melange of cross-cutting subcultures', continually reacting against each other in some more or less cohesive, or divisive, not necessarily stable, equilibrium (Gregory, 1983). In short culture tends to be a mess, which is not amenable to efficient analysis.

Nevertheless it is management's job to make sense of this mess. Their preferred culture must be defined and its coherence ensured. Then things must be so organized that this preferred culture dominates all other subcultures. The coherence and dominance of management's intended culture appeared to be essential qualities of Peters and Waterman's 'excellent' companies. The process of achieving coherence and dominance is often referred to as 'culture management'.

The idea of culture management seems to imply the sort of approach taken by the great and famous originators of such organizations as IBM, Hewlett Packard, NCR, ITT, McDonald's, etc. These businesses all share 'strong', deliberately established and maintained, coherent, dominant 'cultures'. Put another way, each of these organizations appears to have gained the active participation of all their members in fully exploiting their organization's distinctive competence, whatever it happens to be.

Selznick argued that it is vitally important for an organization to define its distinctive competence which then becomes the focal point of the organization's culture (Selznick, 1957). In the case of IBM, for example, it is often suggested that the distinctive competence is to do with providing the customer with reliability and support. IBM's reputation for technological innovation is insignificant, but customer service and support is their distinctive competence and appears to have been absorbed in the hearts and minds of all their employees. An IBM engineer would spend Christmas morning at a customer's installation if need be to ensure the site was operational when required. There is something about the IBM culture which persuades employees to set aside considerations of self-interest in favour of their service to the company. How has IBM achieved it?

Pascale (1985) looked at the way some big firms (including IBM, ITT, Procter & Gamble, Morgan Guaranty, etc.) achieved their so-called 'strong' cultures. He found that these companies all used a systematic process of socialization for their management recruits, based on the following seven steps:

1. Careful selection of entry level candidates, based on apparent ability and compatibility with the corporate culture. This implies that right from selection, potential mavericks are filtered out of the system. Relative youth is also a key factor, recruitment straight from university or after a relatively short period, ensures that recruits are still highly suggestible.

2. After selection recruits are exposed in their first months to a period of 'humility inducing' experience in order to precipitate self-questioning of their prior behaviour, beliefs and values. This is essentially a period of breaking down any potential resistance to accepting corporate values and beliefs. IBM typically put their new recruits through training which puts them under fairly extreme pressure, working through the early hours of the morning on their own material and then going on to help others. Procter & Gamble involved their potentially high flying recruits in colouring in maps of sales territories.

3. The third phase involved 'in the trenches' training in one of the core disciplines of the business such as customer support.

4. Meticulous attention was given to systems for measuring operational results and rewarding individuals according to their performance.

5. Careful adherence was required to the firm's transcendant values, such as the ideals of the firm serving mankind, or providing a first class product for the benefit of society, etc. This enables employees to reconcile personal sacrifices necessitated by membership of the organization.

6. A system of reinforcing folklore is provided through legends

and interpretations of watershed events in the firm's history that validates its culture and its aims.

7. Consistent role models and consistent traits are associated with those recognized as being on the fast track. Firms needed to create high flyers in order to fulfil these role models – the characteristics of high flyers being their visible consistency with corporate values, etc., rather than any inherent super ability.

The success of this seven-step process is apparent in the way employees perform and in particular how they fulfil the firm's expectations in exploiting its distinctive competence. However, such approaches have been widely criticized because they seem to have elements of 'brainwashing', and their use of culture and symbol possibly has parallels in populist political movements. There is potentially a moral problem in deciding how far it is proper for a firm to go in 'socializing' its employees. But there are other problems with the approach which may be even more pressing.

Firstly, it is important to note that the seven stages provide a systematic, integrated programme – there is no suggestion that any one of the steps can be effective on its own. Attempts have been made to implement 'culture programmes' on a more limited front without success. Attempts to create artificial cultures by rewriting the company history, creating artificial company stories, circulating over-zealous statements of corporate mission, all seem doomed to fail. Reynolds described one such case, a 'silicon valley' computer firm, where top management went through the motions of creating a corporate culture. Because the reality differed from the official version they were trying to elaborate, all their attempts were counter-productive and only resulted in increased cynicism and alienation among employees. 'Everyone knew the operative values at Falcon Computer were hierarchy, secrecy and expediency – regardless of what the official culture said' (Reynolds, 1986, p. 51). Corporate integrity can be extremely critical.

The IBM engineer is persuaded to perform beyond what one might regard as the normal call of duty because of a basic belief that the business is in some way working for the greater good of society. This belief, or value, is deliberately instilled and reinforced during the new employees induction programme and is centred around the company's distinctive competence, which is the focus of its differentiation strategy. In IBM's case, according to Pascale, this was customer service. Whether the methods of socialization are acceptable or not, it is clear that the desired result would not be achieved if employees were unable to believe in the basic integrity of the organization's strategy.

At a crude level, corrupt and dishonest management destroy the possibility of corporate integrity. Many managers appear to believe that getting caught is what matters, and since they are not caught their dishonesty is not known about and therefore no harm is done. This is an illusion. A dishonest senior manager may never be brought to book for being dishonest despite the fact that almost every member of the organization knows perfectly well that the position of trust held is regularly abused. It would be most unusual for dishonesty among senior managers not to be known. At the same time, it is equally unusual for it to be openly acknowledged and punished.

At a slightly less basic level, the attempt to motivate employees by imposing a false culture, i.e. one which is espoused by top management but not practised, is also likely to be counter-productive, as it was at Falcon Computer (Reynolds, 1986).

Lack of corporate integrity produces only cynicism and alienation among members. With integrity, the strategy of the business becomes the means of achieving consensus among members and concentration of their efforts.

Even if the seven steps identified by Pascale are all carefully implemented and the 'strong culture' successfully created and maintained, the result may be far from ideal. For example, this may explain why IBM, with all its resources, is not known, in a high technology industry, as a technological leader. Strong culture may be merely the contemporary way of achieving the sort of conformity and obedience that was formerly achieved through more overtly autocratic methods of management.

> The value driven organisation is capable of tight control . . .
> because the shared values provide a common perspective. . . .
> Linkage through a shared strategic vision can replace bureaucratic
> mechanisms of command and control. (Leitko and Szczerbacki,
> 1987, p. 64).

Conformity appears to be the end result of this process of socialization, but conformity is only an aspect of bureaucracy and is inappropriate in times of rapid change because it will stifle innovation.

A more sensitive approach to culture management might involve influencing the cross-cutting of the various subcultures so that they tend to support the culture desired by management. To achieve this management would define some minimum set of cultural characteristics to which all subcultures should be encouraged or persuaded to subscribe. A minimum set might consist simply of an understanding of the purpose of the business and its competitive specialism or its strategic objectives. With this as common ground among all employees, management's cultural role would be firstly to eliminate cultural elements which confuse, or subvert, the understanding and achievement of the purpose and specialism of the business and replace them by cultural elements which clarify and expound. By cultural elements is meant the aspects of culture which are made manifest in symbolic form.

There have been few thorough surveys of culture management, presumably because of the complexity of the subject. One researcher identified general managers who had been successful over a five-year period and found that only a few undertook activities which they themselves felt could be characterized as 'culture management'. However, those that did were among the top performers (Kotter, 1982). The actions they took, which they regarded as culture management, fell into two categories. Firstly, actions related to items such as leadership and motivation, which would have been taken anyway, without any knowledge or understanding of the culture concept. Secondly, actions which could be much better understood as symbolic rather than cultural. The power of organizational symbols is substantial and, unlike culture, they can often be managed effectively.

8.4   Organizational symbolism

When Michael Edwardes took over the running of the insolvent British Leyland motor company it was under the influence of Communist-led shop stewards, headed by Derek Robinson, the Senior Convenor at the Longbridge factory in Birmingham. According to Edwardes, Robinson's 30-month stewardship had resulted in 523 industrial disputes and cost the company 62,000 cars and 113,000 engines. When Robinson opposed Edwardes' recovery plan, which had already been approved by the work-force, he probably saw it as his last chance to wrest power from the management. Edwardes' response to Robinson's opposition was to sack him forthwith, seeing this as *his* 'last chance of gaining manageability at Longbridge' (Edwardes, 1983). The dismissal of Robinson was, above everything else, a symbolic act. In all the subsequent discussions with unions over this dismissal, management never wavered from their original decision because of the symbolic importance that any fudging might have had. It was a watershed event in the history of the company, marking the point when management started to manage and the politically-motivated local stewards lost control. Robinson had become a symbol of Communist control. As such he had to be removed. The story of his removal has itself become a symbol of the firm's step 'back from the brink'.

Symbols are the more or less tangible manifestations of culture. Robinson was a symbol of the numerically insignificant militant Communist subculture at Longbridge. Within his own subculture he was a hero; to other Leyland subcultures he was a villain; to all subcultures he had come to embody symbolic meaning.

Symbols can be anything: people, words, events, stories, actions or physical objects. What makes them symbolic is the fact that they convey meaning beyond their face value.

Many businesses make use of specific events to reinforce culture through symbolic means. The making of long service awards, and the official marking of an employee's retirement can be used to highlight the value the company places on loyalty, its respect for employees and appreciation of their work. Similarly, the making of awards for performance, once largely restricted to prizes for sales achievements, is now becoming more widespread and more imaginative. Actions such as these appear to be far more powerful in their effect than direct and formal statements of what the company stands for and values. In this instance, actions can certainly speak louder than words.

Culture is manifested through stories or myths, many of which identify the roles of heroes or villains at watershed events in the company history. A common story is about the intimidating old President who is affronted by the innocent new employee who insists on the proper exercise of company rules no matter if the assailant does claim to be President. In a benign culture the story goes that the President rewards the employee; in a malign one the result is instant dismissal. Stories about the young employee being rewarded for initiative, or the old employee being rewarded for dogged devotion to duty, are repeated in many different organizations (Martin *et al.*, 1987). Some of the stories are created deliberately in order to communicate a particular symbolic meaning. Others seem to originate from some factual basis and then be amended and embroidered over time, so that they communicate some meaningful point about the culture in question.

Management has no monopoly on the creation of potent symbolic stories. For example, the story was told in the 1970s how, at a Ford assembly plant, a shop-floor operative collapsed and died, and his workmates were forced to carry on working without going to their colleague's assistance for a full ten minutes before the supervisor took any action to see if there was anything wrong with the man (Beynon,

1975). A similar incident had also been reported at another car assembly plant, the only difference being that the length of delay in this latter case was fourteen minutes. The same story has also been repeated in the British steel industry and in iron foundries. It sems reasonable to assume that versions of this story have been told in other organizations as well.

The story, in its various versions, may or may not be based on some incident that actually happened, but it is extremely unlikely to be wholly true. Few managements would wish to behave in such a way, and even if they did, very few would have established such iron discipline that would keep people working in such circumstances. The point of the story is clearly symbolic, intended to illustrate the vicious, exploitative nature of management. Where its source has been identified, the story has emanated from 'organized labour' in the form of local union representatives who have clearly seen themselves as in conflict with management.

Symbols do not have to be created by conflicting subcultures to be dysfunctional to management's desired dominant culture. They can arise directly from management either accidentally or gratuitously. They may even be remnants of a historical position and have become inappropriate over time.

Not all symbols which are deliberately created by management convey the intended meaning. For example, an incompetently, or insincerely, performed long service ceremony, is likely to be counter-productive in that the symbolic meaning it communicates is more or less the exact opposite of that intended. In such cases, the whole institution of long service awards could become symbolic of the cynical disregard management has for its employees.

Old established businesses have been notorious for the labyrinthine status symbols they deployed such as keys to the executive toilets, carpets in offices, size of company car and proximity of parking space, different eating arrangements from the Directors' Dining Room to the Works Canteen, etc. All such symbols convey the simple meaning that hierarchy is what matters, not serving the customer.

An understanding of the dynamic equilibrium of culture in an organization can be used to reinforce the desired or consciously-created subculture. Cultural inconsistencies in an organization can arise both from the head-on conflict of different subcultures and from the unconscious or unintentional 'dropping' of conflicting symbols. By ensuring that symbols of the desired culture convey meanings which are both consistent and dominant they can be made to contribute positively to the exploitation of the firm's competitive specialism.

Moreover, this link between the strategy pursued by an organization and its culture can be further reinforced by the deliberate planned use of the more tangible images of the firm's material symbols, such as its products, its logo, its architecture, etc. The elimination of inconsistent images and the reinforcement of consistent ones inevitably contributes to the dominance of the desired culture over other subcultures, so that a positive strategic equilibrium position is achieved.

Even so, organizational culture is hard to change. Once it has matured into a readily recognizable form it develops a robustness which seems impervious to orthodox approaches to organization development. Deliberate attempts to change the culture have often been highly unsuccessful. Those successes that have been documented (e.g. Tunstall, 1983) have been slow and painstaking, and have generally involved a good many mistakes along the way. Not only is culture itself difficult to change, but the 'stronger' the culture the more it tends to inhibit other organizational change.

The most effective means of changing the culture of a business is through symbolic change, from the obvious and crude but effective firing of top management, to the less dramatic, more subtle detailed changes involving the elimination of conflicting symbols and the creation of new reinforcing symbols.

8.5   Manageable characteristics of culture

Auditing culture is extremely difficult,

> people don't speak of assumptions directly, but rather imply them
> through diverse concrete examples. [Moreover,] some assumptions
> may contradict overtly stated norms, so people are reluctant to
> admit them. [Even if these difficulties are overcome,] the diversity
> and size of many organisations require us to consider how
> representative a culture audit's findings really are [– they may only
> be representative of one or more subculture in the organization]
> (Wilkins, 1983, p. 31).

Kanter (1983) identified an aspect of organizational culture that she called 'empowerment', as being a prerequisite of effective innovation in the large US corporations she studied. Her research compared successful and less successful innovators and found that the successful ones had found a way round their own structures and bureaucratic tendencies through empowerment.

Empowerment comprised three ingredients:

● resources – funds, materials, space, time, etc.
● information – technical and market data, expertise, etc.
● support – endorsement, backing, approval and legitimacy.

For empowerment to operate effectively firms had to have open communications and what Kanter called 'network' forming arrangements which cut across the usual organizational structures.

Communications in an organization are generally described in terms of being open or closed. When an organization enjoys open communications it means that communications, both formal and informal take place across the organization as well as up and down the chains of command. It means that they take place freely between all members of the organization without restraint and protocol. A chief financial officer may talk to a junior sales clerk without risk of causing any emotional disturbance among other organization members. Moreover the junior sales clerk may speak to the president without restraint or inhibition of any kind. Not only *may* these communications take place, but if communications are open, they actually *do*.

Closed communications, on the other hand, mean that communications only occur formally up and down direct lines of command, and mainly down. Communication across the organization would be psychologically loaded and widely perceived as even damaging to career prospects and, consequently, do not occur.

Clearly these descriptions are of extreme cases – in reality organizations generally steer between the two, but tend in one direction or the other.

The other characteristic associated with empowerment is participation, i.e. the degree to which members of the organization are involved in the decision-making process. To some extent, consideration of participation overlaps the structural idea of centralization, but participation goes further into the organization than structure, being a characteristic of the whole organization including parts which may be relatively untouched by the decision-taking style adopted by central management.

Problem-solving groups, task forces, quality circles or any form of shared responsibility team are all vehicles for increasing the degree of participation which appears prerequisite if organization members are to contribute to strategic action. Despite these various widely used approaches to establishing effective participation, there are problems and paradoxes in introducing participative systems – 'participation is something the top orders the middle to do for the bottom!'

Kanter found that participation on job specific issues worked effectively, i.e. improved a firm's effectiveness as an innovator, whereas attempts to provide participation on company-wide issues tended to create alienation and cynicism. Thus the sort of participation which is provided through statute in Europe, particularly Germany, providing for employee representatives on the board of directors, would only be likely to be counter-productive in a firm's attempt to innovate.

Kanter found that the participative operation of effective teams was difficult to achieve. Differences in rank, personal calibre, skills, expertise and knowledge could all upset teamwork – the bureaucratic tendency to hierarchy applied to problem-solving teams just as it did to the mainstream organization. Moreover, the fruits of the participatory process were essentially long term. They were realized in terms of a more adaptive, innovative organization that could respond to, and stay ahead of, the change in its various environments.

8.6 Summary

Structure, culture and symbolism provide a further framework for strategic thinking which emphasizes the paramount importance of people in turning strategy into action thereby achieving concentration, consistency and flexibility.

The original structural concepts of standardization, specialization, formalization, configuration and centralization offer an incomplete description of structure and are not as unambiguous as they are sometimes portrayed.

Mintzberg's extension of the structural concept, though even less readily measured, produces a provocative and potentially usable taxonomy of structural forms. Even allowing for extreme difficulties in accurately measuring structure, some pragmatic prescriptions for management action are apparent.

A valid form of cultural analysis remains extremely problematic. The anthropological approach to analysing culture is not practicable and the validity of less time-consuming approaches to 'culture auditing' is difficult to justify.

The culture of an organization is made manifest in the meanings attached to organizational symbols and this seems to provide the key to culture management.

The creation, shaping and elimination of organizational symbols is a feasible enterprise. To some extent managers may do this intuitively, without overt regard for the symbolic aspect of their action.

Overtly adopting the symbolic perspective could provide management with powerful new insights helping them influence the behaviour of organizational members.

Symbol management (including communications), actions and physical objects (including structural characteristics) can ensure that symbolic meanings reinforce strategy, rather than undermine it.

DISCUSSION CASE: TACHOCHEM PLC

Tachochem PLC was a large long-established holding company which since the 1930s had been regularly referred to as a 'blue chip'. It was a diversified manufacturing group mainly serving the automotive and construction industries. Throughout the post-war years it had found business very easy to achieve – the main job of the sales function was resisting customer pressure for an increase in their monthly allocations.

By the end of the 1960s the world was changing rapidly. Competition had increased dramatically, particularly from overseas, and Tachochem had lost almost half its previous market share. In 1973 the oil price crisis had a devastating effect on demand for all Tachochem's products and the company moved into losses for the first time in its 90-year history.

One of Tachochem's largest subsidiaries was Conchem Ltd which had seven factories manufacturing a variety of building materials and components, employing around 4,500 people. All these factories were grossly under-utilized even before the 1973 collapse in demand, and there was little prospect of volumes ever recovering sufficiently for the production facilities to become profitable again. Clearly some decisive management action was necessary and the top management of Conchem were instructed to make firm proposals to the parent company's Executive Committee, such proposals being to bring Conchem back into profit over a given time period.

Conchem's main site was in Manchester and comprised the original and main factory as well as the Head Office. This main factory accounted for about 30 per cent of Conchem's business, but was a substantial loss-maker largely because of poor factory utilization. There were three other factories each of about half the size of the Manchester one and three further quite small factories. Of all the factories, it appeared only the small ones were profitable, although this position was not completely clear because profitability at plant level was calculated on the basis of a rather arbitrary allocation of overheads. The overhead burden was extremely heavy and was done on the basis of factory floor area.

Conchem's management devised two plans.

1. Scheme A involved the closure of all three small factories and the closure of half the Manchester factory and one other. The plan involved around 2,000 redundancies including 150 from the Head Office and promised to return Conchem to profit after nine months.
2. Scheme B involved the closure of the main site in its entirety plus two of the smallest factories and the moving of the remaining Head Office staff to expanded offices at one of the larger remaining factories. The number of redundancies was similar and though it was expected to take slightly longer to implement the projected profitability was much the same as for Scheme A.

Conchem's board considered which scheme they should recommend to the parent company. Scheme B was a more radical proposal than Scheme A, involving more upheaval, especially for Head Office staff. The financial outcomes as projected were similar. Whilst Scheme A was on paper quicker to implement, there was considerable feeling among Conchem management that the savings were less certain than they would be from Scheme B. Making substantial savings from closing half a factory would be much less certain than the elimination of costs if a site was vacated altogether.

Discussion points
- As Chief Executive of Conchem which do you feel are the most important considerations in this case?
- Is the long term financial viability of the business of paramount importance?
- If so, and bearing in mind that both options indicate similar financial outcomes, which scheme would you recommend?
- What further information would you require in order to firm up your recommendation?

Conchem's Head Office was built in 1932 when the company was at its most successful. The entrance foyer was a large open space with a granite floor and black marble tiles and chromium walls with decorative 1930s-style stained glass windows.

There were four ways out of the foyer. The most impressive was up an elegant sweep of staircase rising to the first floor and a wide pair of light oak and glass doors which gave onto the directors' suite of offices. In addition there were two lifts with brightly polished brasswork. There was also a doorway at the left hand side which led to a long corridor and some back stairs. Use of these various exits was determined strictly according to seniority – only directors used the stairs.

Conchem's senior managers (i.e. those who reported directly to a director) had carpets on their office floors and were delivered trays with glasses and fresh carafes of drinking water in their offices each morning.

The doors to the directors' suite were facing south and thus often had the sun shining through them. They were popularly known as 'the golden gates'. Through the golden gates the carpet was double thick and the walls were adorned with an impressive selection of original impressionist oil paintings.

Discussion points
- Does the above additional information help the process of choosing between Scheme A and B?
- Would knowledge of the Head Office (and there were many more aspects of its culture and symbolism which would be known consciously and subconsciously by the real decision-takers) be likely to influence the decision?
- Should it?
- What would be the likely impact of the items described on the people working in Conchem's Head Office?
- Think of directors, senior managers, junior managers and clerks, and consider the possible different impacts on each group.
- What message do these physical symbols communicate?

Conchem recommended Scheme B to Tachochem, but it was rejected in favour of Scheme A. No reason for this was given formally, but it was rumoured that the Chairman (who had joined the Group working at Conchem as a young graduate trainee manager thirty years earlier) had destroyed Scheme B simply by saying that 'closing its Head Office would be like tearing the heart out of Conchem!'

Discussion point
- Is there any rational justification for this decision?

Tachochem's merchant bank was in the process of moving its premises into a new tower block in the City of London and one of their senior partners had lightheartedly suggested they purchase all Conchem's furnishings for their new offices.

Discussion points
- Was there any rational justification for such an offer?
- How would the message these same symbols communicate be different in the merchant bank office as opposed to at Conchem?

CHAPTER NINE
Strategic thinking frameworks: entrepreneurial strategy

9.1 Introduction

Entrepreneurial strategy seeks to model the approach used by the typical entrepreneur when first setting up a business. The approach encapsulates many elements of other frameworks and seems in some ways derivative from them. However, the entrepreneur came first. Large scale business followed, often trying to recapture the original sense of direction, the concentration of effort and consistency over time, and the flexibility and responsiveness inevitably lost during years of growth and diversification.

The entrepreneur's decision to set up a new business, the first strategic decision, is the bravest of them all. The new business can only be founded on an extensive personal financial commitment, a high degree of uncertainty and a reliance on superhuman personal efforts. Most established businesses would be unable to tolerate any manager who recommended such a reckless course of action. They are simply not equipped to deal with that kind of risk any more, unless the alternative is terminal collapse.

Yet every business that exists today has gone through the start-up decision, so the entrepreneurs have clearly got something right. In terms of strategy, the entrepreneurial approach is direct and simple. The purposes of strategy – direction, concentration, consistency and flexibility – are achieved, it appears, almost instinctively, largely by adherence to the following three principles (Pearson, 1985):

1. Knowing the mission of the business.
2. Identifying its competitive specialism.
3. Concentrating on exploitation of the specialism.

For a small undiversified business these are relatively simple concepts to apply. Moreover, flexibility that causes large scale businesses so much difficulty, is a natural attribute of the small entrepreneur. The critical question is whether by following this entrepreneurial example, larger businesses can recapture the essentially entrepreneurial characteristics.

9.2   Business mission

The business mission in a set-up decision is usually quite straightforward and has to do with satisfying a customer need that is not already catered for. The mission is not to provide the owner with a return on investment. That may be the entrepreneur's reason for setting up the business, but the mission of the business itself is separate from this and prescribes the means of earning that return. If the business satisfies a customer need, customers will pay an economic price for the product. If an economic price is not paid then the business is not satisfying a customer need. This ability to spot the opportunity, the unsatisfied customer need, is the archetypal entrepreneurial skill.

Business mission is the foundation of an effective strategy. New businesses experience a high mortality rate mainly because they have no clear mission. A few fail because they run out of cash as a result of trying to grow too quickly, but not many. More frequently failure arises because there is no unsatisfied customer need. Or the business does not provide an acceptable means of its satisfaction, because the product is too expensive, too poor quality, too late, too heavy, etc. etc.

The original business mission, which was the basis of the set-up decision seems to remain permanently valid in some businesses. Sears, IBM, Marks and Spencer, Hewlett Packard and many others have been well documented. However, for other firms this is not the case. The original mission may become completely invalid, or it may remain relevant to only a small part of the business. After years of faltering progression down various paths, with endless product diversifications, the mission of the business can become completely obscure, the only unifying elements being the common ownership and use of the financial language.

In response to this many big companies are now writing up their company histories for use as case studies in management training (Smith and Steadman, 1981). The company's history can be instructive and give useful insights both as to the firm's current role and even likely future directions. It is also increasingly used to create or reinforce aspects of corporate culture by explaining in symbolic terms some watershed event of the past, or giving exposure to some important role model, very often through stories about the original founder of the business.

However, corporate history is an inadequate substitute for *knowing* the business mission. With no clear knowledge of its mission, any business will inevitably drift. One way to deal with this problem is to formalize a statement of *corporate* mission that everyone in the company can aspire to support. Such statements are likely to include references to employees, customers, the product and technology. Some firms, attempting at the same time to achieve further shaping of corporate culture, go further and include such noble sentiments as honesty and integrity, service to society at large and so on. Some go far beyond the realms of business strategy with declarations of support for the free enterprise system and the American democratic form of government (Pearce, 1982).

Whilst such approaches may be inspirational and make a cultural impact, so far as the business mission is concerned a more succinct approach is likely to be more effective. A simple, direct, unambiguous and, above all, operational statement of business mission is required. 'Our mission is to sell the best quality widgets on the (defined) market' tells everyone where the emphasis of their job should lie. It can help concentrate all their efforts.

The acid test of the set-up decision is survival. If the business survives it is because customers are paying an economic price for the product and that, in turn, is because the product is satisfying a customer need. This is the case even if the need is not known to the business. Mature businesses frequently do not know what need the customer is satisfying in buying the product. Management may think they know; they may even have a unanimously held view. But it is by no means a simple matter. The only person who really knows what need is being satisfied is the customer – and even he may not know the whole story.

If strategy is to be soundly based the business must know exactly what customer need is satisfied by the product. This is the foundation of the business's long term security and must be thoroughly understood. It cannot be done by the usual informal contacts with customers because the conclusions will be unreliable. One form of customer research was indicated in the strategic marketing chapter – only by using reliable research methods will the *real* needs that the customer satisfies be identified.

In some situations, even professional research will not reveal the real mission that the business is fulfilling. A company which has diversified to the stage of incoherence has no single unifying business mission to reveal. Or a business that is drifting – the world may have changed and the business failed to respond – will either have to metamorphose or die. This does not happen to the entrepreneur. Entrepreneurs have contacts. Their fingers are on the pulse. Disasters do not catch them unawares. If there is a change in the market need that their businesses satisfy, they know about it. The entrepreneurial framework seeks to emulate this sensitivity.

9.3 The competitive specialism

Though an understanding of the business mission is the key to survival, it is not in itself sufficient for high performance. That is achieved by exploiting the competitive specialism.

There are many examples in the literature of what happens to firms that ignore their specialism. The adoption of accounting mores and the consequent search for quick returns through diversification and acquisition have led many firms, particularly those in mature low growth industries, to ignore their competitive specialism and its potential for further exploitation.

One firm which typifies this tendency is the car firm, Jaguar. Jaguar's specialism was clearly related to the production and sale of a well-engineered, up-market focused product. But Jaguar barely survived the period when the needs of its state-owned parent forced its attention down the hierarchy onto purely financial objectives. It lost quality and reputation and ceased to produce a product that fulfilled the Jaguar mission. Sales fell, productivity collapsed and the product became almost unsaleable. The vicious cycle was only reversed by a return to the firm's competitive specialism and a new concentration on quality and reliability. In the depths of 1972 Jaguar employed 160 engineers and many more accountants. By 1985 they employed over 600 engineers and were urgently seeking more. This change reflects one of the more obvious practical implications of concentration on the specialism. As a 'born again' quality producer Jaguar is 'sticking to its knitting', exploiting its specialism and concentrating on its original business mission. Whether such a business remains viable in the face of volatile exchange rates remains to be seen, but the strategy, which was subverted during the Leyland years, provides the only credible prospect of success.

There are three ways in which the competitive specialism can be exploited. Firstly, it can be strengthened or intensified so that it is more readily perceived by customers or so that customers accord it a higher value and are therefore prepared to pay a higher premium. Thus, for example, a specialism related to product quality could be intensified by increasing the quality of the product further and/or promoting the quality of the product more effectively. The result will be to increase the actual and perceived level of quality and reduce the price sensitivity of the product.

Secondly, the specialism can be broadened so that it satisfies the needs of more customers. The most obvious way that this can be done is by geographic broadening, but any product which is focused on a narrow segment of the market can potentially have its focus broadened to appeal to other segments.

Finally, the specialism can be prolonged, so that it survives through developing technology and changing consumer tastes. The automobile industry is a particularly good example of how the competitive specialism can be prolonged through all manner of fundamental changes and yet various products or brands continue, their specialisms recognizably in place.

In much of strategic thinking the concepts are fairly simple, the execution sometimes extremely difficult. Exploiting the specialism is a case in point. It is easy to suggest intensifying its value, for example, by increasing the level of quality. However, extreme care needs to be exercised. Not only is it vital to be certain what the specialism is, but it is also essential to know how far it can be intensified. It would be easy to increase quality beyond customer perceptions, i.e. build in unwanted quality. Similarly it would be easy to provide quality at a price that the customer is unwilling to pay. Intensifying the specialism must only be done with care and on the basis of hard information about customer perceptions.

Broadening the specialism also has its dangers. There may well be a trade-off between broadening the specialism and its intensity. A sharply focused specialism is perhaps the easiest to manage. Widening that focus to encompass more market segments risks losing its perceived value to the existing customers. Again extreme care has to be taken and decisions based on solid data.

Similarly with prolonging the life of a specialism. Some specialisms are related to single products, or to single clearly defined markets, which have finite lives. In the face of inevitable decline it may well be essential to accept the death of the business and to invest in something different while funds are still available. This happens occasionally, but far too many products and product lines have been diagnosed as 'yesterday's breadwinners' or 'dogs' and as a direct consequence have been ruthlessly liquidated. The orthodox wisdom of the day prescribed starving such businesses of investment and pricing them out of the market in a curious self-fulfilling prophecy. In many such cases it might have been perfectly feasible to revive the businesses concerned by identifying their specialisms and taking action to prolong them.

Exploiting the specialism, in one of these three ways is therefore the strategic objective at the top of the hierarchy. Pursuit of this objective is entrepreneurial strategy's essential concern.

9.4   The information base

Pursuit of an effective entrepreneurial strategy is mainly through information. Identifying the competitive specialism, known by instinct to the original entrepreneur, has to be mapped through the collection and analysis of information from existing and potential customers. Exploiting the specialism requires a still wider information base. In addition it is vital to be aware of, and respond to, developments in technology which might present both threats and opportunities directly affecting the firm's competitive specialism.

In exploiting the specialism it may from time to time be necessary to completely replace the product. The case of tyres, when radials replaced cross-ply tyres in the 1970s was a case in point (see Chapter 7). The specialism attaches to the brand and not necessarily the technology. Changing the product in order to exploit the specialism will become increasingly frequent as the technological revolution gathers pace and its impacts broaden out. The defender of a doomed product is in an unenviable position. The attacker, who is ahead of the field with the innovation which will further exploit their specialism, can completely change the competitive structure of the industry to their own advantage.

Knowledge of the factors influencing the competitive specialism, as shown in Figure 9.1, is crucial to an effective entrepreneurial strategy.

Developing such an information base is, in practice, a process of selection and concentration on pertinent issues. A fully comprehensive system would be impracticable for most businesses. The extent to which information should be maintained depends on circumstances. For example, in the case of suppliers, if the industry uses a single key raw material controlled by a small number of firms, strategic supplies

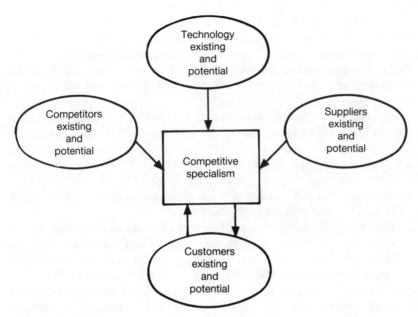

Figure 9.1   *Influences on the competitive specialism.*

may be a key issue. If on the other hand supplies are freely available from a competitive market, the strategic importance of information on individual suppliers is going to be negligible. However, in this era of technological change, the necessity to be fully aware of the technological developments currently impacting, or potentially capable of impacting, on the industry is crucial.

Within each of the four areas, technology, customers, competitors and suppliers, there is a huge and rapidly growing amount of published information already available, together with increasingly effective means of collecting and processing new information. Maintaining a selective and concentrated information base need not be too onerous. The development of information technology has made data more widely available and easier to access and the amount of information in the public domain still appears to be growing exponentially.

Sources of published information are under-utilized because firms, especially small firms, are relucr ⁀t to involve themselves in what at first sight appears to be an infoɪ ̠ation jungle which it might be felt is more properly the field of specialist marketing researchers. But published research on existing and potential technology, on markets and on individual competitors and customers is easily identified and accessed through an increasing number of indexing and abstracting services. In addition, there are now literally thousands of new electronic databases, some offering abstracts as well as the original data itself. The accessibility of such systems is now catching up with the technology and they are becoming more widely used and more readily usable.

In addition to published information strategic management also requires new information, as we have seen, about the perceptions of existing and potential customers. This includes very specific and limited items relating to how customers perceive the products available to them and why they buy what they buy. This information too is available to even the smallest firms and the techniques involved in its collection are not unduly sophisticated.

This selective and specific approach to the building of an information base makes it a practical proposition for all but the smallest firms. Information is the key resource of strategic management. Firms can be completely aware of the state of the art in their own industry. They can readily know enough about available technology, the perceptions of their customers, their competitors and suppliers in order to pursue a soundly-based entrepreneurial strategy of exploiting their competitive specialism.

9.5 Concentration

Entrepreneurial strategy aims to identify relevant innovations which would serve to exploit the competitive specialism. It involves making sure that one-off, discrete investments are taken in a consistent and relevant way which serves the strategic aims of the business. But it also affects the everyday running of the business. It affects the way the Chief Executive works, and it should also affect the way the operative on the shop-floor works. The allocation of resources includes how people allocate their own personal resources of skill, knowledge, effort and enthusiasm. It is a far wider issue than just capital investment or the flows of cash.

In short, entrepreneurial strategy seeks to achieve the maximum concentration of resources and efforts on exploiting the competitive specialism. An organization that adopts the entrepreneurial approach enjoys one great benefit which assists the achievement of concentration: the entrepreneurial strategy concept is very simple. Expression of the competitive specialism is made in deliberately simple and comprehensible, unambiguous terms. Identifying the purpose and specialism of a business may not be such a simple process among all the mess and random noise of the real business world, but conceptually it is simple. And once the competitive specialism is identified, it can be simply communicated so that every member in the organization knows which way they're supposed to be headed.

In most modern businesses concentration is extremely difficult to accomplish. Systems of management, of financial control and of strategic planning, conspire to inhibit any attempts to concentrate. Yet the dispersal of effort and the broad but thin spread of resources, inevitably result in the achievement of very little.

Companies that operate traditional strategic planning systems invariably find concentration almost impossible to achieve. The analysis is carried out in thorough detail, covering every function and every business area and typically results in an allocation of resources that is intended to shore up any weaknesses and exploit any strengths, minimize threats and exploit opportunities. Inevitably it achieves nothing.

Apart from paralysing the existing business, such systems typically also produce strategies of diversification, or more probably acquisition, which achieves a further dramatic loss in concentration and focus.

Such systems seem logical and yet they produce a result which is compromised, indecisive and leads nowhere. But the attraction of such systems goes very deep. They are fundamentally based in an unwritten, taken-for-granted attitude to risk. Few people like to take unnecessary risks. In business the stakes are high, and decision-takers tend to be inherently wary of taking risk. Even without formal SWOT-based planning systems, the investment decision taker, or resource allocator, naturally seeks to avoid risk whenever possible, or at the very least minimize it. This can be done by using various techniques of financial and quantitative analysis which appear to depersonalize the decision and give it a mechanical logic which symbolically processes the risk away.

However, business is by definition at risk, invests in risk and obtains its economic return as a result of risk. Allocating resources to all problems and all opportunities appears superficially to minimize risk. But this is an illusion – in reality it paralyses the business. Concentration might appear to be the risky strategy of putting all your eggs in one basket, but if the competitive specialism of the business has been correctly identified, and if the technology and competitor products have also been accurately assessed, then the selected concentration would be the least risky of all allocations. It is in fact the only action that promises economic results.

The apparent riskiness of concentration nevertheless persists. In multidivisional firms, managers are commonly evaluated, and their future career prospects thus depend, on short term financial measures. An ambitious young manager seeking to establish a track record is unlikely to be willing to take long term decisions and await their outcome which could be some five to ten years later. The time-scales of the executive and the business are not compatible. Controlling business units on the basis of the hierarchy of objectives, i.e. with a minimum performance against short term financial measures and effort concentrated on the strategic objective, could help to avoid this common difficulty.

Many firms which actively seek to encourage long term decision-taking still find it difficult to dispense with traditional attitudes to mistakes. The risk decision-taker who makes a mistake gets punished, one way or another. No matter what the intention is, such firms are in practice supporting an anti-risk climate, which is likely to result in a thin spread of resources rather than concentration.

9.6   Securing effort and enthusiasm

Chester Barnard asserted over forty years ago, that top management had responsibility for communication to 'link the common mission with those willing to cooperate in it'. Communication was the means of turning mission into action. For Barnard executive work was the job of 'maintaining' the organization and involved three prime tasks (Barnard, 1948):

- Formulation of mission and objectives
- Maintenance of organizational communication
- Securing essential services from individuals

The model of strategy outlined above fits Barnard's proposition quite well, the formulation of mission and objectives being seen as the essential first task of strategic management. The concept of mission has been refined into that of exploiting a precisely defined competitive specialism.

The 'maintenance of organizational communication' and 'securing essential services from individuals' are as crucial to the implementation of strategy as they are to the more general role of management. The remainder of this chapter provides an outline of some of the key issues to do with how people may be motivated to put their enthusiasm and effort behind achieving the mission and objectives of the business.

Clearly organizational communication is a substantial part of this. Understanding issues of structure, culture and symbolism (see Chapter 8) are also highly relevant. But personal management, leadership and motivation are also crucial in securing this concentration of effort on strategic ends. Much of the significance of concepts such as structure and culture rests on the fact that they, or aspects of them, impact on behaviour. However, there has been a substantial amount of work within organizational theory, aimed directly at identifying how and, more particularly, why people behave as they do.

In the sections below three main strands of this work are considered, firstly looking at the philosophy or attitude which underlies management's approach to people in organizations, and subsequently looking at the slightly more specific work in the areas of leadership and motivation.

9.6.1 Management philosophy

The phrase management philosophy perhaps sounds a little portentous and is only used with reluctance. The alternative phrase, management attitude, is too slight a concept to convey what is meant here. The philosophy referred to underlies the whole approach of management in their dealings with, and treatment of, people in organizations.

Attempting to create an organizational culture which is falsely based, i.e. which has aspirations not genuinely held by management, has already been shown (e.g. the case of Falcon Computer referred to in Chapter 8) as unlikely to succeed. The inconsistencies become apparent and tend to breed cynicism and alienation among members of the culture. Subsequent attempts at culture management can prove counter-productive.

Thus is seems important for the management philosophy to be consistent with the organization's aspirations, whether these be to run efficiently like a well-oiled machine in precisely determined ways, or to be flexible and responsive to external stimuli and capable of innovation.

Carl Rogers writing on the subject of education and learning expressed widely shared concepts of management philosophy (Rogers, 1969). Whilst borrowing ideas from another discipline can present some specific difficulties, there are sufficient similarities in the role of manager and that of teacher to make the analogies instructive.

Rogers' ideas were consistently based on what he called a 'personal philosophy' which confronted traditional or conventional attitudes to teaching. He said that he had 'found a way of being with students that . . . did not involve teaching so much as . . . the facilitation of learning' (Rogers, 1969).

He was not commending a singular new technique, or a limited change in the curriculum. What Rogers hoped to achieve was a fundamental change in attitude of teachers from the directive, traditional to the student-centred, facilitative, progressive. Such a change implied many and various changes in teaching methods and approaches and, as Rogers emphasized, the changed attitude would inevitably affect everything that the teacher did.

The two approaches to teaching, that Rogers identified as traditional and progressive, are generally expressed in rather extreme terms as being diametrically opposed. As such they are perhaps best regarded as 'ideal types'.

The traditional approach is characterized as authoritarian and directive, with large elements of compulsion or coercion, the method of teaching centring round 'chalk and talk', discipline being maintained by fear and threat and the curriculum being restricted entirely to the essential business of passing exams.

The progressive approach, on the other hand, is characterized by a negotiated curriculum much more loosely related to exams, democratic, student-centred, experiential, discursive teaching methods with discipline being largely held to be a matter of self-discipline, or the lack of it.

In reality, it may be that most teachers and most teaching situations exhibit characteristics from both sides of the divide. There appears to be not so much a dichotomy as a continuum with the extreme ends being as described above.

A comparison can be made between Rogers and his contemporary in organization theory, Douglas McGregor, whose statements of Theory X and Theory Y (McGregor, 1957) reflect a similar dichotomy between the traditional and progressive approaches. McGregor's Theory Y and Roger's facilitative learning share a basic philosophical view of the employee/student which is one of trust and respect. McGregor and Rogers both believed that the two opposing views in their separate fields were actually self-fulfilling prophesies – if you treated people as though they were lazy, untrustworthy and basically irresponsible, then that is how they may be expected to behave. If on the other hand you give them responsibility and trust, then it is asserted, they will respond positively.

The approaches of both McGregor and Rogers seemed deceptively simple to understand, but not so simple to implement effectively. Both have fallen into some disrepute as a result of the naive implementations by some of their followers who thought that managing or teaching was simply a question of being nice to people and that the democratic methods being advocated were simply *laissez-faire*. However, neither McGregor nor Rogers were advocating a soft option – effective student-centred facilitating may be more difficult to achieve than traditional directive teaching. Effective employee-centred management may require more skill and commitment than traditional carrot and stick methods.

In some circumstances the progressive approach has seemed to be less effective than more traditional methods. The same has appeared to hold true in management situations where autocratic methods may be most appropriate for certain conditions. However, where these conditions no longer exist, there would seem to be no valid role for traditional methods.

Rogers' view was that the 'personal philosophy' was all-pervasive. A teacher could not genuinely hold one set of values in one situation and adopt a quite different, even opposing set, in other situations. Values go deeper than that. Rogers was above all else concerned with values, built on the democratic ideal and emphasizing the dignity of the individual, the importance of personal choice, the significance of responsibility, the joy of creativity, etc.

As already noted the same seems to apply in management – superficially held values are an unsatisfactory foundation for an effective organizational culture. A manager's personal philosophy will pervade and influence the whole of the work area, if the values are firmly held.

While philosophy may underlie management's approach to various aspects of organization, it is particularly influential over the way people are led and motivated. These two aspects of organization have also received a lot of theoretical attention and are discussed in more detail below. Management philosophy, if it were identifiable, is nevertheless important in its own right because its impact is so pervasive and because other organizational characteristics may be regarded as vulnerable if underpinned by an inconsistent, or superficially held philosophy.

9.6.2   Leadership

An organization exhibiting a progressive management philosophy may be expected to exhibit a certain sort of leadership. Carrot and stick management, on the other hand, is likely to exhibit characteristics which would be described as traditional.

The job of leadership has been summarized as comprising three key roles (Adair, 1983, p. 33):

- Getting the job done
- Building and maintaining the team
- Developing the individual.

The way these roles are accomplished may well be critical to the firm's effectiveness as an innovator.

The empirical work on leadership is extensive – over 3,000 separate studies by 1979 (House and Baetz, 1979). However, a basic dilemma remains: whether, or to what extent, leaders are born or made. If they are born then theory is not going to be much use – all that can be done is to recruit the appropriate people. Much of the theory disputes this and suggests there are ways of learning to be an effective leader, even though it remains doubtful whether a natural follower can ever be a decisive leader, or a natural autocrat can ever make full use of subordinates.

Adair (1983) quotes an eminent lecturer speaking on leadership at the University of St Andrews in 1934,

> . . . some men possess an inbred superiority which gives them a dominating influence over their contemporaries, and marks them out unmistakably for leadership. This phenomenon is as certain as it is mysterious . . . in every association of human beings . . . there are those who, with an assured and unquestioned title, take the leading place, and shape the general conduct. (Adair, 1983, p. 7)

Many researchers, apparently taking such assertions seriously, have tried to identify the God-given ingredients of 'unquestioned title'. Stogdill (1948, 1974) carried out two surveys of such studies and high-lighted a number of personality traits, abilities and social skills which were identified as being most frequently associated with effective leadership. The most frequently identified traits were:

- Above-average intelligence, but not too far above!
- Initiative, i.e. independence and inventiveness – the ability to see the need for action and the urge to take it.
- Self assurance.

In addition most successful leaders appear to enjoy good health, be above average height or well below it, and come from the upper socio-economic strata of society.

Fiedler (1967) developed a system for categorizing leaders and identifying the sort of tasks and situations in which they would be most effective. His approach has been repeated a number of times and while his method of categorizing leaders (by testing their attitude to their least preferred coworkers) is sometimes regarded as idiosyncratic, the model appears to work. However, his model does not indicate ways in which leaders should adapt their behaviour to be more effective, but simply assumes the leader's personal characteristics are fixed.

A potentially more fruitful line of enquiry has been developed through researching leadership styles. The underlying assumption to these approaches is that it is more important what leaders do than what they are. Leadership *behaviour* is what counts. Leaders are not born but can be developed and trained and may deliberately adopt various leadership strategies.

Lewin *et al.* (1939) published the first classification of leadership styles based on their research at the University of Iowa. They identified three separate decision-taking styles:

- Authoritarian – the leader makes decisions alone and tells subordinates what they must do as a result.
- Democratic – the leader actively involves subordinates in decisions, shares problems, solicits inputs and shares authority for arriving at decisions.
- *Laissez-faire* – the leader avoids taking decisions at all costs and leaves subordinates to make decisions without guidance.

Individuals under democratic leadership were more satisfied, had higher morale, were more creative and more inclined to continue working in the absence of the leader. On the other hand, individuals under authoritarian leadership produced the highest quantity of output. *Laissez-faire* style offered no compensations.

Subsequently researchers at Ohio State University developed an alternative classification based on just two categories of leadership behaviour:

- Consideration – e.g. friendly, consultative, offering recognition, encouraging open communications, supportive and representative of subordinate interests.
- Initiating structure – e.g. planning, coordinating, directing, problem-solving, clarifying subordinate roles, criticizing bad work and pressuring subordinates to perform more effectively.

Researchers have since found that consideration style produces a higher degree of subordinate satisfaction, but whether this is necessarily allied to higher output has never been resolved.

Concurrently with the work at Ohio, researchers at Michigan developed an alternative but similar classification of leadership style:

- Employee-oriented – concerned with welfare and development of employees, engages in two-way communications, supportive, non-punitive, delegates responsibility and authority to subordinates.
- Production-oriented – emphasizes planning, goal-setting and meeting schedules, more likely to give explicit instructions, make use of power, evaluate subordinates and stress importance of production.

Employee-oriented leadership generates a higher degree of satisfaction among subordinates, but there is no evidence, again, that this is necessarily associated with higher output.

This lack of connection between job satisfaction and productivity might seem on the face of it disappointing. However, all the researches indicate that the jobs which are likely to benefit most directly from the factors which make up job satisfaction (e.g. those which permit of initiative and creativity) are not the most susceptible to having their output measured. The connection between, for example, democratic style and high morale and creativity has been made, and the connection between creativity and real productive contribution may be regarded as extremely likely, though inherently difficult to demonstrate empirically. Moreover, this connection is likely to become more pronounced as the nature of employment changes, becoming more technical and professional in the face of the technological revolution.

The path–goal theory of leadership, based on research by Evans (1970, 1974), House and Dessler (1974), House and Mitchell (1974) and House and Baetz (1979), provides yet a further classification of leadership styles that may be adapted to different circumstances:

- Directive leadership – gives instructions and guidance, schedules work and sets standards of performance, rules and regulations.
- Supportive leadership – friendly, supportive leader concerned for well-being of subordinates.
- Participative leadership – consultative of subordinates, solicitous of suggestions, and takes ideas seriously when reaching decision.
- Achievement-oriented leadership – emphasizes excellence in performance and expresses confidence in subordinates, sets

challenging performance goals and encourages subordinates to accept personal responsibility for performance.

Through a series of diagnostic questions this model seeks to identify the most effective leadership style for different management situations. For example, participative leadership is identified as the most effective approach when dealing with a high degree of instability and uncertainty which requires the input from various professional specialists.

Whilst there is a variety of terminology in these various leadership studies, there is a clear and close connection between the styles identified and the management philosophies discussed previously. There is a comparable bi-polar dimension which has democratic, participative, supportive, consideration, employee-centred characteristics at one extreme and authoritarian, directive, task-oriented, initiating characteristics at the other. This dichotomy follows quite closely the traditional–progressive dichotomy identified by Rogers.

Interestingly, there is also considerable overlap between the concept of leadership, defined in this dichotomous fashion, and the previously considered concept of centralization which, too, is dichotomous. A high degree of centralization may well be consistent with traditional (i.e. authoritarian) leadership, while a decentralized organization may be consistent with progressive (i.e. democratic) leadership. A crucial difference in the two concepts lies, of course, in the fact that one is evidenced simply by the compliance or otherwise with certain arbitrary rules, while the other can only be established through more behavioural measures.

9.6.3 Motivation

There appear to be two major strands in the theory of what motivates people at work. Firstly, there are those contributions which have sought to explain motivation in terms of intrinsic human needs, how these various needs will be salient at any given time and how individuals will change their behaviour in order to satisfy salient needs. Secondly, there is evolving theoretical and empirical work on developing a practical model seeking to explain how motivation actually works. These approaches stress the relationship firstly between effort and performance and secondly between performance and reward. To be motivated any individual must perceive that there is a direct connection between their efforts and a certain level of performance. In addition they must perceive that achievement of that level of performance will result in rewards which are desired (i.e. in the satisfaction of needs). The path–goal model, for example, suggests that the critical factors in motivation are:

- Providing subordinates with rewards
- Making the rewards contingent on achieving certain goals
- And helping subordinates obtain the rewards by clarifying the *paths* to the *goals*, i.e. helping them understand what they must do to obtain the rewards.

The key to what constitutes a reward, of course, depends on the individual's needs. Maslow's name has long been associated with the theory of human needs (Maslow, 1943), though, like Herzberg, he has attracted criticism for the unscientific method of his research. Maslow's hierarchy of needs starts with physiological (food, sleep, sex, etc.) at the lowest level, rises through safety needs, love needs, esteem needs and finally, at the top level, the need for self-actualization. Maslow's model suggested that needs had to be satisfied strictly in order, progressing up the hierarchy. Thus physiological needs must be satisfied first. When they are satisfied safety needs become salient. When these are in turn satisfied love needs become operative, and so forth. If at any time a lower level need ceases to be satisfied, it becomes dominant, or prepotent. As soon as it is again satisfied it ceases to motivate.

Maslow's model is simple to understand and seems plausible; it appeals intuitively and seems sound common sense as well as good theory. However, there is no empirical evidence of the five layers of needs, nor of how people move from one layer to another.

Other approaches may be less elegant, but may get nearer the truth. Murray's original work in the 1930s (Murray, 1938), later enhanced by Atkinson (1964) and McClelland *et al.* (1953), suggested there were more than twenty intrinsic human needs, any of which might be potent at any one time. There was no hierarchy and no structured progression from one need to the next. They suggested that needs were primarily learned, rather than inherited, and they tended to be activated by external cues in the environment. This picture of human needs is clearly much less structured than Maslow's. If offers a diversity and flexibility of needs that looks messy, but which may be realistic.

Not all the intrinsic needs in the McClelland group's model are of equal importance. Most attention has been focused on just three needs: the need for affiliation, for achievement and for power. Empirical work on these three suggest they can be useful in identifying individuals who will find different types of situations differentially motivating. Consequently the theory has found frequent application in the design of tests used in selection and recruitment.

Needs for achievement and affiliation appear to have wider application, but the power motive may have little relevance beyond this context. Whilst there is evidence that the need for power has a strong motivational effect in certain individuals, there is no evidence to suggest that a strong need for power is any indicator of effectiveness as a leader. Moreover there are many examples of individuals who appear to get satisfaction from the exercise of power for itself, rather than in the service of some other achievement.

Alderfer (1972) produced a simplified model suggesting just three basic human needs: existence, relatedness and growth. Existence can be taken as similar to Maslow's physiological and safety needs. Relatedness is similar to Maslow's love and esteem needs and also to the McClelland group's need for affiliation. Alderfer's growth need is equivalent to Maslow's self-actualization and the McClelland group's needs for achievement.

Thus it may be possible to draw out some consensus, in the most general terms, from these various theoreticians, that there are perhaps three groups of human needs which might motivate behaviour:

- Basic needs: existence, physiological, safety, etc.
- Social needs: love, esteem, affiliation, relatedness, etc.
- Growth needs: achievement, self-actualization, etc.

There is no suggestion that these needs have a hierarchical arrangement of the sort proposed by Maslow. The only further assertion that can be made is the simple statement that a satisfied need is not a motivator of behaviour. Thus, if basic needs are satisfied, motivational systems will only be effective if they offer satisfaction of one or both of the other two needs. Furthermore, it seems probable that social needs are generally likely to fall into the category of what Herzberg called hygiene factors, with growth needs being the real motivators. Management's job then would be to ensure that work provides opportunities to satisfy social needs, but that beyond this, motivation is achieved through opportunities to grow and achieve.

This conclusion, that people are motivated by social and achievement needs contrasts starkly with earlier, carrot and stick approaches to motivation. As McGregor pointed out,

the carrot and stick method of motivation works reasonably well under certain circumstances. The *means* of satisfying a man's physiological and, within limits, his safety needs can be provided or withheld by management. Employment itself is such a means, and so are wages, working conditions and benefits. By these means the individual can be controlled so long as he is struggling for subsistence. Man lives by bread alone when there is no bread. But the carrot and stick theory does not work at all once man has reached an adequate subsistence level and is motivated primarily by higher needs. (McGregor, 1957, p. 27)

If this was pertinent in 1957, it is probably much more pertinent now when living standards have improved so much further. It is sometimes argued that the higher levels of unemployment that have recently emerged are revitalizing the carrot and stick. This may be true for the unemployed, but the basic needs for the vast majority of those at work have probably long been satisfied, and probably remain so.

Herzberg identified positively motivating factors as including achievement, recognition of achievement, work itself, responsibility and advancement. Herzberg had actually found that pay and working conditions, along with company policy and administration, technical supervision and interpersonal relations with one's supervisor were ineffective as motivators, but could be the source of serious job dissatisfaction and therefore demotivation (Herzberg *et al.*, 1959).

Herzberg's research has received some criticism over the years because of the potentially unreliable method he used and the fact that the findings have rarely been accurately replicated. Nevertheless, his factors are consistent with the other theoretical contributions to motivation at work.

The effectiveness of motivational systems seems therefore to depend on whether they provide opportunities for the satisfaction of social and achievement needs or whether the organization adopts simple carrot and stick methods seeking to motivate through fear and economic reward. As with leadership, there is some consistency between this dichotomy and the divide identified in management philosophy described by the terms 'progressive' and 'traditional'.

9.6.4   Communication

Kanter identified open communications and 'network' forming arrangements which cut across the usual organizational structures as prerequisites of effective innovation.

Open communications and the other aspects of entrepreneurial management, philosophy, leadership and motivation are all elements in creating an organization where the individual member is both free to use their own initiative and is well disposed to doing so in a way which serves corporate needs. Within them, however, there is no element of strategic direction. This is provided by the analysis of mission and competitive specialism. For the freedom and motivation of individual members to be used effectively, the mission and competitive specialism must therefore be effectively communicated.

Thus it is not sufficient merely for organizational communication to be open, communication itself has a specific mission. It it not just 'management by walking about' (Peters and Austin, 1985). The message is a vital ingredient, not merely the communication process. The object is to convert objectives into action. In the case which has been developed here, that means making everyone in the organization aware of the specialism of the business so that all efforts can be concentrated on its exploitation. Without this communication, concentration is not possible because people are unlikely to know the strategy by intuition. Communication of strategy and objectives throughout the organization is crucial.

To be effective the message must be unambiguous. This is a simple enough idea, even obvious, but there is a natural human tendency to deliver conflicting messages and ambiguity, nicely encapsulated by the slogan, 'Be innovative and take risks. But be careful.' Ambiguity of this sort, deliberate or not, can be, and often is, compounded by the message sender totally ignoring the inconsistencies and making them undiscussable by the means of communication (e.g. through mixed status meetings).

The message must also be short and simple if it is to have any impact. The competitive specialism must be capable of communication in brief, unambiguous statements. Statements about specific strategic actions, whether investments or divestments, need similarly to be brief and easily understood.

The message should be communicated in every possible way: in formal statements of strategy, in house journals, newsletters, notice boards, employee accounts, product literature, advertising, public relations, bonus payment schemes, product training seminars, induction programmes, briefing sessions, consultation meetings, social gatherings and any other medium available.

In the particular case of strategy there is often an additional problem of confidentiality. There is a natural tendency to feel the need to preserve confidentiality, despite all the clear benefits from open communication. On some occasions there may be some specific element of strategy which has to remain under wraps until a particular time, but this is very much the exception. The temptation to treat strategy automatically as confidential must be resisted.

The mission of communication is to give all members the sense of direction of the business so that the decisions they all take, and the efforts they all make, are made in a consistent manner so that the business continues to fulfil the customer's perceived need by continuing to exploit its specialism. Every member of the business, from boardroom to shop-floor, takes such decisions and therefore should know what the strategy is and where the business is headed.

9.6.5 Participation

Participation in relevant decision-making has already been briefly discussed in Chapter 8. It is no soft option. The participative operation of effective teams is difficult to achieve. Differences in rank, personal calibre, skills, expertise and knowledge can all upset teamwork – the bureaucratic tendency to hierarchy applies to problem-solving teams just as it does to the mainstream organization.

The fruits of the participatory process are essentially long term and are realized in terms of a more adaptive, innovative organization that can stay ahead of the change in its environments.

A high degree of participation fits naturally alongside the other progressive elements described above, while low participation is consistent with traditional style.

9.7   The limits of customer orientation

The concepts of entrepreneurial strategy are in themselves simple and logical. They are based on systematic data collection and rational decision-taking. The thinking is cold-blooded and analytical. Business is customer-oriented because it pays, not because there is a passion for the customer.

There is an idealism in much current literature, a plea for an overriding dedication to the customer, an almost fanatical enthusiasm for the concept of service. Tales of such dedication are repeated about the strong culture companies, and in particular about their founders. Much of the literature about corporate culture is couched in these terms.

But business is calculating. The creation of strong cultures as a way of influencing the behaviour of members is calculated. The analysis of customer perceptions of product attributes is systematic and the aim is accuracy and precision. The aim of product positioning is to maximize the competitive advantage. The development of the information base is to guarantee the future prosperity of the business. The concentration of resources is to ensure that there is no strategically irrelevant expenditure. The aim of communication is to ensure that the efforts of all the firm's members are similarly focused. The aim of entrepreneurial strategy is to deliver value to the customer as efficiently as possible and to avoid all waste.

Create the customer, but don't give the business away. The aim in the supplier–customer relationship must be to achieve the larger long term slice of the negotiable surplus. This means measuring precisely what the customer values and giving it in measured terms and never gratuitously giving a penny more. If the value supplied exceeds the customer's requirement, i.e. what the customer values and is prepared to pay for, then it represents waste just as surely as if the money was poured down the drain. The only purpose in producing a differentiated product is to earn a price premium over and above the general market level.

This simple point is made in these basic terms to emphasize the fact that, despite the current dogma, there are limits to customer orientation. Business exists to serve the customer, that is its mission. But it also competes directly with the customer for the economic surplus arising from their mutual transactions. This is a calculated relationship, with little room for excess or simple idealism.

9.8 Summary

Entrepreneurial strategy is based on the simple tenet that every business was created to satisfy a customer need.

It is essential to know, as the entrepreneur does, exactly what the need is that the business satisfies.

Entrepreneurial strategy is based on three factors:

1. Definition of the *mission* of the business, i.e. identifying the market need the business satisfies.
2. Identification of its unique competitive specialism – the distinctive competence for which customers are prepared to pay a premium.

3. Concentration of effort and resources on the exploitation of that competitive specialism.

The competitive specialism can be exploited in three ways:

(a) by intensifying it,
(b) by broadening it, and
(c) by prolonging it.

Entrepreneurial strategy is information intensive being based on knowledge of existing and potential technology, customers, suppliers and competitors.

The conversion of entrepreneurial strategy into action is achieved through people who must have the freedom to use their own initiative, be motivated to use that initiative for the strategic aims of the business and therefore must have those strategic aims communicated to them.

Entrepreneurial strategy is customer-oriented, but it is calculating, not passionate – there are economically defined limits to customer orientation.

DISCUSSION CASE: VENTURE FINANCE INTERNATIONAL LTD

Venture Finance was a successful and growing banking subsidiary of a Hudson Trust Inc., a financially-oriented multinational conglomerate. As its name implies, the bank's main mission was to provide venture capital facilities to the corporate sector. However, following a number of acquisitions, the bank had developed a strong high street retail activity with personal, rather than corporate, customers. The Venture Finance shop-front was non-traditional and highly distinctive and, it was thought, it had contributed significantly to the success of the business.

Hudson Trust regarded its own role as being to decide the broad strategy of its subsidiary companies and to hold the purse strings, but otherwise to give subsidiary company management maximum autonomy.

So far as strategy was concerned, Hudson was anxious that Venture Finance appeared to be drifitng away from its original role in providing venture capital in return for equity. This role was attractive to the parent company because each investment represented a low risk prototype for their own acquisition activities. A number of such investments had eventually become full scale acquisitions and two had subsequently been floated with full stock exchange quotations. For Venture Finance management, however, it appeared to be easier to achieve the financial performance targets set by Hudson by expanding the personal loans and retail business.

Discussion points
- As a senior Hudson Trust executive how would you propose to encourage Venture Finance to fulfil the strategic role required of it?
- Should Hudson seek to define that strategic role, or is it a matter solely for Venture Finance management?
- Is it important to Hudson what strategic role Venture Finance fulfils, or is it more important whether the business is successful?
- What inducements or controls can be put in place to lead Venture Finance to give their business the emphasis required by Hudson?

Hudson control their subsidiary businesses through a simple monthly reporting procedure. Each monthly report is provided on a single side of A4 paper and basically designed to show how the business performed against target – targets were set at the start of the year and represented a highly demanding level of performance. The report includes a number of key financial performance ratios, a precise three-month cash flow forecast with six- and twelve-month projections and a mandatory statement of any items in the annual rolling budget which are now expected to be inaccurate by a factor of 10 per cent or more. These monthly reports form the basis of the parent company's assessment of the business as a prospect for future investment, and of the top management as prospects for future advancement. The key to providing satisfactory returns was never to give surprises, even nice ones. An unexpectedly high positive cash flow, for example, would be treated by Hudson as an instance of incompetence by subsidiary company management. The nature of venture finance made it much more 'lumpy' and prone to surprises than the more predictable personal retail business.

Venture Finance has been approached by a well-known computer software firm promoting a system which is designed to aid the process of taking personal loan decisions. It is an expert system which asks a series of simple questions about the borrower and generates recommended lending limits. It is pointed out that the software speeds up the process of loan decisions because it eliminates the need to use any judgement or discretion in routine decisions which account for around 80 per cent of all loans. In Germany, it was pointed out, counter staff had been trained how to use the system and then took over the routine loan decision role from branch management who were thus freed to develop new business.

Discussion points
- As Chief Executive of Venture Finance what is your attitude to this new computer software?
- Is it important or simply a matter for branch managers?
- Does it have any strategic implications?
- Could it help your prospects for promotion within Hudson?
- As a Venture Finance branch manager how do you regard the new system? Is it a threat or an opportunity?
- The German example was illustrated with a photograph of a branch manager on a golf course 'developing new business' having been given the 'free' time by the new system. Do you regard this as a realistic situation for Venture branch managers?
- If not, why not?
- As a counter clerk at a Venture Finance branch, what is your attitude to the new system?

A further technological development relevant to Venture Finance is the availability of automatic cash dispensing machines. They are now both reliable and relatively cheap. Venture Finance has not used them because it felt that its role as a corporate lender meant they were inappropriate. Investing in them had not been proposed to Hudson because of the tension over the bank's strategic role.

It was, however, clear that automatic cash dispensing machines could free quite a lot of counter staff time. This could be devoted to learning and operating the new computerized personal loan system, which could then free branch management to devote more time and effort to developing new corporate business.

Discussion points
If the full potential offered by these two new systems was properly understood, how would you expect the following groups to react to a proposal to invest in them:

- Hudson Trust management?
- Venture Finance top management?
- Venture Finance branch management?
- Venture Finance counter staff?
- Proceeding with the investments might require some changes in jobs and in the way branches are organized. Do these represent any significant problems?

Venture Finance requested permission from Hudson Trust to make the investments in both items. The justification for the use of automatic cash dispensers was based on the savings to be achieved in counter staff and by the assumed loss of retail business if the investment was not made. The justification of the computerized loan system was based on its use by branch management to speed up their routine work thereby freeing them to devote more time to improving the quality of their non-routine loan decision-making.

Hudson approved the required capital expenditures and loan software and cash dispensing machines were duly placed in each branch. Typically, the result in the branches was that a junior counter clerk was made redundant and the branch manager practised with the loan deciding programme but failed to use it for real.

Discussion points
- What had gone wrong?
- Who was at fault?
- What could be done to put it right?

Note
Venture Finance used the new technology simply to reduce costs by getting rid of some counter staff. They used the new technology to *reinforce* the existing way of doing things.

This is a peculiarly British response. All things being equal, most of us would prefer things to stay the way they are. The purveyors of the new technology recognize this to the extent that they often use 'minimum requirements for organizational change' as a major selling point in UK markets. Consequently, we continue to lag behind in our exploitation of the new opportunities provided by technology.

CHAPTER TEN

Relating strategy
to its context

10.1 Introduction

Some nine different strategic thinking frameworks have been outlined in previous chapters. None of them provides the whole answer to strategic analysis and formulation. Each makes a distinctive contribution to the overall view and each has particular relevance to particular circumstances.

This final chapter aims to provide some pointers as to how strategic thinking and management may best be related to its context. This will not be a question of selecting the most appropriate tool for the job, but rather one of recognizing the realities of context and shaping a strategic management approach which may embody aspects of several of the frameworks described.

It may be that the desired outcome of business strategy is an instantly recognizable position. A currently successful position strategy is achieved, for example, by McDonald's. The achievement and reinforcement of that position, to both internal and external stakeholders, owes much to the application of the cultural and symbolic perspective. However, this does not mean that such a company does not also make overt use of the technology and innovation and strategic marketing perspectives. Effective business strategy will not be achieved by simplistic application of tools and techniques, but by a process of individual shaping which will make use of thinking about the strategic problem from several different perspectives, depending on the strategic context.

Two particular aspects of context to be considered in strategic thinking are the environment and the business organization itself.

10.2 The environmental context

The opening pages of this book highlighted a few of the critical factors in the contemporary environment which are likely to affect all businesses. These include the technological revolution, the increasingly short term orientation of capital and the progressive globalization of markets. Of these perhaps the most important for most businesses is the revolution in technology.

Looking forward through the next decade, the first two trends appear likely to continue. Technology has been widely forecast to continue its current phase of rapid development until at least the turn of the century, if not indefinitely. Similarly, the short term orientation of traditional capital markets appears likely to continue, although this may be mitigated to some extent by the opening up of new forms of finance which do not carry these imperatives.

Globalization of markets appears less certain. There are fundamental reasons for this to continue: the intrinsic economic benefits of international ade and the escalation of technological development costs requiring ever larger markets for their justification. However, the results of globalization are not necessarily equitable, particularly if some participants are not playing to the same rules. Many argue that this is the case with Japan. If this view predominates and Japanese markets remain effectively closed, the current trend to globalization may go into reverse.

One further aspect of the business environment in the 1990s which is likely to have a crucial impact on business strategy, is the 'green' issue. On the one hand, most existing industries will be constrained by new green legislation in some respect or another. On the other hand, the demand for green products probably represent the most exciting predictable growth potential of all.

These broad environmental aspects form a backdrop for the more detailed analysis of specific industries covering growth, volatility, technological development, competitive structures and the many other items identified in Chapter 5.

Given this thumbnail environment analysis, the strategic thinking frameworks carry the alternative implications as summarized in Table 10.1.

The frameworks which appear to provide the greatest insights into the development of strategy in the present overall circumstances are the technology and innovation framework, strategic marketing, structure, culture and symbolism and entrepreneurial strategy. Of

Table 10.1   *Contexts and frameworks.*

	Situational characteristics	
	1. Rapid technological development. 2. Increasingly competitive markets. 3. Increasing short term financial returns.	
Strategic thinking framework	Relevance	Strategic implications
Long range budgets	Limited	Limited.
SWOT-based planning	Limited	Tends to result in loss of concentration and dispersal of effort and diversification.
Life cycles	Limited	Illusory and ambiguous.
Portfolios	Growth phase only	Milk and/or divest mature businesses. Invest in young, fast growth firms with high market share.
Competitive strategy	Direction	Use technological innovations to become cost leader, or seek differentiated position in order to reduce competition.
Strategic marketing	Direction	Ensure that customer needs are known and their satisfaction is the focus of attention.
Technology and innovation	Direction Flexibility	Focus on technological developments in order to ensure that there are no surprises and that innovation may be used to maximum strategic effect.
Structure, culture and symbolism	Concentration Consistency	Engage the 'hearts and minds' of all employees on the defined strategic aims of the business.
Entrepreneurial strategy	Direction Concentration Consistency Flexibility	Combines much of the above. Defines direction and concentrates effort on exploiting the competitive specialism of the business.

these the first two appear to be crucial, defining technology and innovation as a means of implementing strategy towards strategic marketing ends, i.e. direction. Culture and symbolism represent enabling or reinforcing factors, i.e. to achieve concentration and consistency, while the entrepreneurial model offers an alternative which to some extent encapsulates the other frameworks and might be more appropriate for a relatively small, or single product line, business.

The thrust of strategy in these technologically and competitively volatile times will therefore be to use technological developments in order to exploit (i.e. broaden, intensify or prolong) the competitive specialism of the business.

10.3   Organizational context

The other aspect of context which is critical to the effectiveness of any particular strategic approach relates to the business organization itself. There has been a great deal of research seeking to identify the organizational characteristics which appear to be prerequisite to success in an era of change.

10.3.1   Previous research

For most of this present century British business has been losing the technological war. British engineers and technologists may be the equal of any, but industry after industry has lost its technological leadership and consequently economic and market leadership also. As far back as the early 1950s the British government funded a major piece of research to try and find out why this was happening, 'in the belief that the application of science in industry is necessary to economic progress and should . . . be one of the most important objects of national policy' (Carter and Williams, 1956).

Their main findings identified the characteristics of what they called 'the technically progressive firm', i.e. one that was 'keeping close to the best which could reasonably be achieved in the application of science and technology'. These characteristics included the following:

Good external communications
- High quality of incoming communications
- Deliberate survey of potential ideas
- Willingness to share knowledge
- Willingness to take new knowledge on licence and to enter joint ventures
- Readiness to look outside the firm
- Readiness to look ahead
- Effective selling policy
- Good technical service to customers

Good internal communications
- Effective internal communications and coordination

Positive attitude to science and technology
- High status of science and technology in the firm
- Use of scientists and technologists on board of directors

Recruit and train high quality people
- Sound policy of recruitment for management
- Ability to attract talented people
- Willingness to arrange effective staff training
- High quality chief executives
- Adequate provision for intermediate managers
- Good quality intermediate managers
- Ability to bring the best out of managers

Professional management
- Consciousness of costs and profits in R&D
- Ingenuity in getting round material and equipment shortages
- Use of management techniques
- Identify outcome of investment decisions
- Rapid replacement of machines

High rate of expansion

There were five characteristics which were tested and found not to be associated with innovativeness. These were:

- Membership of an industry with a strong scientific or technological background.
- Adequate buildings or site.
- Scientific or technological training of *the* key personality in the firm.
- Resistance to innovation on the shop-floor.
- Adequate finance.

Since that classic research there have been several thousand further studies, mainly corroborative of Carter and Williams' findings. For example, Burns and Stalker (1961) found that the most successful innovators paid closest attention to their market and did not concentrate exclusively on the research and development aspect. Similar findings were confirmed by Myers and Marquis (1969).

Project SAPPHO (Scientific Activity Predictor from Patterns with Heuristic Origins) (1972) also confirmed much of the Carter and Williams research. The SAPPHO research was carried out in two science-based industries, chemicals and instruments, and concentrated its attention on new product innovation; it identified the following factors as being associated with successful product innovation:

1. Understanding user needs.
2. More attention paid to marketing.
3. Development work carried out more efficiently.
4. More effective use of outside technology and scientific advice.
5. Individuals responsible for innovation were more senior and had more authority.

Robertson (1973) confirmed the SAPPHO findings and summarized the root causes of innovation failure as 'the neglect of marketing research and preconceived ideas about market needs'.

Similarly, successful innovations have been identified as depending on:

- direct links between research and development and marketing,
- planned programmes of innovation, and
- technically effective and market oriented management (Chisnall, 1985).

Various other studies (e.g. Hopkins, 1981 and Cooper, 1982) have broadly confirmed the SAPPHO findings in identifying key activities associated with successful innovation. These include the following:

1. Good contact with the firm's product markets (to know accurately user's requirements) and its technological environment (to know the state of the art).
2. Good internal cooperation and coordination between engineering (R&D), production and marketing.
3. Careful planning and control.
4. Efficient development work.
5. The will on the part of top management to innovate.
6. Provision of good after sales service and user education.

Rogers (1983) reported more than 3,000 separate studies in this area and a recent project, based on this solid foundation, has crystallized some of the main findings in a simple matrix model (Pearson, 1989a).

The organizational characteristics which have been found critical to success can be collected into two clusters. One cluster is related to the way the organization is managed and the degree to which people in the organization have the freedom to use their own initiative and creativity. This cluster has been referred to as 'organizational style'. The other cluster is related to the firm's strategy: how well founded it is and how well people in the organization know, understand and support that strategy. This cluster of characteristics has been referred to as 'strategic focus'.

Strategic focus appears to be the motivator of change, while organizational style is the facilitating characteristic. In part these two characteristics reflect the basic management dilemma referred to in Chapter 7, balancing the needs of individuals in an organization for freedom and space, with the requirements of the organization for structure and order. If the appropriate organizational style could be combined with the right strategic focus, the business might be expected to be both innovative and competitive in exploiting its specialism. Positioning a business with the appropriate focus and style is thus the key strategic action.

The components of style and focus were not identified simply as a result of a statistical relationship. In addition, they exhibited two essential characteristics. Firstly, they influenced the way people in an organization behave. Secondly, they lend themselves to being controlled by management. Only if they both influence behaviour *and* can be managed are they of any practical use.

10.3.2 Organizational style

The components of organizational style, which have already been described in some detail, are:

- Management philosophy
- Leadership
- Motivation
- Participation
- Communications

Each of these components has a substantial theoretical background. Other variables which were related to the structure and culture of the organization were also included in the original research project but were eliminated either because of difficulties in their subsequent management or because their influence on behaviour was uncertain.

Progressive	Organizational style	Traditional
Open Democratic Theory Y Holistic High	Communications Leadership style Management philosophy Motivation systems Participation	Closed Autocratic Theory X Mechanistic Low

Figure 10.1 *The dimension of style.*

Each of the individual characteristics of style is measured along a single dimension. In the case of management philosophy, for example, it runs along a continuum which could be labelled Theory Y at one end and Theory X at the other. Similarly, communications can be assessed in terms of being open or closed. Leadership style can be democratic or autocratic; participation, high or low; and motivation systems could focus on the growth and social needs at one end being labelled 'holistic', or fear and economic rewards at the other end, being labelled 'mechanistic'.

Theory Y management philosophy, open communications, democratic leadership, a high degree of participation, and holistic motivation systems, all appear to be at the same end of a continuum. Traditional philosophy, closed communications, autocratic leadership, little participation, and mechanistic motivation systems all appear to be at the opposite end of the same continuum.

The characteristics are thus all capable of being assessed along the same dimension which in aggregate can be labelled 'progressive' at one extreme and 'traditional' at the other as in Figure 10.1.

10.3.3 Strategic focus

The characteristics of strategic focus were found to be as follows:

- Generic strategy
- Functional orientation
- Long term vision
- External communications
- Corporate integrity

In the main the theoretical pedigree of these characteristics is not as extensive as those of style, though each has been discussed previously in this text.

Dispersed	Strategic focus	Concentrated
Low Inactive Accounting Cost leadership Unclear	Corporate integrity External communications Functional orientation Generic strategy Long term vision	High Active Marketing Differentiation Clear

Figure 10.2   *The dimension of focus.*

Each of the individual characteristics of focus is measured along a single dimension. In the case of generic strategy, for example, it runs along a continuum which could be labelled differentiation at one end and cost leadership at the other. Similarly, functional orientation can be assessed in terms of being accounting or marketing. External communications can be active or inactive; long term vision, clear or unclear; and corporate integrity, high or low.

A differentiation strategy, marketing orientation, active external communications, clear long term vision and high corporate integrity, all appear to be capable of concentrating the strategic focus and thus they are all at the same end of the continuum. Cost leadership, accounting orientation, inactive external communications, unclear long term vision and low integrity all appear likely to result in loss of

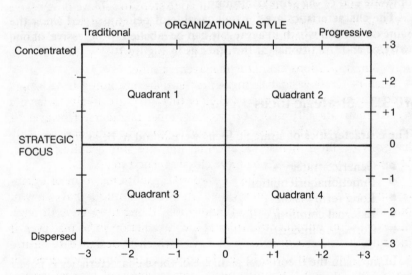

Figure 10.3   *The organizational style and strategic focus matrix.*

concentration and thus appear to be at the opposite end of the same continuum.

The characteristics are thus all capable of being assessed along the same dimension which, in aggregate, can be labelled concentrated at one extreme and dispersed at the other, as shown in Figure 10.2.

The two clusters of characteristics can be put together to form a simple two dimensional matrix as can be seen in Figure 10.3.

10.3.4   The style and focus matrix

The matrix positions are important in themselves, but the individual characteristics which comprise a company's style and focus profiles are, in terms of management action, even more important. Two companies with identical style scores are likely to have different scores at the level of individual organizational characteristics and therefore require different management action in order to change the overall position in regard to style.

It may be anticipated that the more innovative companies would be positioned in Quadrant 2, the progressive–concentrated area of the matrix. The label, 'innovating team', seems to encapsulate the essence of the progressive–concentrated quadrant, the teamwork being facilitated by the progressive style and the target for innovation by the concentrated focus.

Some managements take very deliberate steps to achieve progressive style, putting a lot of effort into internal communications involving both regular consultation meetings with employees and formal briefings involving every member of the organization in effective two-way communications along the management line.

Such progressive management practices are becoming increasingly widely used and the general belief is that they are likely to have a strong motivational impact on organizational members. However, it seems likely from this research that such approaches do not necessarily have any result in themselves and that they are only enabling factors. Strategic focus appears to be more closely related to results.

A Quadrant 1 firm tending towards the traditional form of organizational style can still be innovative. As previous studies have shown, bureaucracy is the antithesis of innovation. Being innovative through the exercise of bureaucratic rules is a contradiction in terms, even if the rules have been drawn up in a way which is designed to ensure a high degree of strategic focus. In contrast, the autocracy does not necessarily contain this fundamental contradiction of innovativeness.

It may be extremely inhibiting to members of the organization and make it very difficult for *them* to be innovative. However, the autocrat has maximum freedom. An autocrat can make the rules, take instant and personal decisions, pass instructions to subordinates and anticipate rapid and total compliance.

The effectiveness of an autocracy as an innovator depends more or less entirely on the innovativeness and effectiveness of the autocrat. It is possible, in certain circumstances, for the autocrat to provide the organization with the strategic focus required to be innovative. However, such circumstances are specific and limited, firstly, to small organizations (which are frequently the creation of a single person who presides over every aspect during the early phase of growth), and secondly, to organizations in crisis, as was the much quoted case, for example, with Jaguar Cars Ltd in 1980 when, week-to-week survival seemed uncertain and its new Chief Executive had little alternative but to adopt an authoritarian style.

For companies not in crisis, if they are successful they will rapidly become too big for the personal autocratic structure and management arrangements will need to be changed to cope with the new circumstances. Such change will necessitate repositioning the business in Quadrant 2.

The Chief Executive of one Quadrant 1 firm recognized the problem and had become interested in the subject of organizational culture. He saw the possibility of creating a 'strong culture' company as the best solution (Pearson, 1989a and b). The precise meaning of 'strong culture' in this context is not completely clear, though it seemed probable that the strong culture was seen in some way as inducing a high degree of motivation among organization members to support his role as Chief Executive.

The traditional–concentrated quadrant of the matrix appears to accommodate three different types of organization, the autocracy, the bureaucracy and the strong culture. Of these it seemed apparent that the autocracy could be innovative depending on the nature of the autocrat. Bureaucracies would be incapable of the flexibility to innovate. Strong cultures, though not fully defined, would seem, for the same reasons, to be equally unlikely to be able to innovate effectively.

Companies positioned in the dispersed half of the matrix appear unlikely to be effective innovators whatever their organizational style. This is because either they espouse strategic aims which are incapable of concentrating resources and efforts in business terms, or they have no consistent set of strategic aims at all. In the former category are firms driven by purely financial targets such as returns on capital employed, margins, etc. These firms fall into the traditional–dispersed quadrant. Dominated by financial considerations, they are likely to have a rigid, though not necessarily autocratic, style. According to Hayes and Garvin (1982) a company driven by financially stated aims tends to be a liquidator, going down what they identified as 'the disinvestment spiral'. They might espouse a strategy of cost leadership. By definition there can only be one cost leader per industry sector and as a consequence the unsuccessful intended cost leaders almost inevitably follow down the same path as the liquidators.

Other firms falling into the dispersed half of the matrix, may have a less clear and consistent set of strategic aims. Companies positioned in the progressive–dispersed quadrant may sometimes appear to have clearly stated aims, but still change 'from day to day'. The consequence of this is that members of such a company are unaware of the strategic aims, or at least the current ones, and consequently the companies are unable to concentrate action and resources consistently in order to achieve the strategic aims.

Some companies may find themselves on the borders, not exhibiting any extremes of progressive style or dispersed focus. Employees of one such company described the company's management as 'nice guys, but . . .' and went on to suggest that they were insufficiently decisive and unprepared to be ruthless.

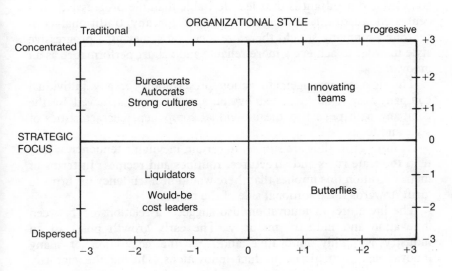

Figure 10.4   *Contents of the four quadrants of the matrix.*

One company in the research study reported above appeared to be a more stereotypical example of the dispersed–progressive quadrant, one of the interviewees describing the company as a 'butterfly – always flitting from one project to another' with no consistency over time. In this case it seemed clear that innovativeness was possible through a progressive style, but in the absence of a strategic focus, the company failed to be innovative.

During the course of the research a number of descriptive terms were used by interviewees to describe their own organization. Qualitatively, though imprecisely, these terms may adequately describe the characteristic firm for each quadrant of the matrix as shown in Figure 10.4.

Whilst it is again emphasized that the matrix is an aggregate device, the annotations serve as shorthand for certain intuitively recognizable organizational types representative of the four quadrants.

There is no evidence of innovativeness being associated with a dispersed strategic focus. It appeared to be a prerequisite of innovativeness that a firm be positioned in the concentrated area of the matrix. For a company positioned in the dispersed area, the prerequisite management action in order to be an effective innovator, would therefore be to achieve a concentrated strategic focus.

A progressive style was not necessarily a prerequisite of innovativeness, but the autocratic innovator is less robust and reliable, for reasons already identified, than the innovating team. The traditional–concentrated quadrant is thus less desirable than the progressive–concentrated quadrant. Management action for any traditional–concentrated company should therefore focus on achieving a progressive style in order to achieve a more reliable and robust performance as an innovator.

The detailed management action prescription for any individual company would be indicated by the specific score achieved by the company with regard to the individual component characteristics of style and focus.

As firms grow they are subject to certain inevitable tendencies; they tend to create rules and structures, routines and recipes. In terms of matrix position this implies that there would be a tendency for firms to 'drift' towards the traditional side of the matrix.

The literature on innovation also suggests a relationship between innovation and industry maturity. The early growth phase of an industry is highly innovative and sees the generation of many innovations, particularly product innovations. During the maturity phase, the emphasis on innovation reduces and its focus changes to the

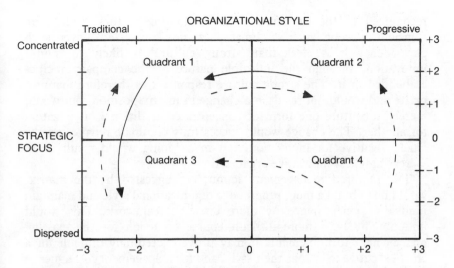

Figure 10.5   *Natural tendencies and management thrusts. Solid arrows: direction of natural organizational tendency; broken arrows: required direction of management initiatives.*

production process with an increasing emphasis on cost reduction. In terms of the matrix position this seems to imply that there would be a tendency for firms to 'drift' ultimately towards the financially-oriented traditional–dispersed quadrant.

The direction of these natural tendencies is indicated in Figure 10.5, together with the directions of management thrusts required to counteract these tendencies and to achieve the most advantageous positioning for effective innovation.

The direction of these natural tendencies is probably widely accepted and understood. However, the appropriate management responses may be less well understood. For example, a chief executive of the innovative autocrat type previously referred to, understood the vulnerability of the position as an autocratic innovator, but did not have a clear concept of the innovative team. Had innovation not been recognized as important, the manager may well have regarded bureaucratization as an acceptable way of depersonalizing the leadership position in the company.

Innovation was recognized as a crucial ingredient of the company's success and bureaucracy was overtly recognized as inconsistent with innovation. The response was to aim for a 'strong culture' in order to get into 'the hearts and minds' of all members. The permanency and robustness of culture, which is one of the basic characteristics recognized in the literature as differentiating culture from more transient concepts such as climate, was not recognized. Given such permanency it is clear that 'strong culture' is likely to inhibit innovation, through the inflexible nature of the company recipes embedded in it. The strong culture response was therefore inappropriate and would not result in a change in matrix position, but would merely substitute one form of concentrated–traditional organization for another. The change would successfully eliminate reliance on the chief executive for innovation, but in so doing would result in an increasingly less innovative organization.

The required management action, as suggested by the matrix, would be to build a more progressive organizational style and maintain innovative performance by more effective teamwork. This would undoubtedly be a more difficult course of action for the existing management to implement. It may prove exceedingly difficult for a chief executive to change their style, and for management colleagues to respond by changing theirs accordingly. The means to achieving it would clearly lie through a process of education and training.

Another company in the research also tended to be relatively traditional. It was a subsidiary company of a multinational group, whose central policy was described as 'maximizing subsidiary company autonomy'. The avowed aim of this policy was to overcome the natural tendencies to bureaucracy which come with size and maturity by letting the small subsidiary businesses take their own decisions. The parent company philosophy was well known by subsidiary company members. One interviewee explained 'what looks like local autonomy from head office, looks like dictatorship from here'. The point that was being made was that autonomy devolved to the local managing director who, as a consequence, had total control within that part of the organization. This individual freedom for the managing director could be used by different individuals in different ways including, as this particular interviewee suggested, a wholly autocratic style of management.

In summary the style and focus model seems to suggest that,

- it is more important to communicate a particular message, than it is to have generally open communications;
- that it is more pertinent to know exactly which way decisions should be taken than to be able to participate in taking them either way;
- that it is more important to know what aspects of your job

contribute directly to strategy than to have the freedom to choose what actual jobs you do.

These conclusions were highlighted by the 'butterfly' company, which probably had more open communications than any of the companies in the research sample, but appeared to communicate no useful message regarding strategy or innovation.

Finally, the model suggests that strategic focus *must* be concentrated for a firm to be an effective innovator, whereas it is merely *better* for a firm to have a progressive organizational style.

10.4   Conclusion

This final chapter has made some tentative suggestions as to the relevance of the different strategic thinking frameworks for different circumstances defined by both environmental and organizational characteristics.

The discussion of organizational characteristics has focused on a simple matrix model which, in many ways, encapsulates much of the thinking outlined in previous chapters. The organizational characteristics which appear to be critical for a business that is going to prosper in today's environment are firstly a clear strategic focus and secondarily a progressive organizational style.

This means that the firm should:

1. Have a strategy based on differentiation as opposed to cost leadership,
2. Have a marketing orientation,
3. Have a clear and well-informed long term vision, or direction
4. Have active external communications with technology suppliers, customers and competitors,
5. Maintain high corporate integrity.

In addition, unless the firm is able to rely on the offices of an innovative though autocratic chief executive, it should also:

6. Be managed according to the underlying philosophy of Theory Y, not the soft option of simply being nice to people, but the

exacting option of thrusting responsibility and authority down the line,

7. Be managed democratically,
8. Motivate people by satisfying their social and growth needs,
9. Have open communications,
10. Encourage and experience a high degree of participation by all members in strategically significant decisions.

Such a progressive–concentrated business will be well placed to use the various strategic thinking frameworks outlined in this book in a discriminating and sensitive way in order to make the most of the opportunities it creates.

References

Adair, J. (1983), *Effective Leadership*, Gower.
Alderfer, C. P. (1972), *Existence, Relatedness and Growth*, Free Press.
Ansoff, H. I. (1965), *Corporate Strategy*, McGraw-Hill.
Atkinson, J. W. (1964), *An Introduction to Motivation*, Van Nostrand.
Barnard, C. I. (1948), *Organization and Management*, Harvard University Press.
Baumol, W. J. (1959), *Business Behaviour, Value and Growth*, Macmillan.
Baumol, W. J. (1986), 'Entrepreneurship and a century of economic growth', *Journal of Business Venturing*, vol. 1.
Beynon, H. (1975), *Working for Ford*, EP Publishing.
Boston Consulting Group (1968), *Perspectives on Experience*, Boston Consulting Group.
Bower, M. (1966), *The Will to Manage*, McGraw-Hill.
Brech, E. F. L. (1957), *Organisation: The framework of management*, Longman.
Bright, J. R. (1983), *Practical Technology Forecasting*, Industrial Management Center Inc.
Burns, T. and Stalker, G. M. (1961), *Management of Innovation*, Tavistock.
Burrell, G. and Morgan, G. (1979), *Sociological Paradigms and Organizational Analysis*, Heinemann.
Carter, C. F. and Williams, B. R. (1956), *Industry and Technological Progress: Factors governing the speed of application of science*, Oxford University Press.
Chakrabarti, A. K., Feinman, S. and Fuentevilla, W. (1978), *Industrial Product Innovation: An international comparison*, Industrial Marketing Management.
Chambliss, L. and Peston, R. (1987), 'A day of drama in world markets', the *Independent*, 21 October.
Chandler, A. D. (1962), *Strategy and Structure*, MIT Press.
Chandler, A. D. (1977), *The Visible Hand: The managerial revolution in American business*, Harvard University Press.
Channon, D. F. (1973), *The Strategy and Structure of British Enterprise*, Macmillan.

Child, J., Ganter, H. D. and Kieser, A. (1987), 'Technological innovation and organizational conservatism' in Pennings, J. M. and Biutendam, D. (eds), *New Technology as Organizational Innovation*, Ballinger.

Chisnall, P. M. (1985), *Marketing: A behavioural analysis*, 2nd edn, McGraw-Hill.

Cooper, R. G. (1982), 'New product success in industrial firms', *Industrial Marketing Management*.

Coyne, K. P. (1986), 'Sustainable competitive advantage: what it is and what it isn't', *Business Horizons*, February, vol. 29, pp. 54–61.

Cyert, R. M. and March, J. G. (1963), *A Behavioural Theory of the Firm*, Prentice Hall.

Deal, T. E. and Kennedy, A. A. (1982), *Corporate Cultures*, Addison-Wesley.

De Bono, E. (1978), *Lateral Thinking*, Penguin.

Dewhurst, H. A. (1970), 'The long range research which produced glass fibre reinforced tires', *Research Management*, May, vol. xiii, pp. 201–8.

Drucker, P. F. (1955), *The Practice of Management*, Heinemann.

Drucker, P. F. (1964), *Managing for Results*, Harper & Row.

Drucker, P. F. (1985), *Innovation and Entrepreneurship*, Heinemann.

Edwardes, M. (1983), *Back from the Brink*, Collins.

Emery, F. E. and Trist, E. L. (1965), 'The causal texture of organizational environments', *Human Relations*, vol. 18, pp. 21–32.

Evans, M. G. (1970), 'The effects of supervisory behaviour on the path goal relationship', *Organisational Behaviour and Human Performance*, vol. 5, pp. 277–98.

Evans, M. G. (1974), 'Extensions of a path goal theory of motivation', *Journal of Applied Psychology*, vol. 59, pp. 172–8.

Fayol, H. (1916), *Administration Industrielle et Générale*, Pitman.

Fiedler, F. E. (1967), *A Theory of Leadership Effectiveness*, McGraw-Hill.

Foster, R. N. (1986), *Innovation: The attacker's advantage*, Summit.

Fredrickson, J. W. and Mitchell, T. R. (1984), 'Strategic decision processes: comprehensiveness and performance in an industry with an unstable environment', *Academy of Management Journal*, vol. 27, pp. 399–423.

Gordon, W. J. J. (1961), *Synectics*, Harper & Row.

Green, P. E. and Tull, D. S. (1970), *Research for Marketing Decisions*, Prentice Hall.

Greenley, G. E. (1986), 'Does strategic planning improve company performance?', *Long Range Planning*, vol. 19, pp. 101–9.

Gregory, K. L. (1983), 'Native-view paradigms: Multiple cultures and culture conflicts in organisations', *Administrative Science Quarterly*, September, vol. 28, pp. 359–76.

Hall, P. D. (1969), 'Computer systems' in Wills, G., Ashton, D. and Taylor, B. (eds), *Technological Forecasting and Corporate Strategy*, Bradford University Press.

Hall, W. K. (1980), 'Survival strategies in a hostile environment', *Harvard Business Review*, September–October, pp. 75–85.

Hamermesh, R. G. (1986), *Making Strategy Work: How senior managers produce results*, Wiley.

Hayes, R. H. and Garvin, D. A. (1982), 'Managing as if tomorrow mattered', *Harvard Business Review*, May–June, pp. 71–9.

Hayes, R. H. and Abernathy, W. J. (1980), 'Managing our way to economic decline', *Harvard Business Review*, July–August, pp. 67–77.

Heller, F. A. (1988), 'Working models on the shop floor', *Times Higher Education Supplement*, 29 January, p. 15.

Herzberg, F., Mausner, B. and Snyderman, B. B. (1959), *The Motivation to Work*, Wiley.

Hodder, J. E. (1986), 'Evaluation of manufacturing investments: A comparison of US and Japanese practices', *Financial Management*, Spring, pp. 17–24.

Hogg, S. (1986), 'A dance to the music of economic time', *The Times*, 17 June, p. 17.

Hopkins, D. S. (1981), 'New product winners and losers', *R&D Management*, May.

House, R. J. and Baetz, M. L. (1979), 'Leadership: Some generalizations and new research directions' in Staw, B. M. (ed), *Research in Organizational Behaviour*, JAI Press.

House, R. J. and Dessler, G. (1974), 'The path goal theory of leadership: some *post hoc* and *a priori* tests' in Hunt, J. G. and Larson, L. L. (eds), *Contingency Approaches to Leadership*, Southern Illinois University Press.

House, R. J. and Mitchell, T. R. (1974), 'Path–Goal theory of leadership', *Journal of Contemporary Business*, vol. 3, pp. 81–98.

Johne, F. A. (1985), *Industrial Product Innovation: Organisation and management*, Croom Helm.

Jones, H. (1974), *Preparing Company Plans*, Gower.

Kanter, R. M. (1983), *The Change Masters: Corporate entrepreneurs at work*, Allen & Unwin.

Kennedy, A. (1983), 'The adoption and diffusion of new industrial products', *European Journal of Marketing*, vol. 17, no. 2, pp. 31–88.

King, J. (1967), *Can Research Evaluate the Creative Content of Advertising?*, Market Research Society Annual Conference.

Koehler, W. (1938), 'Closed and open systems' in *The Place of Values in the World of Fact*, Liverwright.

Kondratiev, N. D. (1935), 'The long waves in economic life', *The Review of Economic Statistics*, November.

Kotler, P. (1984), *Marketing Management: Analysis, planning and control*, Prentice Hall.

Kotter, J. P. (1982), *The General Managers*, Free Press.

Kudla, R. J. (1980), 'The effects of strategic planning on common stock returns', *Academy of Management Review*, vol. 23, no. 20, pp. 5–20.

Lawrence, P. R. and Lorsch, J. W. (1967), *Organization and Environment*, Harvard University Press.

Leitko, T. A. and Szczerbacki, D. (1987), 'Why traditional OD strategies fail in professional bureaucracies', *Organisation Dynamics*, Winter, pp. 52–65.

Lenz, R. C. (1983), 'How to project technological development through trend extrapolation', *Technology Forecasting*, October.

Lewin, K., Lippitt, R. and White, R. K., (1939), 'Patterns of aggressive behaviour in experimentally created "social climates"', *Journal of Social Psychology*, vol. 10, pp. 271–99.

Madison, A. (1982), *Phases of Capitalist Development*, Oxford University Press.

Martin, J., Feldman, M. S., Hatch, M. J. and Sitkin, S. B. (1987), 'The uniqueness paradox in organisational stories', *Administrative Science Quarterly*, vol. 28, pp. 438–53.

Maslow, A. (1943), 'A theory of human motivation', *Psychological Review*, vol. 50, pp. 370–96.

McClelland, D. C., Atkinson, J. W., Clark, R. A. and Lowell, E. L. (1953), *The Achievement Motive*, Van Nostrand.

McGregor, D. M. (1957), 'The human side of enterprise', *Adventure in Thought and Action*, Proceedings of the Fifth Anniversary Convocation of the School of Industrial Management, Massachusetts Institute of Technology.

Meyer, A. De, Nakane, J., Miller, J. G. and Ferdows, K. (1989), 'Flexibility: The next competitive battle – the manufacturing futures survey', *Strategic Management Journal*, 10.

Miller, D. (1988), 'Relating Porter's business strategies to environment and structure: analysis and performance implications', *Academy of Management Journal*, vol. 31, no. 2.

Miller, E. J. and Rice, A. K. (1967), *Systems of Organisation*, Tavistock.

Mintzberg, H. (1981), 'Organization design: fashion or fit', *Harvard Business Review*, January–February, pp. 103–16.

Mintzberg, H. (1983), *Structure in Fives: Designing effective organisations*, Prentice Hall.

Mintzberg, H. (1987), 'The strategy concept', *California Management Review*, Fall, pp. 11–32.

Murray, H. A. (1938), *Explorations in Personality*, Oxford University Press.

Myers, S. and Marquis, D. G. (1969), *Successful Industrial Innovations: A study of factors underlying successful innovations in selected firms*, National Science Foundation.

Norburn, D. and Schurz, F. D. (1984), 'The British board-room: time for a revolution', *Long Range Planning*, vol. 17, no. 5, pp. 35–44.

Pascale, R. (1985), 'The paradox of "corporate culture": reconciling ourselves to socialisation', *California Management Review*, vol. xxvii, no. 2, pp. 26–41.

Pearce, J. A. (1982), 'The company mission as a strategic tool', *Sloan Management Review*, Spring, pp. 15–24.

Pearson, G. J. (1985), *The Strategic Discount: Ways to an entrepreneurial strategy*, Wiley.

Pearson, G. J. (1989a), 'Factors which facilitate and hinder innovation in a mature industry', PhD thesis, Manchester Business School.

Pearson, G. J. (1989b), 'Promoting entrepreneurship in large companies', *Long Range Planning*, vol. 22, no. 3, pp. 87–97.

Peters, T. J. and Austin, N. (1985), *A Passion for Excellence*, Random House.

Peters, T. J. and Waterman, R. H. (1982), *In Search of Excellence*, Harper & Row.

Pettigrew, A. (1979), 'On studying organisational culture', *Administrative Science Quarterly*, vol. 24, no. 1, pp. 570–81.

Piatier, A. (1984), *Barriers to Innovation*, Frances Pinter.

Pinchot, G. (1985), *Intrapreneuring*, Harper & Row.

Porter, M. E. (1980), *Competitive Strategy: Techniques for analysing industries and competitors*, Free Press.

Porter, M. E. (1984), *Competitive Advantage: Creating and sustaining superior performance*, Free Press.

Porter, M. E. (1987), 'From competitive advantage to corporate strategy', *Harvard Business Review*, May–June, pp. 43–59.

Prescott, J. E., Kohli, A. K. and Venkatramen, N. (1986), 'The market share–profitability relationship: an empirical assessment of major assertions and contradictions', *Strategic Management Journal*, vol. 7, pp. 377–94.

Project SAPPHO (1972), *Success and Failure in Industrial Innovation*, Science Policy Research Unit, University of Sussex.

Pugh, D. S., Hickson, D. J., Hinings, C. R. and Turner, C. (1968), 'Dimensions of organisation structure', *Administrative Science Quarterly*, vol. 13, pp. 65–105.

Pugh, D. S., Hickson, D. J., Hinings, C. R. and Turner, C. (1969), 'The context of organisation structure', *Administrative Science Quarterly*, vol. 14, pp. 91–114.

Ramo, S. (1980), *America's Technology Slip*, Wiley.

Ray, G. F. (1980), 'Innovation as the source of long term economic growth', *Long Range Planning*, April, vol. 13, pp. 9–19.

Reynolds, P. C. (1986), 'Corporate culture on the rocks', *Across the Board*, October, pp. 51–6.

Rickards, T. (1985), *Creative Decision-Making*, Tudor Rickards & Associates.

Roberts, K. J. (1986), 'How to define your market segment', *Long Range Planning*, vol. 19, no. 4, pp. 53–8.

Robertson, A. (1973), 'The marketing factor in successful industrial innovation', *Industrial Marketing Management*, no. 2.

Robinson, R. B. and Pearce, J. A. (1983), 'The impact of formalized planning on financial performance in small organizations', *Strategic Management Journal*, vol. 4, pp. 197–208.

Rogers, C. R. (1969), *Freedom to Learn*, Charles Merrill.

Rogers, E. M. (1983), *Diffusion of Innovation*, 3rd edn, Free Press.

Rumelt, R. P. (1974), *Strategy, Structure and Economic Performance*, Harvard Business School Press.

Schein, E. H. (1984), 'Coming to an awareness of organisational culture', *Sloan Management Review*, Winter.

Schoeffler, S. (1977), *The PIMS Letter on Business Strategy*, no. 2, The Strategic Planning Institute.

Schumpeter, J. A. (1939), *Business Cycles: A theoretical, historical and statistical analysis of the capitalist process*, McGraw-Hill.

Selznick, P. (1957), *Leadership and Administration*, Harper & Row.

Shanklin, W. L. (1983), 'Supply side marketing can restore "Yankee ingenuity"', *Research Management*, May–June, vol. xxvi, no. 3, pp. 20–5.

Shaw, W. C. (1981), *How to do a Company Plan*, Business Books.

Simon, H. A. (1986), 'How managers express their creativity', *Across the Board* No. 3.

Skinner, W. (1986), 'The productivity paradox', *Harvard Business Review*, July–August, pp. 55–9.

Smircich, L. (1983), 'Concepts of culture and organisational analysis', *Administrative Science Quarterly*, vol. 28, pp. 339–58.

Smith, G. D. and Steadman, L. E. (1981), 'The present value of corporate history', *Harvard Business Review*, vol. 59, no. 6, pp. 164–73.

Stogdill, R. M. (1948), 'Personal factors associated with leadership: A survey of the literature', *Journal of Psychology*, vol. 25, pp. 35–71.

Stogdill, R. M. (1974), *Handbook of Leadership: A survey of theory and research*, Free Press.

Suzuki, R. (1979), 'Worldwide expansion of US exports – A Japanese view', *Sloane Management Review*, Spring.

Trist, E. L. and Bamforth, K. W. (1951), 'Some social and psychological consequences of the long wall method of coal getting', *Human Relations*, vol. 4, pp. 3–38.

Tunstall, W. B. (1983), Cultural Transition AT&T, *Sloan Management Review*, Fall, pp. 15–26.

Twiss, B. (1986), *Technological Forecasting*, 3rd edn, Pitman.

Urwick, L. F. (1947), *The Elements of Administration*, Pitman.

Utterback, J. M. (1976), 'Innovation in industry and the diffusion of technology', *Science*, 15 February.

Weber, M. (1947), *The Theory of Social and Economic Organisation*, Free Press.

White, J. (1984), 'Corporate culture and corporate success', *Management Decision*, vol. 22, no. 4.

Wilkins, A. M. (1983), 'The culture audit: A tool for understanding organisations', *Organisational dynamics*, Autumn, pp. 24–38.

Williamson, O. (1973), 'Managerial discretion and business behaviour' in Gilbert, M. (ed.), *The Modern Business Enterprise*, Penguin.

Woodward, J. (1958), 'Management and technology', *Problems of Progress in Industry*, no. 3, HMSO.

Reference notes

Adair, J. (1983), *Effective Leadership*, Gower.
This is an easy read and provides a lot of material which is widely used for training junior and middle management. It does not set out to be particularly innovative.

Alderfer, C. P. (1972), *Existence, Relatedness and Growth*, Free Press.
These three intrinsic needs represent the distillation of a lot of work on motivation.

Barnard, C. I. (1948), *Organization and Management*, Harvard University Press.
An early classic which contains quite a lot of ideas which are still fresh. Peters and Waterman (1982) suggested that Barnard was in fact one of the most influential of management theorists.

Baumol, W. J. (1959), *Business Behaviour, Value and Growth*, Macmillan.
Baumol suggested that the separation of management from ownership resulted in discretion for managers to pursue their own goals, i.e. to maximize their own utility, rather than simply to maximize profits for the owners. Sales maximization seemed a plausible proxy for manager utility since the bigger the firm the higher were managerial salaries and perks; banks were more willing to finance large and growing businesses; personnel problems were easier to deal with when sales were growing; and large and growing sales lent prestige to managers, whereas profits simply went into the pockets of shareholders. Though this may all be 'plausible', it is still only quite a small step on the road to reality.

Boston Consulting Group (1968), *Perspectives on Experience*, Boston Consulting Group.
This publication provides the empirical details on which the portfolio approach to strategy was originally based. Many subsequent papers and articles, including Boston's own 'special commentaries' elaborated aspects of the portfolio approach and often tended to overlook the empirical basis which implies substantial limitations on the validity and usefulness of portfolios.

Burns, T. and Stalker, G. M. (1961), *Management of Innovation*, Tavistock.
A classic study of how the electronics industry failed to get established in the smoke stack industrial areas of Scotland. They introduced the terms mechanistic and organic organizations to describe firms that were rigid, bureaucratic and unable to innovate on the one hand and firms that were open flexible and well suited to volatile environments on the other.

Burrell, G. and Morgan, G. (1979), *Sociological Paradigms and Organisational Analysis*, Heinemann.
A thoroughly academic work which promises a satisfying theoretical framework for viewing the whole of management theory, but in the event disappoints since the practical value of such work seems limited.

Carter, C. F. and Williams, B. R. (1956), *Industry and Technological Progress: Factors governing the speed of application of science*, Oxford University Press.
A classic early innovation study. Carter and Williams's team of researchers visited 269 different firms, developed 152 usable general case studies, 4 industry-wide case studies and 5 innovation specific case studies. The research was substantial as well as being the first. Their main findings identified the characteristics of what they called 'the technically progressive firm', i.e. one that was 'keeping close to the best which could reasonably be achieved in the application of science and technology'.

Cyert, R. M. and March, J. G. (1963), *A Behavioural Theory of the Firm*, Prentice Hall.
A well-known study which sets out to describe how it actually is, rather than the academic studies of how it theoretically is. This introduced the ideas of satisficing, coalitions and organizational slack.

Drucker, P. F. (1955), *The Practice of Management*, Heinemann.
Early Drucker, now rather dated – the parts that have stood the test of time have been repeated in 1974.

Drucker, P. F. (1964), *Managing for Results*, Harper & Row.
This was perhaps Drucker's most influential book. He clearly recognized the power of what, twenty-five years later, we call differentiation.

Drucker, P. F. (1985), *Innovation and Entrepreneurship*, Heinemann.
Late Drucker, portentous though still substantial.

Edwardes, M. (1983), *Back from the Brink*, Collins.
A fun read.

Emery, F. E. and Trist. E. L. (1965), 'The causal texture of organisational environments', *Human Relations*, vol. 18, pp. 21–32.
The Tavistock Institute published a number of well-known empirical studies examining the interdependence of social, economic and technical systems. These included Trist and Bamforth's study of the impact of new technology in British coal mining, and Miller and Rice's study on Indian textile workers. The 'causal texture' is a theoretical development from these various empirical works.

Fiedler, F. E. (1967), *A Theory of Leadership Effectiveness*, McGraw-Hill.
This is a widely quoted study which has been widely used in leadership training.

Foster, R. N. (1986), *Innovation: The attacker's advantage*, Summit.
The ideas behind this book come mainly from operations research and technological forecasting of the 1940s and 1950s.

Fredrickson, J. W. and Mitchell, T. R. (1984), 'Strategic decision processes: Comprehensiveness and performance in an industry with an unstable environment', *Academy of Management Journal*, vol. 27, pp. 399–423.
This found a negative relationship between comprehensiveness of planning and performance measures such as an average return on assets and sales growth.

Gordon, W. J. J. (1961), *Synectics*, Harper & Row.
A classic study of creativity. Synectics is a sophistication on the traditional brainstorming technique.

Green, P. E. and Tull, D. S. (1970), *Research for Marketing Decisions*, Prentice Hall.
This standard work is regularly updated and is now in its 6th edition. See especially Chapter 7, 'Multi-dimensional scaling of perception and preference'.

Greenley, G. E. (1986), 'Does strategic planning improve company performance?', *Long Range Planning*, April, vol. 19, pp. 101–9.
This reviewed current published research data and found 'the research

published to date, relative to manufacturing companies, is far from conclusive in establishing a relationship between strategic planning and company performance'.

Hall, W. K. (1980), 'Survival strategies in a hostile environment', *Harvard Business Review*, September–October, pp. 75–85.
This reports an interesting study which is worth reading.

Hayes, R. H. and Abernathy, W. J. (1980), 'Managing our way to economic decline', *Harvard Business Review*, July–August, pp. 67–77.
Seminal article, definitely worth reading.

Hayes, R. H. and Garvin, D. A. (1982), 'Managing as if tomorrow mattered', *Harvard Business Review*, May–June, pp. 71–9.
This article follows on from Hayes and Abernathy's (1980) influential paper 'Managing our way to economic decline' and examines in detail the technical reasons why the adoption of orthodox accounting mores and processes leads naturally and inexorably to a process of disinvestment and competitive decline.

Hodder, J. E. (1986), 'Evaluation of manufacturing investments: A comparison of US and Japanese practices', *Financial Management*, Spring, pp. 17–24.
An interesting study.

Kennedy, A. (1983), 'The adoption and diffusion of new industrial products', *European Journal of Marketing*, vol. 17, no. 2, pp. 31–88.
This is a review article of particular interest to students of innovation.

Koehler, W. (1938), 'Closed and open systems' in *The Place of Values in the World of Fact*, Liverwright.
This was an early attempt at showing how the properties of systems influence the way they operate. Much of general systems theory seems intuitively valid to many widely differing situations, but the models, like Koehler's candle, should be viewed with some suspicion as explanations of particular cases. Undoubtedly they have pointed to new and interesting ways of thinking, but the level of generalization explicit in general systems theory makes it inappropriate as a basis for deciding particular action.

Kotler, P. (1984), *Marketing Management: Analysis, planning and control*, Prentice Hall.
A standard marketing textbook.

Kudla, R. J. (1980), 'The effects of strategic planning on common stock returns', *Academy of Management Review*, vol. 23, no. 20, pp. 5–20.
This suggests there is no relationship between formal planning and common stock returns.

Lawrence, P. R. and Lorsch, J. W. (1967), *Organization and Environment*, Harvard University Press.
An important piece of research which was one of the early contributions to what became known as 'contingency theory', i.e. there is no single best way, it all depends.

Maslow, A. (1943), 'A theory of human motivation', *Psychological Review*, vol. 50, pp. 370–96.

232   Reference notes

Frequently quoted hierarchical model of intrinsic human needs is tantalizingly plausible but lacks any significant supporting empirical evidence.

McGregor, D. M. (1957), 'The human side of enterprise', *Adventure in Thought and Action*, Proceedings of the Fifth Anniversary Convocation of the School of Industrial Management, Massachusetts Institute of Technology.
A much maligned exposition of Theory X and Theory Y. Lots of naive interpretations of Theory Y have failed. Theory Y management is not a soft option – Theory X is much easier to adopt as a manager, but a competent Theory Y application is likely to be more effective.

Meyer, A. De, Nakane, J., Miller, J. G. and Ferdows, K. (1989), 'Flexibility: The next competitive battle – the manufacturing futures survey', *Strategic Management Journal*, 10.
Though only published in 1989, this report of an ongoing survey was first written in 1987 and refers to data on 1986. Thus it is already somewhat dated. However, the points it makes regarding flexibility and the European and American approach to it, are only likely to be even more pressing now than they were three years ago.

Mintzberg, H. (1981), 'Organization design: fashion or fit', *Harvard Business Review*, January–February, pp. 103–16.
This article is a succinct examination of various organizational structures and their strengths and weaknesses.

Peters, T. J. and Austin, N. (1985), *A Passion for Excellence*, Random House.
A rather less thoughtful follow-up to *In Search of Excellence*, rich in supporting anecdotes which proclaims three secrets of long term excellence – superior customer service, constant innovation and making full use of the abilities of every company employee.

Peters, T. J. and Waterman, R. H. (1982), *In Search of Excellence*, Harper & Row.
The best-seller, now much derided because a number of the chosen 'excellent' companies subsequently failed to perform. Nevertheless this seems to be a significant contribution to management literature, relating good theory to good practice. Identifies eight distinctive characteristics of the excellent companies:

- A bias for action
- Keeping close to the customer
- Granting autonomy and enabling entrepreneurship
- Achieving productivity through people
- Being hands-on and value driven
- Sticking to the knitting
- Keeping a simple form and lean staff
- Operating simultaneous loose–tight properties.

Robinson, R. B. and Pearce, J. A. (1983), 'The impact of formalized planning

on financial performance in small organizations', *Strategic Management Journal*, vol. 4, pp. 197–208.
This found no relationship between formal planning and profit margins and ROE ratios.

Williamson, O. (1973), 'Managerial discretion and business behaviour' in Gilbert, M. (ed.), *The Modern Business Enterprise*, Penguin.
Williamson broadened the definition of managerial utility from sales revenue to include salary, security, power, status and professional excellence. Other than salary, these items are not readily quantifiable, so Williamson used various more or less measurable proxies. From this rather more realistic beginning the model is then forced into obscurity by the use of classical maths.

Index

Abernathy, W. J. 101, 102, 137
accounting philosophy, 2, 14
acquisition, 2, 88, 122, 182
Adair, J., 191–2
adhocracy, 159
Alderfer, C. P., 197
Atkinson, J. W., 196
Austin, N., 16, 199

Baetz, M. L., 192, 194
Baumol, W. J., 4, 46
Beynon, H., 170
Bower, M., 32
Boston Consulting Group, 75–82, 112, 115, 138
boundary management, 47
brainstorming, 140, 141
Brech, E. F. L., 11
Bright, J. R., 132
budgeting, 56–64
bureaucracy, 10, 12–14, 16, 157, 159–61, 168, 215, 216, 219
Burns, T., 10, 17,
Burrell, G., 163
business portfolios, 79–88, 92, 93,
business positioning, 121–2
business strategy, 41–3, 45, 93, 105
business strength, 84–5, 92, 100
business unit, 50–2, 87
buyers' bargaining power, 95

capital planning, 58
Carter, C. F., 209–10
cash cow, 2, 80–2,
centralization, 11, 156–7, 173
Chakrabarti, A. K., 136
Chandler, A. D., 11, 154
Channon, D. F., 155
Chisnall, P. M., 211
communication, 11, 162, 173, 188, 198–200, 209, 210, 212, 213, 214

company audit, 59–60
company history, 180–1
competition avoidance, 31–2
competitive advantage, 102, 104, 135
competitive forces, 93–6
competitive rivalry, 93–4
competitive specialism, 122, 179, 182–4, 187
competitive strategy, 98–107, 112, 118, 126, 208, 213, 214
competitor analysis, 96–8
concentration, 23–4, 25, 28, 64, 99, 112, 153, 179, 186–8, 208
configuration, 154, 156–8
consistency, 24, 25, 64, 99, 112, 153, 179, 208
Cooper, R. G., 211
corporate integrity, 167, 168, 213, 214
corporate strategy, 40–2
cost leadership, 31, 98–103, 107
cost of capital, 144–5
creativity, 138–42
culture, 30, 32–3, 64, 134, 136, 153–5, 161–74, 208, 216, 219
culture management, 165–9
customer, 30, 47, 48, 93, 113, 114, 116–18, 120, 122, 181
customer perceptions, 115–21
Cyert, R. M., 46, 63

DCF, 143–8
Deal, T. E., 165
De Bono, E., 139
development budgeting, 62–4
differentiation, 94, 95, 99–100, 103–4, 107, 113, 118, 121, 214
direction, 22–5, 30, 64, 104, 105, 107, 112, 126, 153, 179, 208
directional policy matrix, 82–3
discount rate, *see* hurdle rate
disinvestment spiral, 1, 102, 217

235